MW00910287

Literature in the Early American Republic

EDITORS
Matthew Wynn Sivils, *Iowa State University*
Jeffrey Walker, *Oklahoma State University*

ADVISORY EDITOR
Lance Schachterle, *Worcester Polytechnic Institute*

EDITORIAL ASSISTANT
LuElla Putnam D'Amico, *Whitworth University*

EDITORIAL ADVISORY BOARD
Stephen Carl Arch, *Michigan State University*
Allan M. Axelrad, *California State University, Fullerton*
John Bryant, *Hofstra University*
David Cody, *Hartwick College*
Robert Daly, *State University of New York, Buffalo*
William Merrill Decker, *Oklahoma State University*
Benjamin F. Fisher, *University of Mississippi*
Wayne Franklin, *University of Connecticut*
Kay Seymour House, *Emeritus, San Francisco State University*
Mark L. Kamrath, *University of Central Florida*
William P. Kelly, *City University of New York*
Kent Ljungquist, *Worcester Polytechnic Institute*
Robert D. Madison, *University of Arkansas*
Barbara Alice Mann, *University of Toledo*
John P. McWilliams, Jr., *Middlebury College*
Dennis Moore, *Florida State University*
Wesley T. Mott, *Worcester Polytechnic Institute*
H. Daniel Peck, *Vassar College*
Leland S. Person, *University of Cincinnati*
Thomas L. Philbrick, *Emeritus, University of Pittsburgh*
Judith Richardson, *Stanford University*
Zabelle Stodola, *University of Arkansas at Little Rock*
James Wallace, *Boston College*
Signe O. Wegener, *University of Georgia*

Literature in the Early American Republic

Annual Studies on Cooper and His Contemporaries

VOLUME 6

Editors
Matthew Wynn Sivils
Jeffrey Walker

AMS Press, Inc.
New York

LITERATURE IN THE EARLY AMERICAN REPUBLIC
ANNUAL STUDIES ON COOPER AND HIS CONTEMPORARIES

ISSN 1938–5773

Literature in the Early American Republic: Annual Studies on Cooper and His Contemporaries is an annual, peer-reviewed journal that welcomes a wide range of submissions on the literary culture of the United States from the adoption of the Constitution in 1789 to the death of James Fenimore Cooper in 1851. We also seek submissions addressing (or establishing critical editions of) unpublished archival manuscripts (letters, diaries, poems, and other documents) of cultural or literary relevance to the period. Studies devoted to works by minority figures and other historically underappreciated writers, as well as articles dealing with the works and influence of James Fenimore Cooper, are central to our mission.

Please format essays in accordance with *The Chicago Manual of Style* (16th ed.), especially sections 14.14–67 and the *LEAR* "House Style Guide." As all submissions undergo review by outside readers, the author's name should appear only on the cover page. An author whose essay is selected for publication will be asked to provide a brief abstract and biographical statement. Whenever available, authors should use as their primary texts those scholarly editions approved by the Modern Language Association Committee on Scholarly Editions. For example, in the case of Cooper, authors should use those editions approved by the "Writings of James Fenimore Cooper" and published by AMS Press and SUNY Press.

We require submissions be made electronically as Microsoft Word documents attached to a single e-mail and sent simultaneously to Wayne Franklin (wayne.franklin@uconn.edu) and Jason Berger (jason.berger@usd.edu).

Please direct inquiries concerning subscriptions to AMS Press, Inc., Brooklyn Navy Yard, 63 Flushing Avenue-Unit #221, Brooklyn, NY 11205-1073, or e-mail inquiries to orders@amspressinc.com.

Copyright © 2014 AMS Press, Inc.
All rights reserved

International Standard Book Numbers
Set ISBN-10: 0-404-63910-0
Set ISBN-13: 978-0-404-63910-5

Vol. 6 ISBN-10: 0-404-63916-X
Vol. 6 ISBN-13: 978-0-404–63916-7

All AMS books are printed on acid-free paper that meets the guidelines for performance and durability of the Committee on Production Guidelines for Book Longevity of the Council on Library Resources.

AMS PRESS, INC.
Brooklyn Navy Yard, 63 Flushing Avenue-Unit #221
Brooklyn, NY 11205-1073, USA
www.amspressinc.com

Manufactured in the United States of America

Contents

Preface

THE sixth volume of our award-winning *Literature in the Early American Republic: Annual Studies on Cooper and His Contemporaries* (*LEAR*) is complete, and we are very pleased to present ten original essays penned by seasoned veterans and a bevy of talented newcomers. These ten address the development of political print networks and competing literary politics in the early Republic; the paternal and maternal elements of George Washington's character; the role of the arid West in the prose of George Catlin and Washington Irving; two essays on Brockden Brown, one examining the agrarian gothic and the relationship between land and class in *Wieland*, and the other offering a fictionalized account of Brown's drawing and its relationship to narrative practice; and five new essays on Cooper: the social upheaval arising from tenants threatening landowners during the anti-rent strife of the 1840s; his use of the words *aristocracy*, *aristocrat*, and *aristocratic* in his fiction; the developing role of globalization in his novels; and two essays on *The Last of the Mohicans*, the first, an investigation of how Cooper casts Magua as a Romantic satanic rebel, and the second, a study of the "Last Man" stories and the inevitable question; Who *is* the "last" of the Mohicans?

We open the sixth volume with Steven Carl Smith's portrait of bookshop owner John Ward Fenno and his attempt to stake a claim to the political corner of the early American book trade. Hawking mostly London-imported books and periodicals, Fenno tried to connect American readers to a larger transatlantic, particularly British and especially conservative and Republican, literary network. Portraying quite a different ideology, Jillmarie Murphy's provocative analysis, "Maternal Fathers; or, The Power of Sympathy: Phillis Wheatley's Poem to and Correspondence with 'His Excellency General Washington,'" explains how Wheatley treated the paternal and maternal side of George Washington's character. Murphy shows how Wheatley used female imagery in her poem, and accompanying letter, to emphasize the general's compassion and empathy as he leads the struggle for America's independence during the Revolutionary War. Matthew J. C. Cella shows a different kind of spirit surfacing in the prose of George Catlin and Washington Irving. In their "Western Narratives," Catlin's *Letters and Notes* and Irving's *A Tour on the Prairies*, both writers investigate "Disturbing Hunting Grounds" as they ponder geocultural change in the arid West. As the prairies and the bison-hunting grounds suffer because of western expansion, Catlin and Irving express ambivalence toward the geographical and cultural changes those patterns anticipate and offer a template for those changes.

In a somewhat similar vein, Tyler Roeger identifies an "Agrarian Gothic" in Charles Brockden Brown's use of "Carwin, Class Transgression, and Spatial Horrors" in *Wieland*. In Brown's novel, Carwin is used to demonstrate how agrarianism takes the form of a gothic transgression; hierarchies of rural owner and rural worker become frighteningly blurred, and property ownership generates potentially devastating effects on class identity and space. Megan Walsh continues the discussion of Brown, but her emphasis features "*Wieland*, Illustrated," as she explains how Brown uses "Word and Image in the Early American Novel." Because Brown made drawings in the same notebook in which he composed *Wieland*, Walsh explains, the novel offers a fictionalized account of drawing and its relation to narrative. *Wieland* illustrates Brown's belief that not only word but also image must fully surface in narratives of early America.

The importance of the word resurfaces with Allan M. Axelrad's "James Fenimore Cooper, American English, and the Significance of *Aristocracy* in a Republic," the first of five essays on the works of the Burlington, New Jersey, native. An active participant in the postcolonial project of constructing an American English, Cooper found the words *aristocracy*, *aristocrat*, and *aristocratic* problematic because of their association with the old regime. To that end, Cooper took great care when using them in his fiction, and the results are surprising. Less surprising, at first glance, are his views on "Foreign Friendship." When Sarah Sillin examines "James Fenimore Cooper and America's International Origins," she concentrates on the tropes of sympathy and friendship in two early novels, *The Pilot* and *The Prairie*. However, while she discovers that Cooper's early novels evoke optimism regarding American participation in globalization, she learns that Cooper later expresses a less than optimistic feeling of an American's ability to generate international friendships in *The Deerslayer*. Certainly little friendship exists in the story found in Lance Schachterle's analysis of "Patriotism and Caste" in *The Chainbearer*," "Cooper's Fifth Revolutionary War Novel." Cooper shows how Mordaunt Littlepage, son of the hero of *Satanstoe*, defends his landownership by marrying the Chainbearer's niece, who has fallen from shabby gentility to manual work, carrying chair for her uncle. The novel foregrounds the social revolution and upheaval the nation faced less than a century after its political independence.

In the first of two final Cooper essays, both dealing with *The Last of the Mohicans*, Donna Richardson examines "Cooper's Revision of *Paradise Lost* and of Romantic Satanism" showing how Cooper casts Magua as a Romantic satanic rebel who justly criticizes Europeans for trying to play God. Respecting codes and practices of other cultures requires personal sacrifice, yet only Uncas fully bears this cross. And he dies. John Hay, however, questions Uncas's role as the last man of the Mohicans in "Narratives of Extinction" when he enters the debate about such stories, typified by Mary Shelley's *The Last Man*. Unlike Shelley's ambiguous "lastness," Cooper uses the Last Man, Hay argues, to help white readers understand Native American history.

We editors once again thank the members of our editorial board and other colleagues whose expertise and willingness to read these essays multiple times, to pen their evaluations in detail, and to help shape the final content of each essay have resulted in another first-class collection. We also appreciate those at our own institutions whose generosity supported this sixth volume of *LEAR*. At Oklahoma State, Jeffrey Walker thanks Carol Moder, his Department Head, for continually championing the journal while at Iowa State, Matthew Sivils once again thanks his Department Chair, Barbara Ching, for her ongoing support.

Finally, this is the last volume of *LEAR* we two editors will produce, for much like Natty Bumppo, we must move on, casting ourselves as "foremost in that band of [Editors], who [have opened] the way for the march of the [best scholarship on the literature of the early American republic] across the continent." But never fear, as we "move westward towards the setting sun," a duo of new editors—Wayne Franklin, of the University of Connecticut, and Jason Berger, of the University of South Dakota, will settle the territory and carry forth the standards that have made *LEAR sui generis*. For *LEAR*'s first six volumes have amply demonstrated that the heretofore "unpublishable" longer essay, the critical edition of historical and literary documents, and the comprehensive and invaluable bibliographical survey, the forgotten staples of first-class scholarship, have once again found a home, and that its critical essays deserve the epithet "learned." And while we like to think of *LEAR* as modern as the minute, we value scholarship that, in the words of our CELJ adjudicator, "will have real staying power and will not lose its relevance once a new literary theory du jour takes over."

To that end, we editors want to thank three people at AMS Press whose unflagging support has helped make *LEAR* the *best new journal* in print: Gabe Hornstein, President of AMS Press, who printed books of the very highest quality, regardless of cost; David Ramm, our Editor-in-Chief, who solved every seemingly impossible editorial problem with savoir faire; and Donna Brantlinger Black, whose indefatigable copyediting erased all our editorial sins and helped make *LEAR* a model of clarity. All three—as well as their staff at the Brooklyn Navy Yard—have improved this annual beyond our ability to properly thank them one more time. But we will do it anyway. Thank you, everyone.

The Editors

Abstracts

A RASH, THOUGHTLESS, AND IMPRUDENT YOUNG MAN": JOHN WARD FENNO AND THE FEDERALIST LITERARY NETWORK

Steven Carl Smith

Hawkish bookshop owner John Ward Fenno succeeded his father as editor of a prominent Federalist newspaper in Philadelphia before relocating to Manhattan. Once characterized by Philadelphia publisher Mathew Carey as a "rash, thoughtless, and imprudent young man," Fenno and his brief time as a dealer in political texts in New York City presents a compelling case study of the development of political print networks and competing literary politics in the early republic. Fenno's estate inventory and his correspondence with one of his retail shopkeepers reveal his small Manhattan bookshop as a meeting place for local Federalists; from this politicized space, Fenno initiated a national political project to counter the influence of the Republican newspaper network that helped sweep Thomas Jefferson into the presidency in 1800. In New York, Fenno staked a claim to the political corner of the early American book trade, and as many of his books and periodicals were London imports, he also attempted to connect American readers to a larger transatlantic, particularly British and especially conservative, transatlantic literary network. Yet because he died in 1802, that literary network never quite materialized.

MATERNAL FATHERS; OR THE POWER OF SYMPATHY: PHILLIS WHEATLEY'S POEM TO AND CORRESPONDENCE WITH "HIS EXCELLENCY GENERAL WASHINGTON"

Jillmarie Murphy

Contemporary scholars recognize Phillis Wheatley's 1775 poem to George Washington as a call to freedom rather than a tribute to

Washington; however, Wheatley's poem and accompanying letter, with Washington's response to each, reveal much more. Her verse functions as an early conflation of masculine and feminine virtue and, thus, highlights a paradoxical development between the paternal and the maternal aspects of Washington's character at the time of the American Revolution. Wheatley's glorification of powerful female imagery throughout her poem serves to emphasize the necessity of Washington's compassion and empathy as he leads the struggle for America's freedom.

DISTURBING HUNTING GROUNDS: NEGOTIATING GEOCULTURAL CHANGE IN THE WESTERN NARRATIVES OF GEORGE CATLIN AND WASHINGTON IRVING

Matthew J. C. Cella

Two western narratives, George Catlin's *Letters and Notes* (1841) and Washington Irving's *A Tour on the Prairies* (1835), chart early American attitudes concerning the value and future prospects of the arid West. As outsiders, both Catlin and Irving were drawn to the bison hunting-grounds of the western tribes, extolling the aesthetic value and economic viability of the indigenous geocultural landscape. Both writers also expressed ambivalence about what they saw as the inevitable upheaval of this landscape, due to frontier progress and, thereby, both offered a template for negotiating one of the seminal aspects of western American experience: geocultural change.

AGRARIAN GOTHIC: CARWIN, CLASS TRANSGRESSION, AND SPATIAL HORRORS IN *WIELAND*

Tyler Roeger

The effect of an agrarian economy is an issue of troubling speculation in Charles Brockden Brown's *Wieland; or, The Transformation. An American Tale.* In Brown's novel, through the character of Carwin, agrarianism takes the form of a gothic transgression in which hierarchies of rural owner and rural worker become frighteningly blurred. Amidst growing early American discourses on agrarianism, the gothic relationship in Brown's *Wieland* between class and land is far more than a simple reconsideration of property, and *Wieland* reveals a developing form of property ownership that has potentially devastating effects on class identity and space.

Wieland, Illustrated: Word and Image in The Early American Novel

Megan Walsh

The drawings Charles Brockden Brown made in the same notebook in which he first composed *Wieland* argue for a reading of the novel in which disputes over narrative authority play out through the experiences of visual representation. The novel offers a fictionalized account of drawing as it relates to narrative practice, evidence of the literary significance of Brown's own visual experiments and of the pressing need to integrate more fully a word and image methodology with the study of the early national literary culture.

James Fenimore Cooper, American English, and the Signification of *Aristocracy* in a Republic

Allan M. Axelrad

Cooper was a thoughtful observer and an active participant in the postcolonial project of constructing an American English language. After the Revolution, the signification of words such as *aristocracy*, *aristocrat*, and *aristocratic* became particularly problematic because of their unique association with the old regime. While most everyone agreed that anything to do with aristocracy, aristocrats, or aristocratic behavior was unrepublican, there was considerable disagreement about what these words actually signified. These words signified something unique to Cooper, and he was adamant about using them correctly.

Patriotism And Caste in *The Chainbearer*: Cooper's Fifth Revolutionary War Novel

Lance Schachterle

Cooper argued to his British publisher Richard Bentley that the theme of *Chainbearer* (1845) was "revolution," by which, this essay argues, he meant the social upheaval of tenants threatening landowners during the anti-rent strife of the 1840s. In *The Chainbearer*, Cooper depicts how Mordaunt Littlepage, Revolutionary War veteran and the son of the hero and heroine of *Satanstoe*, struggles to oppose a Vermont squatter, Aaron Thousandacres. For Cooper, this struggle recalls the Revolution of 1775–81 in defending the rights of property owners as defined in the US Constitution. With the help of the Dutch Chainbearer Andries Coejemans and the "just Onondago" Susquesus, Littlepage successfully defends his landownership. But Cooper interestingly tweaks the rigidity of class structure by having Littlepage marry the Chainbearer's niece, who has descended from shabby gentility to living by manual work, carrying chain for her uncle. Thus the novel foregrounds Cooper's sense of what revolutions the country was facing in the generations after the Revolutionary War established political independence.

Foreign Friendship: James Fenimore Cooper and America's International Origins

Sarah Sillin

Tropes of sympathy and friendship characterize James Fenimore Cooper's changing vision of international relations in *The Pilot* (1824), *The Prairie* (1827), and *The Deerslayer* (1841). Cooper's novels from the 1820s evoke optimism regarding US participation in the global sphere, suggesting that closer ties to the British, Native Americans, and Spanish creoles will benefit the nation through trade, cultural exchange, and expansion. Increasingly, however, Cooper's later work conveys his concerns that Americans' failure of feeling—evidenced by the nation's violent colonial history—threatens to undermine valuable international friendships.

Cooper's Revision of *Paradise Lost* and of Romantic Satanism in *The Last of the Mohicans*

Donna Richardson

Rather than simply echoing Milton by equating Magua with Satan, as previous criticism suggests, Cooper casts Magua as a Romantic satanic rebel who justly criticizes the Europeans for trying to play God. Cooper also revises the discourse of Romantic satanism itself; he depicts satanic self-deification on a cultural level as an ethnocentrism that implicates characters who try to confront it in language practices and institutional injustices beyond their understanding. To redeem this ideological fall, it is necessary to respect the codes and practices of other cultures, as well as to engage in personal sacrifice, and the only character who fully bears this cross of cross-culturalism is Uncas.

Narratives of Extinction: James Fenimore Cooper and The Last Man

John Hay

"Narratives of Extinction" reads James Fenimore Cooper's *The Last of the Mohicans* (1826) as a "Last Man" tale informed by the contemporaneously emerging discourse of biological extinction. British writers of the era envisioned the natural extinction of the human race and developed a literary vogue for Last Man stories, epitomized by Mary Shelley's novel *The Last Man* (1826). In Shelley's hands, "lastness" ended only in ambiguity and interminable mediation. Asking, "Who *is* the last of the Mohicans?" this essay argues that Cooper used the unstable figure of the Last Man to allow white readers to establish narrative continuity with the country's Native American history.

"A Rash, Thoughtless, and Imprudent Young Man": John Ward Fenno and the Federalist Literary Network

Steven Carl Smith
Providence College

IN December 1798, on yet another cold night in Philadelphia, John Ward Fenno was startled by rustling about the porch step of his home on Chestnut Street. "There came last night to my House two ruffians," he wrote the next day in his paper, the *Gazette of the United States,* "one of whom lurked about the porch, while the other, as I stood at my own door, struck me on the head with a bludgeon." After absorbing the initial blow at the hands of the assailant, whom he later identified as a "United Irishmen," Fenno retreated into the office of the *Gazette* and seized a piece of printing equipment to fend off further violence. He later reflected that shrinking back may have saved his life, considering it a "fortunate" decision, and that to have attempted retaliation would have had dire consequences; "I should have been murdered," he concluded.[1]

This was not John Ward Fenno's only brush with violence. The denouement of Fenno's career as a political hack involved his rivalry with Benjamin Franklin Bache. The grandson of Benjamin Franklin and editor of the Jeffersonian *Aurora,* Bache was the foremost voice in a vibrant, and growing, Republican newspaper network.[2] The bad blood began when the elder John Fenno traded rhetorical jabs with Bache's *Aurora* in the pages of his *Gazette of the United States.* As caustic as the

Literature in the Early American Republic: Annual Studies on Cooper and His Contemporaries
Volume 6, 2014. Copyright © 2014 by AMS Press, Inc. All rights reserved.

rhetoric between Fenno's *Gazette* and Bache's *Aurora* was, the enmity between the two men reached a boiling point in early August 1798.

In a series of scathing editorials, Bache implicated the Fennos in a massive forgery scheme in which the Philadelphia Federalist Joseph Thomas was accused of stealing nearly $20,000. "We understand that the recent discovered scheme of swindling and forgery, has but barely budded," so went the *Aurora*, and that the "branches of this grand affair promise to appear in several quarters of the Union in a short time." Referring to the elder Fenno as "that *mercenary scoundrel*," Bache insinuated that the editor of the *Gazette of the United States* was somehow involved in Thomas's scheme and that, due to the damning evidence Bache was putting forth, Fenno and, by extension, Federalists had little by way of political morality. Infuriated, young Fenno stormed into the *Aurora*'s Market Street office demanding that Bache retract his accusation that his father covered for Thomas:

> *Fenno's* young sprig plucked up courage enough to go as far as the office of the *Aurora* yesterday evening, in order to deny that his *pappy* was the friend of *Jozey Thomas*—the lad was accompanied by a gentleman, who acknowledged he had reason to be ashamed of the youth's behaviour. *Fenno's* young lady in breeches came to require the name of the writer that called his papers a *mercenary scoundrel,* and to demand *satisfaction* for his being billed Jozey Thomas's friend—but when the person he was offended with rose from his seat, behold the "poor little foolish, fluttering thing"—literally ran away with his mouth full of froth, and its knees trembling![3]

Naturally, the Fennos had a remarkably different interpretation of the shakedown. Young Fenno maintained that he had visited the *Aurora* to correct the ways in which his father had been spoken of "in villainous terms." The young man portrayed himself as having assumed an imposing countenance, so much so that Bache—that "mean and contemptible coward"—had stood trembling and quaking before the "lad" he had abused. In a striking contrast to Bache's story, in his version of the events, young Fenno had stood his ground and had told Bache that, if "he neglected to recant the obnoxious terms, that I should treat him as a scoundrel, and that he was a lying, cowardly rascal." Taking exception to Fenno's thinly veiled threat, the other men in the office had "bristled up" while Bache had "doubled his fist, and made some shew of striking a blow at me."[4] It was at this time that Fenno's unnamed companion had insisted they withdraw.

The quarrel in Bache's office, and the competing narratives that appeared in the *Aurora* and the *Gazette of the United States*, would be resolved only by a clash in the streets of Philadelphia. On the very day that the *Gazette* and the *Aurora* published their rival stories, the two men happened upon one another at Fourth and Market Street. Enraged not only by Bache's language toward his father but also by the way he was characterized as a drooling, inarticulate ne'er-do-well, Fenno—at least in Bache's recounting of the incident—"muttered up courage enough last evening" and lunged at Bache "with *tooth* and *nail*." A violent scrum ensued during which young Fenno apparently bit and scratched his antagonist. Bache, however, gave himself the last word, pointing out that he "got in return a sound rap or two across the head and face" of Fenno.[5] Similar to the previous incident, Fenno's retelling of the brawl was quite different. Casting Bache as that "villain whose detestable propensities present to an Indignant world, a combination of vice and depravity, which both in degree and variety, challenge the whole annals of mankind," John Ward Fenno reminded readers of the *Gazette* that Bache had derided his father as a "MERCENARY SCOUNDREL" and reported that this "crying affront, which struck with the force of thunder to the heart" had sent young Fenno into a rage. Young Fenno was convinced that he must "resort to prompt revenge," and while on a leisurely stroll with his younger brother, he ran into Bache, who just so happened to be walking on Fourth Street "with his bludgeon, accompanied by John Beckley":

> Upon which I immediately proceeded towards him; and after advancing full in his view, for about one third of the square, came up with him. He drew back, and brandished his club—I advanced and seizing him by the collar, struck him at the same instant in the face, and repeated my blows as fast as possible. He repeatedly attempted to push his stick in my face; but having closed in with him, his arms were so cramped, that his attempts proved very feeble. The scuffle issued in my driving him against the wall, when I should have soon wrested the club from his hand—had not his companion, very improperly seized my left hand,

> and disengaging it from round his body, held it fast. Bache instantly drew off. My attempts to get at him again were rendered ineffectual by those around, one of whom seized me round the body, and held me fast, while Bache sneaked home, his nose barked, and his sconce covered with blood, conspicuous marks of Jacobin valour. I had no weapon, but my fist and received no hurt in the transaction. It is not without reluctance that I further intruded upon the public. The active misrepresentations of Bache and his partisans, seemed to call for a true statement of the affair.[6]

1. Philadelphia Life

The assault at his Philadelphia home and the long-standing quarrel with Bache were typical moments in John Ward Fenno's life in Philadelphia. As the editor and political middleman for Philadelphia Federalists, through succeeding his father at the helm of the *Gazette of the United States*, John Ward Fenno was clearly in over his head. Born in Boston in March 1778 and the oldest of fourteen, Jack, as he was affectionately called by his family, was trained as a printer by his father. Despite this formal training, Jack Fenno was also provided with a classical education, first at Mr. Payne's Academy in New York and later at the University of Pennsylvania. Jack's ultimate ambition was to read for the bar, but his father's sudden death during the yellow fever epidemic of 1798 forced him to take over the *Gazette of the United States*. Jack Fenno kept the business in the family, at least early on. To make up for the exodus of journeymen and apprentices due to the outbreak, Fenno's younger brothers Charles and George provided much-needed help with the production of the paper until he sold the paper and left for New York in 1800; he opened a small bookshop soon thereafter.[7]

Once characterized by the Philadelphia publisher Mathew Carey as a "rash, thoughtless, and imprudent young man," John Ward Fenno and his brief career as a political bookseller in New York City shed light on the development of political print networks and competing literary politics in the early Republic. At first glance, the opening of a small Broadway bookshop seemed a mundane move for a political actor of Fenno's standing, but the establishment of Jack Fenno's bookshop in New York was a decidedly political affair. As a newcomer to an already-saturated New York print market, Fenno made his bookshop into an accessible public space for the city's Federalists in an increasingly Jeffersonian world.[8]

In recent years, Federalists have enjoyed a revival among historians and literary scholars alike. Many studies—dubbed "Founders Chic" by historian David Waldstreicher—tend to be quasi-celebratory and narrowly organized around a single politician in an effort to legitimate, or even rescue, Federalist contributions to the formation of the early American state. Still others, beginning with the collection of essays edited by Doron Ben-Atar and Barbara Oberg, seek to look beyond the influence of luminaries and father figures by placing Federalists within a larger political context, in conversation with scholars of the new political history, who, while focusing on political actors beyond the narrow purview of the so-called "Founders," nonetheless seek to understand the day-to-day political lives of early Americans. More recently, historian Philip J. Lampi, building on his lifetime of research on early American elections, has called for a Federalist redux of sorts. Lampi argues against the pervasive scholarly assumption that Federalist influence dwindled rapidly in the early nineteenth century, an assumption articulated most recently by Sean Wilentz, who depicts the post-1800 Federalists as a party in steady decline that had disappeared entirely by 1815. Lampi makes the case that Federalists still had considerable pockets of influence even after Jefferson's election in 1800. Bridging the gap between historians seeking to reimagine, and thus add greater texture and nuance to, the Federalists and those of the new political history are literary scholars interested in the cultural construction of politics. William C. Dowling, Catherine O'Donnell Kaplan, and Bryan Waterman place Federalist politics, in particular their opposition to the French Revolution and policies put forth by President Thomas Jefferson, into a wider literary context by studying a cadre of conservative litterateurs, including Joseph Dennie, William Dunlap, Charles Brockden Brown, and men active in social clubs, particularly the Philadelphia Anchor Club and New York Friendly Club.[9]

It is against this backdrop of shifting cultural and political milieus that Fenno operated his New York bookstore and a national

Federalist literary network. Unlike other New York publishers, such as Evert Duyckinck, who, I suggest elsewhere, were interested in neither literary nationalism nor political culture but rather in making money by selling cheap books to a national market, Fenno staked a claim to the political corner of the early American book trade. And although he passed away long before it could be fully implemented, Fenno's distribution network connected American readers to a larger transatlantic, particularly British and especially conservative, literary culture. In order to combat the Jeffersonian threat he perceived, Fenno contracted retail agents dotted around the early American landscape who agreed to hawk his hawkish books and periodicals.[10] This essay, then, is situated at the intersection of the new political history and literary history, and it contributes to scholarship that attempts to make sense of the ways in which middling political actors helped to shape the politics of everyday life in New York and the early Republic.

2. For Sale by J[ohn] W. Fenno

John Ward Fenno left Philadelphia in a hurry. In two separate letters, Fenno asked protégé Asbury Dickins to ship the remnants of the wardrobe he left behind in Philadelphia to his New York residence. In July 1800, Fenno concluded his note to Dickins by imploring him, "[S]end me my boots & c." Two months later, in August 1800, Fenno again raised the specter of his missing threads: "Has there been no opportunity by sea or land, for the Costumes . . . Boots & c.?" Fenno had good reason to flee Philadelphia in such haste. Shortly after taking over the *Gazette of the United States* in September 1798, he was slapped with a $5,000 libel suit by Alexander Dallas, the secretary of Pennsylvania. Fenno did not contest the case. While reeling from lawsuits and fending off assaults, both physical and rhetorical, from his rivals a few blocks away at the *Aurora*, Fenno had grown disillusioned at the state of American politics leading up to the election of 1800. Indeed, merely to *speculate* on a potential Jeffersonian presidency worried him a great deal. Writing to his friend Joseph Ward in March 1800, Fenno bristled at the prospect of a Republican administration. "Reflection and Experience have convinced me that it will be in vain to look for a moral principle or fidelity to engagements," he wrote, "in the conduct of any Republican govt. whatsoever."[11] In May 1800, months before Jefferson's triumph, he sold the *Gazette of the United States* to Caleb Wayne. Seemingly retired from political life, he opened a bookstore in New York City shortly thereafter.

After arriving in New York, with or without his shoes, Fenno opened in the First Ward a bookshop that he hoped would become a gathering place for the city's Federalists. In an advertisement that appeared in *The New-York Gazette and General Advertiser*, Fenno announced that his new shop stocked "engravings, elegantly printed in colours . . . just received from London." With this advertisement, Fenno tipped his avidly pro-British hat by celebrating a number of prints that commemorated British victories in the Napoleonic and Anglo-Spanish Wars. In particular, Fenno feted Horatio Nelson's victory at the Battle of the Nile, noting that he had in stock four plates, including images of the "blowing up of l'Orient by the fire of the Bellerophon and vanguard" and "Zealous Capt. Hood's" pursuit of "le Genereux, le Guilliaume Tell, la Justice and la Diane." Fenno pointed out that this collection of prints would eventually form a "compendious Naval History of the War."[12] The following January, Fenno appealed yet again to Manhattan's Anglophiles by offering a number of engravings, "among which are Portraits of the most distinguished worthies of Great Britain"—Samuel Johnson, Lord Mansfield, Lord Kenyon, Lord Camden, and Lord Loughborough, among others.[13]

Fenno's choice for a storefront at 141 Broadway presents an interesting case study of competing literary politics. Less than two hundred feet from his new Broadway shop was the bookstore owned by Hoquet Caritat, a French national championed by Paine, promoter of French Enlightenment philosophy, steadfast defender of the French Revolution, and proponent of Thomas Jefferson's administration—all things that would have made Jack Fenno's skin crawl. Caritat's store at 153 Broadway at the City Hotel was a gathering place to read and discuss the latest imported philosophical tome. It is in this location, and due in no small way to the atmosphere of collegiality and intellectual exchange going on between the stacks, that Caritat remade, and expanded, his shop into a circulating library and center of importation and distribution of European texts, especially the writings of the French *philosophes*, the *Encylopédie*, and books celebrating the French Revolution.[14]

Caritat was ostensibly constructing a network devoted to the distribution and discussion of French Enlightenment philosophy and, by extension, Jeffersonian Republicanism. While it may seem highly unusual that a hawkish, petulant High Federalist such as Jack Fenno would establish his own shop down the street, Fenno's decision to do so was most likely a strategic political and business maneuver, for Fenno had a propensity to counter Republican politics in a confrontational way. It is within this context that his wordy book catalog comes into focus. Caritat's bookstore and circulating library catalog, *The Feat of Reason and the Flow of the Soul*, provided for subscribers and consumers alike a detailed, partially annotated list of the books to be found at 153 Broadway; only occasionally did Caritat allow his voice to interject in this carefully constructed text.[15]

John Ward Fenno designed his catalog to mock *The Feat of Reason and the Flow of the Soul*; in doing so, he created a contrast to the books in Caritat's store. In the relatively brief catalog, Fenno annotated twenty-eight entries, inserting his own editorial voice in order to criticize the French Revolution. Whereas Caritat imagined New York intellectuals of all political stripes gathering to discuss his latest imports, Fenno appealed to like-minded conservative Federalists. Fenno's catalog, then, was a highly charged document that effectively transformed his bookshop into a politicized space, insofar as it would have been unlikely for a Jeffersonian, or, at the very least, someone with pro-French sympathies, to be a welcomed customer. For example, Fenno described Napoleon Bonaparte's *Egyptian Correspondence* (1799) as a "very curious and interesting display of Gallic Perfidy" and M. Mercier's *New Picture of Paris* (1800), as offering the finest description of "the present deplorable state of that metropolis." Fenno avidly promoted the *Anti-Jacobin, or Weekly Examiner*, to which he added, "to this work, the finest wits and geniuses of England, regularly contributed," concluding, naturally, that it was "of course, one of the most ingenious productions of the present day." No text in the catalog better reveals Fenno's political sympathies than François-Alexandre-Frédéric la Rochefocauld-Liancourt's *Travels Through the United States* (1799). While he offered *Travels Through the United States* for sale, Fenno derided the very notion of the text: "[T]the amusing delusions of this Sansculotte, double-faced *Duke*, being blended with much curious research, and some ingenious speculation, will be found to possess a degree of interest sufficiently ample to award perusal."[16] Liancourt's travel narrative, in Fenno's telling, was not worthy of legitimate discussion, yet he still encouraged New Yorkers to purchase the book from him, if only out of comic relief.

Jack Fenno's loathing of all things French even reached to authors and texts that would have been considered politically and religiously moderate. In a letter to Asbury Dickins, Fenno noted several books he had recently sent to Philadelphia while also complaining about former mentor William Cobbett. Fenno's dissatisfaction at that time with Cobbett, however, paled in comparison to the contempt he reserved for Stéphanie Félicité du Crest de Saint-Aubin, comtesse de Genlis, author of a popular collection of short comedies for children, whose books he had received from London contacts: "I have never yet seen a number of the Porcupine," he wrote, "& as to the books noted at the time of your mention, I suppose the person by whom I sent them is as fatigued himself with them." The following sentence of the letter took a vicious turn, as Fenno mentioned that he had forwarded several copies of "~~*Theatre of Education*~~ Little Bruyère by that bitch of a whore the *Comptesse de Genlis*."[17] Fenno's remark was not without an embedded narrative, revealing deeply rooted political and gendered animosities. Mme de Genlis, while having been born into old nobility, nonetheless grew up in poverty because her father had lost the family's estate during her early years. An opportunistic marriage to the soon-to-be comte de Genlis allowed entrance to the royal court as *dame d'honneur*. In 1772, her political and social fortunes shifted considerably as a result of a brief affair with the Duc de Chartes, Phillippe Egalité, who appointed her to be *gouverneur* (head tutor) for his sons, including Louis-Phillippe, thus making her the first woman to be responsible for educating royal princes. Tacitly supportive of the French Revolution, she fled France for Switzerland, and later London, after the fall of the Girondins in 1793 at the outset of the Reign of Terror that would claim her husband. She would go on to support herself by way of the pen, writing a number of popular novels and educational tracts, including *The Theatre of Education* (1781) and *Le Petit La Bruyère* (1802).[18] After receiving Mme de Genlis's texts from London, Fenno, it seems, reacted against the very notion that women could earn a living by the pen, as he had done.

3. *A Look Inside Jack Fenno's Bookshop*

Jack Fenno's death, which hit suddenly in 1802 after a bout with yellow fever, was a solemn affair for his family. After gathering the entire Fenno clan at his side, Jack embraced his siblings and encouraged them to not dismay at his passing.[19] After his untimely death at age twenty-four, Jack Fenno's assets, both public and private, had to be tallied for legal purposes. The assets under question consisted not only of the stock in his Broadway bookshop—namely, books in various stages of production and a host of stationery and writing instruments—but also the items in Fenno's home, just upstairs from his store. Both aspects of Fenno's material life as a bookseller and would-be litterateur were accounted for in a fifty-four page inventory composed by Ezra Sargeant (himself a printer in New York, likely brought in by the city's board of assessors as a material expert), John Morgan, and John Rodman. The estate inventory provides for scholars a window into the economic life of a bookshop owner in the early Republic. By categorizing the generic list of books and presenting a variety of assessments, I note in this section of the essay what New Yorkers would have likely encountered on a visit to Fenno's shop in 1802.

Table 1 provides a breakdown of the total stock in John Ward Fenno's store. The fluidity of valuation is a consistent problem in any analysis of Fenno's estate, as Sargeant, Morgan, and Rodman drafted the assessment using both dollars and pounds sterling. This difficulty aside, noticeable immediately is the concentration, both in stock and in valuation of stock, in texts of various stripes: Fenno's store had 9,624 printed items under the broad categories of books, pamphlets, periodicals, and chapbooks. By comparison, Fenno possessed a great number of stationery items, but had very little capital tied up in selling pencils and paper. His primary focus was selling books and, as will be demonstrated below, his shelves were weighted with political texts of interest to the city's Federalists.

While Fenno stocked a wide variety of texts, ranging from the eponymous pocket editions and chapbooks to a variety of reference and educational texts, it is clear that clientele walked into his shop expecting to find literary texts, broadly defined. Table 2 shows the total book stock in Jack Fenno's store at the time of his death in 1802.

Table 1: Total Stock in John Ward Fenno's Bookstore, 1802

	Itemization of Stock		Valuation of Stock	
	(*N*)	(%)	($)	(£)
Books	6,922 (611)	19.5	5,897.37	1,057 13s 03d
Monthly Publications	2,191 (1)	6.1	109.11	--
Pamphlets	343 (18)	0.9	--	39 15s 10d
Pocket Books	168 (17)	0.4	618.12	--
Stationery	883 (1)	2.4	26.06	240 01s 5d
Writing Instruments	24,988 (4)	70.3	--	26 08s 12d
TOTAL	35,495 (652)	99.6	$6,650.66	£1,363.17.11

Note: Numbers in parentheses under "Itemization of Stock" represent the number of titles. *Source*: Estate Inventory of John Ward Fenno, John Ward Fenno Papers, The Library of the New-York Historical Society.

Table 2: Total Book Stock in John Ward Fenno's Store

	Itemization of Stock		Valuation of Stock	
	(*N*)	(%)	(£)	(%)
Belles Lettres	5,021 (399)	70.8 (65.3)	655 04s 05d ($4,052.74)	62.0 (62.2)
Chap Books	760 (--)	10.7 (--)	62 0s 05d	5.8 (--)
Education	149 (39)	2.1 (6.3)	£22 04s 18d ($95.83)	2.0 (1.4)
Professional	294 (112)	4.1 (18.3)	£128 04s 10d ($616.94)	12.1 (9.4)
Reference	126 (27)	1.7 (4.4)	£128 01s 07d ($59.50)	11.8 (0.9)
Religious	572 (34)	8.0 (5.5)	63 15s 06d ($1,072.36)	5.9 (16.4)
Pocket Book	168 (--)	2.3 (--)	($618.12)	(9.4)
TOTAL	7,090 (611)	99.7 (99.8)	£1,060.13.13 ($6,515.49)	99.6 (99.7)

Note: Numbers in parentheses under "Itemization of Stock" represent the number of titles and the percentages of total titles. *Source*: Fenno Estate Inventory, NYHS.

The estate inventory reveals that belle-lettristic texts, aside from a fair number of religious volumes he kept on hand, formed the foundation of his business. Within this broad category, Fenno also stocked a number of periodicals. As shown in Table 3, Fenno had thirty-one titles on hand in 1802. Foremost ideologically were several British publications critical of the French Revolution. Fenno, for instance, had on hand two copies of a two-volume set of the *Anti-Jacobin*; *or, Weekly Examiner*, containing thirty-six issues of the London weekly. Groundbreaking and widely read during its brief existence, *The Anti-Jacobin* has been considered by scholars to be one of the most effective periodicals at combining literature with politics. *The Anti-Jacobin*, according to Kevin Gilmartin, was intended by editors George Canning, John Hookham Frere, George Ellis, and William Gibson to push back against sympathy for France and its revolution. Next to the *Anti-Jacobin* on the shelf, Fenno's patrons would have found seven sets of the *Anti-Jacobin Review and Magazine*. A monthly publication, the *Anti-Jacobin Review*, like the similarly titled *Anti-Jacobin*; *or, Weekly Examiner*, was a concerted attempt by British conservatives to subvert, even promote the persecution of, Gallic radicals and their supporters. In their prospectus, the editors of the *Anti-Jacobin Review* advocated the use of the press to control the "vehicles of JACOBINISM" that had been allowed to spread like a virus. "The press has been too long an engine of destruction," wrote the editors, and it should, in their view, "be rendered a means of preservation, and an instrument of protection." As estimable as they made their aims seem, the editors of the *Anti-Jacobin Review* advocated the shuttering of radical voices, including a push to prosecute Thomas Paine in a criminal trial as a symbolic way to silence "the tongues' of the Jacobins." Likewise, Fenno stocked the *British Critic*, yet another reactionary British journal—and, in this case, a High Church publication—critical of the French Revolution. In addition to periodicals damning the French Revolution, Fenno stocked texts that celebrated British culture. For example, Fenno offered fifteen volumes of *The Annual Register*, a compendium publication produced annually in London that summarized the past year's major developments in politics, economics, and literature.[20]

In addition to a variety of conservative London periodicals, Fenno relied on the London publishers to supply books for his shop. Even though American booksellers became increasingly less reliant on imported books after the Revolutionary War, a number of shopkeepers, Fenno included, continued to import British texts in the early nineteenth century. In fact, Fenno preferred books imported from London to those produced in the United States: American books, in his estimation, were "so damnably high charged as to frighten the poor American bookmonger." Fenno, though, recognized that New York printers would eventually supply his shop because, he concluded, the continued political strife in Europe would threaten international commerce. "The trade of importing must be suspended till the War is Over," he confided to Dickins, referring to the wars of the French Revolution. He confessed that a shipment from London aboard the sloop *Katy* would surely be "the last that will come . . . to so large an amount."[21]

Fenno stockpiled philosophical and political works imported from London that catered to Federalist patrons. Much like the selection of periodicals, as noted in Table 3, 34.8 percent of Fenno's stock of belles lettres consisted of literary texts broadly conceived to be works of political philosophy or contemporary political treatises. Many of the titles were works on political economy, in particular commentary authored by noted Britons. Foremost were the twenty-three copies of *The Works of the Right Honourable Edmund Burke* (1792) and eight copies of *Burke's Tracts: A Letter from the Right Honourable Edmund Burke to a Noble lord, on the Attacks made Upon Him and His Pension, in the House of Lords, by the Duke of Bedford and the Earl of Lauderdale* (1796). Fenno also stocked four copies of *Beauties of the Anti-Jacobin* (1799), a compendium of essays by George Canning, John Hookham Frere, George Ellis, and William Gifford that had originally appeared in *The Anti-Jacobin; or, Weekly Examiner*. Also on the shelves were two copies of John Locke's essays, one copy of Adam Smith's *The Wealth of Nations* (1776) and the collected works of Alexander Pope.[22]

A portion of Fenno's stock originally lined the shelves of William Cobbett's Philadelphia bookstore. Formerly an enlisted man in the British Army, Cobbett found himself in the United States after running afoul of corrupt officers by loudly protesting against the abuse of fellow enlisted men. Cobbett fled to Philadelphia by way of France.

Table 3: Total Book Stock of Belles Lettres in John Ward Fenno's Store, 1802

	Itemization of Stock		Valuation of Stock	
	(*N*)	(%)	(£)	(%)
Advice	19 (5)	0.3 (1.2)	3 18s ($18.50)	0.4 (0.4)
Architecture	50 (12)	0.9 (3.0)	30 11s 14d	4.4 (--)
Biography	81 (30)	1.6 (7.5)	29 08s 08d ($137.25)	4.1 (3.3)
Classics	107 (29)	2.1 (7.2)	17 07s 18d ($291.67)	2.6 (7.1)
Cooking	230 (1)	4.5 (0.2)	7 13s 04d	1.0 (--)
Essays	190 (58)	3.7 (14.5)	126 08s 12d ($281.22)	18.8 (6.9)
Fiction	143 (31)	2.8 (7.7)	26 06s 11d ($163.00)	3.8 (4.0)
Gardening	3 (2)	0.0 (0.5)	2 11s 6d	0.3 (--)
Geography	22 (7)	0.4 (1.7)	1 07s 0d ($123.50)	0.1 (3.0)
History	390 (66)	7.7 (16.5)	141 15s 08d ($581.50)	21.1(14.3)
Music	47 (4)	0.9 (1.2)	4 18s ($56.61)	0.6 (1.3)
Periodicals	294 (31)	5.8 (8.0)	35 08s 11d ($515.74)	5.3 (12.7)
Philosophy	1,748 (19)	34.8 (4.7)	6 11s 02d ($611.74)	0.7 (15.0)
Plays	218 (9)	4.3 (2.2)	42 14s 12d ($92.90)	6.4 (2.2)
Poetry	272 (33)	5.4 (8.2)	94 00s 13d ($195.37)	13.9 (4.8)
Travel	120 (42)	2.3 (10.5)	85 15s 01d ($285.75)	12.7 (7.0)
Misc. Texts	1,087 (20)	21.6 (5.0)	9 14s 01d ($700.99)	1.2 (17.2)
TOTAL	5,021 (399)	99.1 (99.8)	£664.04.06 ($4,052.74)	97.4 (99.2)

Note: Numbers in parentheses under "Itemization of Stock" represent the number of titles and the percentages of total titles. *Source*: Fenno Estate Inventory, NYHS.

While in Philadelphia, however, Cobbett took a different track by assuming the ardently pro-British pen name Peter Porcupine. Cobbett, as "Porcupine," was the author and editor of satirical pamphlets and a newspaper, *Porcupine's Gazette.* Friend to John Ward Fenno's father while he still edited the *Gazette of the United States*, Cobbett, according to historian Jeffrey L. Pasley, "belligerently opposed the Republicans and all their doings" while supporting Great Britain and criticizing the French Revolution. Cobbett was, in Pasley's estimation, "a character assassin and hatemonger sui generis" who engaged in the most outlandish of "journalistic thuggery" against Bache and Republican politicians.[23] Sargeant, Morgan, and Rodman, for reasons not easily understood, wrote up a separate section in the estate inventory that lists texts once possessed by Cobbett. It is not clear whether these texts were marked as having been owned by Cobbett or whether Fenno had physically separated them from other books in his store. The only distinguishable characteristic unique to these texts was that they had been part of a separate entry in Fenno's inventory. Table 4 delineates the total stock Fenno inherited from Cobbett after the Porcupine fled the United States for London. The Cobbett leftovers, whether cordoned in a corner, celebrated in some way by their new owner, or integrated into the general stock, represent a microcosm of Fenno's store and may have been a guiding force for young Fenno as he built up Gotham's premier Federalist and Anglophone bookshop. As with the store writ large, much of the stock handed down by Cobbett was tied up in belles lettres, as well as professional and religious texts. The percentages of Cobbett's texts that ended up in Fenno's store, however, vary between the number of copies and titles. For example, 49.8 percent of Fenno's belle-lettristic titles were originally owned by Cobbett, but the total number of Cobbett copies made up only 24.4 percent of Fenno's overall belle-lettristic stock. A similar disparity results when comparing the number of religious texts: 58.8 percent of the religious titles came from Cobbett, but only 26.3 percent of the total copies.

Like many booksellers in early America, Fenno stocked books in various stages of production. In addition to bound books, he had on hand a variety in boards and in sheets. What is striking in this instance is the number of copies stored in sheets, as is specified in Table 5. Fenno most likely kept so many texts in sheets—in this case 44.6 percent of his overall book stock—due to space constraints in his shop, as books in sheets could be either stacked or rolled and, if sold, sent to one of the local bookbinders for completion.[24]

Breaking down John Ward Fenno's estate inventory provides an avenue for understanding the ways in which a bookseller operated a

Table 4: Total Book Stock left over from William Cobbett, 1802

	Itemization of Stock		Valuation of Stock	
	(*N*)	(%)	($)	(%)
Belles Lettres	1,227 (199)	73.1 (62.5)	$2,669.14	63.0
Education	98 (24)	5.8 (7.5)	$92.33	2.1
Professional	188 (67)	11.2 (21.0)	$641.69	15.1
Reference	14 (8)	0.8 (2.5)	$52.25	1.2
Religious	151 (20)	8.9 (6.2)	$780.73	18.4
TOTALS	1,678 (318)	99.8 (99.7)	$4,236.14	99.8

Source: Fenno Estate Inventory, NYHS. Numbers in parentheses under "Itemization of Stock" represent the number of titles and the percentages of total titles.

Table 5: Book Stock in John Ward Fenno's Bookstore, in Boards and in Sheets, 1802

	In Boards			In Sheets		
	Itemization		Valuation	Itemization		Valuation
	(*N*)	(%)	(£)	(*N*)	(%)	($)
Belles Lettres	107 (34)	2.1	171 17s 10d	2,740 (6)	54.5	1,105.00
Education	3 (2)	2.0	2 05s 08d	--	--	--
Professional	20 (9)	6.8	36 04s	--	--	--
Reference	19 (7)	15.0	57 18d	--	--	--
Religious	25 (2)	4.3	51 04s	350 (2)	61.1	220.00
TOTALS	174 (54)	2.5	318 10s 17d	3,090 (8)	44.6	1,325.00

Source: Fenno Estate Inventory, NYHS. Numbers in parentheses under "Itemization of Stock" represent the number of individual titles. Percentages listed in this table are the percentage of each category based on total book stock per category listed in Table 2.

retail shop in the early Republic. While the political makeup of Fenno's shop was made clear in the catalog he published soon after arriving in New York, the assessment composed after his death reveals the lengths he went to make his store an important access point for like-minded conservative Anglophones. Indeed, it is likely that the city's Federalists flocked to Fenno's shop to meet with the former editor of the *Gazette of the United States* and to discuss his latest London imports after reading the catalog and hearing about his arrival in newspapers, taverns, coffee shops, and street corners.

4. Asbury Dickins, John Ward Fenno, and the Federalist Literary Marketplace

At the time of his death in 1802, Jack Fenno had a number of retail shopkeepers on commission scattered throughout the early United States. While the account books that would have provided a better understanding of Fenno's interstate literary network do not exist, Sargeant, Morgan, and Rodman, at some point during their assessment, sat down at his desk, opened his ledgers, and tallied all of his unsettled local, regional, and national accounts. Their efforts to generalize Fenno's print network is summarized in Table 6. The assessors did not include in their assessment the total number of transactions between Fenno and his retail agents or the number of titles or copies Fenno sent to each bookseller. Rather, the men most likely copied the transaction histories from the ledgers, noting only the dollar amount for the outstanding balance due. Overall, they noted sixty-five accounts labeled as "Books on Commission," "Unsettled," "In Dispute," and "Failed." Of this total, I have been able to identify thirty-five, either by the inventory itself or through cross-references in newspaper advertisements. Aside from the twelve New York booksellers on account with Fenno, and the six in Philadelphia, 51.3 percent of Fenno's commission accounts were in locations beyond the mid-Atlantic. Fenno had one agent—John Neilson—in Providence on the hook for $17.25 and another–Anthony Henry in Halifax, Nova Scota–who still possessed books totaling $79.25. Fenno had two additional accounts outside of the United States, an "unsettled" affair with a "Capt. Williamson" of Geneva, Switzerland, for $2.00, and $316.21 still owed him by his friend and mentor, William Cobbett, who had returned to England in 1800. Many of Jack Fenno's unsettled commission accounts, however, lay in the South. In total, Fenno had thirteen southern booksellers on commission in five towns and cities, totaling more than $330.00—or 11.5 percent of the overall amount in question. As pointed out in

Table 6: Unsettled Accounts by Region, 180

Region, City, State	Accounts		Stock Received	
	(*N*)	(%)	($)	(%)
Mid-Atlantic				
New York, NY	12	34.2	307.08	10.6
Philadelphia, PA	6	17.2	1,817.00	63.2
TOTAL	17	51.4	2,124.08	73.8
New England				
Providence, RI	1	2.8	17.25	0.6
TOTAL	1	2.8	17.25	0.6
International				
Geneva, Switzerland	1	2.8	2.00	0.0
Halifax, Nova Scotia, Canada	1	2.8	79.25	2.7
London, England	1	2.8	316.21	11.0
TOTAL	3	8.5	397.46	13.8
South				
Alexandria, VA	3	8.5	38.50	1.3
Baltimore, MD	5	14.2	139.25	4.8
Charleston, SC	2	5.7	87.50	3.0
Norfolk, VA	2	5.7	60.75	2.1
Washington, DC	1	2.8	9.32	0.3
TOTAL	14	36.9	335.32	11.5
OVERALL TOTAL	35	99.6	2,874.11	99.7

Source: Fenno Estate Inventory, NYHS.

Table 6, $139.25 of stock was shipped by Fenno to Baltimore, and a considerable portion of that stock was tied up in the firm of Campbell, Conrad & Co. Additionally, Fenno had an unsettled account of $37.50 with Ryan St. John, as well as smaller amounts owed him by Robert Walsh, William Taylor, and Samuel Cole. Of his South Carolina accounts, William P. Young still owed $55.00 while Nathaniel Fitz was in debt to Fenno for the amount of $32.50. Last, of the Virginia accounts, B. Pollard & Co. of Alexandria possessed $58.75 worth of Fenno's stock.[25]

Not surprisingly, a considerable amount of Fenno's fledgling print network was tied up with Philadelphia booksellers. In total, six booksellers held 63.2 percent of the debts still owed Fenno at the time of his death. Of this portion, $1,719.50 was held by two booksellers: Asbury Dickins and John Conrad. As the patriarch of an interstate publishing family, Conrad had outposts in Baltimore, Petersburg, and Norfolk. As historian Rosalind Remer notes, the Conrad family built a sizeable publishing business in the early years of the nineteenth century, becoming a leading distributor of schoolbooks, literature, and a "wide array of miscellaneous imprints." The Conrad's success was not immune to the ebbs and flows of the market, however, as they succumbed to a "spectacular bankruptcy" in 1813.[26]

Asbury Dickins traveled, or at least aspired to do so, in the same circles as influential early republic litterateurs. By age twenty-one, Dickins's Second Street bookshop had become, according to the English traveler John Davis, a "rendezvous" for a great many of Philadelphia's "sons of literature." The oldest lad of the Methodist clergyman John Dickins, Asbury—named after the Methodist itinerant and bishop Francis Asbury—eschewed the path preferred by his father, choosing instead a life among men "of Affluence, Men of Liberality, and Men of Letters." Dickins was, however, according to historian Peter J. Parker, little more than a "snob, a social climber, and a Federalist toady."[27] Snobbery and ambition aside, Dickins was an important conspirator in John Ward Fenno's literary and political designs. While established in New York, Fenno used his Philadelphia connections—Dickins in particular—to develop a national distribution network, thereby connecting conservative consumers to a transatlantic British literary culture.

Dickins and Fenno had a complicated financial relationship independent of their literary scheming. Fenno got himself into dire straits while helping his friend and mentor William Cobbett. Still reeling from the guilty verdict rendered against him in the libel suit brought by Benjamin Rush, Cobbett decided to extricate himself from the American political scene and take his chances in London. Short on funds, Cobbett called on his old friend Jack Fenno, who in turn hit up Asbury Dickins for cash, to help cover his legal fees and relocation costs. Dissatisfied with the level of support Dickins offered,

Fenno panicked and obtained a loan from the Manhattan Company. This was apparently an uncomfortable arrangement for Fenno. "At present I cannot stir," he wrote to Dickins, "for my note is in the Manhattan Bank—they are all Jacobins, & I can have no reliance for a renewal—1381 dolls. in amount."[28] Dickins, however, ignored Fenno's repeated requests to assist their friend.

Fenno and Dickins were invested in the literary career of Joseph Dennie. Dickins worked with Dennie to publish *The Port Folio*—an influential Federalist literary magazine that created, according to historian Catherine O'Donnell Kaplan, a "profoundly oppositional community" in opposition to Jeffersonian Republicanism—while Fenno served as a vital cog in the distribution network. Fenno was confident that he, Dennie, and Dickins would have great success extending the ligaments of Federalism. He declared to Dickins that "whenever Mr. D. sees fit to come forward in seriousness & commence with his publications," he would make "exertions to promote the success of his book." Dennie was one of a handful of men worth his time and resources insofar as he would commit to aiding in the publication and distribution of the magazine. On this note, Fenno reasoned: "I do not choose to commit myself upon the abortive projects of other men." Despite Dennie's talent, Fenno had grown weary of his apparent lack of initiative. Writing to Dickins in August 1800, Fenno complained that Dennie "ought, by this time, to be half through the Press," and given the uninspiring pace, he doubted "whether he has a page ready for the Press."[29]

Prospects for the Federalist literary network seemed high after Dennie and Dickins established *The Port Folio* in 1801. Responding to Dickins's query about how best to construct a feasible system by which to circulate *The Port Folio*, Fenno suggested to Dickins that he contact a number of reliable Federalist booksellers who would take on the journal. "The subject which you suggest to my consideration will prove one of the most delicate points in the construct of your establishment," Fenno wrote to Dickins in February 1801.

> I tell you from experience that you cannot be too cautious in appointing your agents. I would recommend to you Geo. Hill at Baltimore, and Augustine Davis of Richmond, to whom you are welcome to use my name. I think 2.5 per cent an adequate compensation for collecting

> $5 each from 20 people - tho I think it likely that you may have to give 5. When I printed the Gaz. I made particular agreements on the best terms I could, without any particular standard. I would have you to look well to a man's ability as well as honesty, and select men either rich or in good business: I lost more by the poverty of agents than by dishonesty. Indeed, I do not see what need you have of a great number of agents. The two whom I have mentioned, with White at Boston, appear to me adequate to every purpose. If you extend your views to the Southern air, W.P. Young at Charleston is a proper man.[30]

Dickins evidently took Fenno's guidance seriously. Soon thereafter, he wrote to George Hill—a rotund Baltimore bookseller whom Fenno once referred to as "that hog of a fellow"—with the proposition of establishing a commission account to distribute *The Port Folio* in the Chesapeake Bay region. While little correspondence or accounts exist among Hill, Dickins, and Fenno, two surviving letters indicate that Dickins's attempt to extend Fenno's network into the Chesapeake Bay was halfhearted at best. Writing in June 1801, Hill requested to have $200 assigned to his credit. Perhaps wanting to stroke Dickins's ego, Hill praised the books Dickins had sent him: "When I get a little more leisure I will tell you the success of your Goods sent me on commission and perhaps slip you a few more dollars." Less than a month after this letter, however, Hill chastised Dickins for his failure to respond: "I wrote yours of the 18th inst . . . begging you to acknowledge receipt of the money," Hill argued. "Why this is not done in course I know not," he contined, insisting, "when I send you cash again I will take care to guard against such disappointment."[31]

Fenno seemed particularly concerned with Dickins's inability to get *The Port Folio* out to subscribers—himself included—in a timely manner. While acknowledging in January 1801 the potential success of the paper by assuring Dickins he had few doubts that "a very handsome subscription will be had" in New York for the magazine, he pressed the issue of reliability. "Care must be taken, however, to forward the numbers with more punctuality," he wrote; "tho published Saturday, they never reach us until Thursday. You should see to this." Fenno's constant criticism of *The Port Folio*'s distribution in his letters to Dickins would remain a constant obsession. "For God's sake send on your papers earlier," Fenno begged a month later, pointing out that, "instead of coming on Monday, they never reach us 'till Wednesday, & others not till Thursday." Fenno insisted that the slow pace of production and distribution should have been corrected, as it seemed, to him at least, to be a short-term problem. "While your establishment was new men overlooked inequalities," he pointed out, "but believe me," he continued, "the continuance of those inequalities . . . will materially affect the interests of the concern." By the end of February, Fenno was still hot about not receiving his copies, even though he simultaneously bragged of his prowess at securing subscriptions for the journal in New York. "The papers still come on very irregularly," he noted. "We are now at Thursday, without the paper on Saturday last, tho' I suspect the mail of this day to bring it." Fenno's concerns spilled into July, as he wrote about an Albany subscriber who had paid him five dollars for *The Port Folio,* which, incidentally, he "never received." And yet despite this frustration, this particular subscriber paid Fenno again, requesting a full run of the magazine "from 1st no." The problems continued into August, as subscribers began complaining not only to Fenno but also to men working for the Post Office. "No Port Folio this week," he wrote, demonstrating palpable annoyance. "The fellows in the Post Office here (not the best natured persons in the world) swear & fret not a little at being men they are by enquiries, from the subscribers." Nevertheless these hiccups in production and distribution were temporary. *The Port Folio*'s surviving account books—not to mention its longevity on Dennie's watch, long after Fenno and Dickins were no longer part of the concern—show that subscriptions spanned the entire early American landscape from New England to the South and into Kentucky.[32]

In addition to stocking and distributing Dennie's *Port Folio*, Fenno's store, as noted above, was an important clearinghouse for political newspapers, books, pamphlets, and periodicals.[33] In October 1800, Asbury Dickins received "by the Sloop *Patience*" twelve copies of the *British Critic*, six of the *Anti-Jacobin*, six of the *Gentleman's Magazine*, and six volumes each of the first through the fifth run of the *Anti-Jacobin Review.* The periodicals Fenno sent to Dickins, similar to the books that lined his shelves, were London imports; unsurprisingly, prices were almost prohibitively high even for the cheapest of shopkeepers due to the rising tensions in Europe. Fenno writes, "You will observe that the bound vols. are charged 25 cents higher than we have been in the habit of selling them," as the price in England has "been raised . . . 6 pence a number, in consequence of the advance of the price of paper." In this letter, Fenno asked Dickins, in a condescending tone, to tie up some loose ends for him in Philadelphia. In so doing, Fenno knew full well that it would bring more walk-in business to Dickins's shop—stocked with books Fenno had sent him—and, potentially, additional subscribers for Fenno's conservative distribution network. "I send you a number of the above works for persons who subscribed to me in Philadelphia," Fenno wrote, adding that he would make "no apology for putting you to the trouble of delivering these, as I know you will do it with cheerfulness, and I hope besides, that it may be of advantage to you, by bringing customers for other articles in your shop." Further, this particular shipment reveals the way in which Fenno dealt with his retail agents insofar as he considered Dickins, and others like him, to be public representatives of his business. He instructed Dickins to make a public pronouncement of his status as a retail agent clerking in Fenno's network. "Please have this note published in Wayne's paper" (referring to the *Gazette of the United States*): "J.W. Fenno acquaints those Gentleman who subscribed through him for the British Periodicals works; and those who sent out orders for miscellaneous books, either thro' him or Wm. Cobbett, that Mr. Dickins will deliver their Books, at his store in Second Street, opposite Christ Church."[34]

Despite Fenno's continued support, which bordered on obsession, Dickins began to contemplate an escape due to mounting debt he had incurred. Once Dickins had unfolded and read a hastily composed July 1801 note from Fenno that begged him to forward two volumes of the *Index to the Annual Register* "as soon as this gets to hand," Dickins imagined his flight from Philadelphia. On the reverse of the paper, on either side of his Second Street address, Dickins scribbled the word "London" ten times in two sloppy columns, with one halfhearted "Lond" falling below his panicked scrawl on the right-hand side. It was not long after this July 1801 letter that Dickins's tortured fantasy would become reality and he would flee his creditors, many of whom were part of Fenno's network. On 26 October 1801, he received a letter from C. W. Hare: "It is with pain," the letter opened, "that I find myself in some measure compelled to send you the enclosed Notice":

Samuel Blodget v. Asbury Dickins	}	Supreme Court Pennsylvania December Term, 1801 Action on the Case

> You will please take notice that unless you enter special bail in the above case in the sum of fifteen thousand dollars on or before Wednesday next at twelve o'clock at noon at the office of Edward Burd, Esq in Fourth Street near Walnut capias ad respondendum will be issued against you at the suit of the above mentioned Samuel Blodget.

Dickins did not stick around to go through with the legal proceedings. The day after receiving the summons, Dickins granted power of attorney of his estate to Thomas W. Armat; Joseph Dennie gave witness to the transfer. Hours later, Dickins traversed the Delaware River to New Castle, a small town just south of Wilmington, where he hopped a ship to Liverpool. Much like Fenno's abrupt departure from Philadelphia two years earlier, the move was so sudden that Dickins's attorney was put in the awkward position of shipping clothes and providing his client with cash. According to Armat's records, he sent along "To Cloaths at Newcastle—50," in addition to "Pocket 20 Guineas - $93.33."[35]

And just like that, before Fenno and Dickins could fully develop a Federalist literary network in a Republican nation, Asbury was gone, leaving his friend and patron high and dry. Obviously furious, Fenno began the difficult task of reclaiming books, stationery, and periodicals sent to Dickins while simultaneously trying to recoup cash owed him on the commission account. Both Fenno and John Rodman drew up detailed debt sheets that ended up in Armat's hands. "You have on the other side a general statement of my a/c against A. Dickins," he wrote to Rodman in January 1802, though he admitted that, "without documents that could be furnished only by Dickins himself," he was thus unable to "come at any thing like the true Balance." The total

Table 7: Asbury Dickins's Outstanding Debts due John Ward Fenno, 24 May 1802

Dr.	Amount ($)	Cr.	Amount ($)
To Cash at Sundry Times to 13 May 1801	520.75	By Cash Received & Sundries at different times	1,507.25
To Sundry American Publications	651.25	By Sundry Books	1,341.90
To Sundry Books Purchased	1,139.58	By Proceeds of Sundry Books sold on Commission	160.20
To Sundry Prints on Commission, at cost, without charges	318.95	By Cash	1,000.00
To Sundry Books Sent to Mr. Dickins for Sale on Commission	2,756.26		
TOTAL	$5,386.79 -4,008.85		$4,008.85
AMOUNT STILL OWED JW FENNO	$1,377.94		

Source: Assessment drawn by John Rodman, 24 May 1802, Loudoun Papers, Box 27, HSP.

debt owed by Dickins was $1,303.32. After Fenno's death, Rodman drew up yet another assessment. This document does not paint a flattering portrait of Asbury Dickins as an upstanding retail agent. The debt sheet—reproduced in Table 7—indicates that Fenno provided Dickins with at least $3,075.21 worth of books and prints—the latter, apparently, at cost—during the course of their business arrangement. And while Dickins seems to have returned a portion of the unsold stock to the tune of $1,341.90 worth of "sundry books," Fenno received only $160.20 from Dickins for books actually sold on commission, hardly a profitable return given the size of the overall investment. All told, even after Fenno's death, Dickins was still in considerable debt to his friend and patron.[36]

The debt owed by Dickins concluded a year in which Fenno continually asked Dickins to draw up a statement of profits so that Fenno could tend to his accounts. "Business is deplorably dull, with everybody," Fenno complained to Dickins in March 1801. He noted that he was "in daily expectation of two vessels with books & c. for me" and expressed great concern that "one of them is reported to be carried into France." Fenno, though, voiced his greatest dissatisfaction with Dickins's inability to keep an accurate account: "I wish you would make out a statement of your sales on the Comm. a/c as I want to close several affairs, particularly with Mr. Boucher, for the sale of his books." Dickins eventually disputed Fenno's estimation of the debt still owed. Writing from London while in self-imposed exile, Dickins pleaded his innocence with his attorney: "I owe Pratt 1500 dollars, which I am to repay whenever it be convenient," but "Fenno," he wrote, "must be mistaken; it is impossible he should be accurate in his statement." Armat, however, indicated to Dickins that his fortunes in Philadelphia were indeed bleak:

> Have only one moment to say that your note to John Vaughn is this day protested for non payment & that he has intimated a determination to send it to London to collect of you there. The Demands upon you are to the amount of ten thousand Dollars . . . Fenno has taken away the books he sent you on Commission & says there is still 1700 Dollars due . . . your Books throw no light on it there being but 4 Entries & ascertained what is due on the Port Folio – if Ten Thousand Dollars are due the Property will not more than Pay it – if that. In the Interim, You are not safe from Wynne & Schoey . . . I know not what you have left for it but flight.[37]

5. *Conclusions*

John Ward Fenno's attempt to create a national distribution network, consisting of Federalist booksellers dotting the early American landscape and hawking his hawkish books and periodicals, was, ultimately, a failure. His grand scheme was cut short by his untimely death and, to a lesser extent, by the incompetence of his Philadelphia partner, Asbury Dickins, who shirked not only Fenno but numerous other business partners and spent the remainder of his days in debtors' prison. Fenno left dozens of commission accounts in limbo, the fragmentary remains of what he likely thought of as a counterpoint to the network of Republican newspapers that catapulted Jefferson to the presidency in 1800.[38] There was urgency in Fenno's endeavor to publicize and distribute texts that supported his ideas and, subsequently, the cause of Federalists in early America, yet this urgency was hardly realized.

NOTES

The author would like to thank Jeff Pasley, Michelle Morris, Marly Ramsour, Matt Sivils, Jeff Walker, and the anonymous readers for *LEAR* for their helpful comments and suggestions during the writing of this essay. An earlier version of this essay was presented at the 2013 Business History Conference, and the author would like to thank Joe Adelman and Sharon Murphy for their comments and questions. The author would also like to acknowledge the many institutions who supplied generous grants to fund the research: a PEAES Fellowship from the Library Company of Philadelphia, a Gilder Lehrman Fellowship, a Short-Term Fellowship from the New York Public Library, a Reese Fellowship from the American Antiquarian Society, the New York State Library's Cunningham Research Residency, and a Mellon Dissertation Fellowship from the McNeil Center for Early American Studies.

1. *Gazette of the United States*, 21 December 1798.

2. For a discussion of the development of the Republican newspaper network and its contribution to the development of party politics in the new nation, see Pasley, "Two National 'Gazettes,'"; and "*The Tyranny of Printers*," chap. 1.

3. *Aurora, and General Advertiser*, 7 August 1798. For a narrative of this strange affair, see Tagg, *Bache and the Philadelphia Aurora*, 349–51. For more on Bache and the Fennos, see Nerone, *Violence against the Press*; J. A. Smith, *Franklin and Bache*; and Stewart, *The Opposition Press*.

4. *Gazette of the United States*, 8 August 1798. For a discussion of the overtly masculine politics of honor, see Ellis, *Founding Brothers*, chap. 1; Freeman, "Reinterpreting the Burr-Hamilton Duel"; Freeman, *Affairs of Honor*; Freeman, "The Burr-Hamilton Duel"; Greenberg, *Honor and Slavery*; and Rorabaugh, "The Political Duel in the Early Republic".

5. *Aurora, and General Advertiser*, 9 August 1798.

6. *Gazette of the United States*, 9 August 1798. A former indentured servant, John Beckley, according to Pasley, became one of the early Republic's first professional political campaigners, working for Thomas Jefferson's presidential campaign in 1796. He was rewarded for his hard work in 1802 when Jefferson appointed him as the librarian to Congress. See Pasley, "'A Journeyman, Either in Law or Politics.'" See also Marsh, "John Beckley," 54–59; and Cunningham, "John Beckley."

7. For the best biographical treatment of John Ward Fenno, see Hench, "Letters of John Fenno and John Ward Fenno, 1779–1800," 299–368; and Remer, *Printers and Men of Capital*, 36.

8. For a discussion of the New York print marketplace in the early republic, see Steven Carl Smith, "A World the Printers Made," esp. chaps. 1 and 2.

9. For the unambiguous critique of recent Founder-centric studies, see Waldstreicher, "Founders Chic as Culture War." For new approaches to the study of political history in the early republic, see Pasley, Robertson, and Waldstreicher, *Beyond the Founders*. For a reevaluation of the Federalists, see Ben-Atar and Oberg, *Federalists Reconsidered*. For older, yet still-relevant, studies of the Federalists, see Banner, *To the Hartford Convention*; Fischer, *The Revolution of American Conservatism*. For important works of synthesis, see Elkins and McKitrick, *The Age of Federalism*; Wood, *The Creation of the American Republic*; and Wood, *The Radicalism of the American Revolution*.

Lampi, "The Federalist Party Resurgence,"; Wilentz, *Rise of American Democracy*, 114, 165. Lampi writes that Federalists, after Jefferson's election, "are still often assumed to have been old-fashioned gentlemen, beholden to deference and hierarchy, and unable to compete or attract popular support in an increasingly democratic political environment. It is undeniable, of course, that the Federalists never again won the presidency. Yet by focusing on the presidency, the more complicated story of the Federalists' continuing vitality—and their ability to remain competitive in places for at least two decades after Jefferson's election—has been minimized or overlooked." Lampi also points to recent work on political culture and that states despite focusing on "the full range and robustness of Federalist ideas, rhetoric, and political understanding," scholars have "failed to displace the traditional narrative that insists on the inevitability of Federalists' electoral decline" (255–56). See Kerber, *Federalists in Dissent*; Waldstreicher, *In the Midst of Perpetual Fetes*; and Grasso, *A Speaking Aristocracy*. For an excellent story on Lampi's life and research, see Mangu-Ward, "The Orphan Scholar."

Dowling, *Literary Federalism*; Kaplan, *Men of Letters in the Early Republic*; Waterman, *Republic of Intellect*. For work on Charles Brockden Brown, see Barnard, Kamrath, and Shapiro, *Revising Charles Brockden Brown*; Waterman, "The Bavarian Illuminati, the Early American Novel, and Histories of the Public Sphere"; Waterman, "Charles Brockden Brown"; and Watts, *The Romance of Real Life*. For works important to understanding literary Federalism and its opposition to Jeffersonian Democracy in the context of the party politics of the 1790s, see Kerber, *Federalists in Dissent*.

10. Steven Carl Smith, "'Elements of Useful Knowledge'"; S. C. Smith, "A World the Printers Made," chap. 5. For a discussion of the transatlantic literary culture in early America, see especially Kelley, "'While Pen, Ink & Paper Can Be Had.'" See also Radway, "Interpretive Communities and Variable Literacies."

11. John Ward Fenno to Asbury Dickins, 25 July 1800, Loudoun Papers, 1696–1939, Collection 1971, Box 27, Historical Society of Pennsylvania, Philadelphia, PA (hereafter HSP); Fenno to Dickins, 7 August 1800, Loudoun Papers, Box 27, HSP; for a discussion of the libel cases facing John Ward Fenno, see Hench, "Letters of John Fenno and John Ward Fenno," 303; Fenno to Joseph Ward, 30 March 1800, cited in Hench, "Letters of John Fenno and John Ward Fenno," 233.

12. *The New-York Gazette and General Advertiser*, 4 October 1800.

13. *The Daily Advertiser*, 1 January 1801.

14. The physical and economic space Fenno inhabited in New York was crawling with members of the trade, so much so that Fenno relocated from his first shop, situated at Hanover Square, to Broadway soon after settling. For Fenno's first

appearance in New York, see *The New-York Gazette and General Advertiser*, 4 October 1800. Because relocation for men in the publishing trade was no small job, and even moving around the corner in the commercial city was an involved affair, it seems likely that Fenno was squeezed out of Hanover Square for any number of reasons, ranging from economic competition from his neighbors on Pearl and Water Streets to personal and political rivalries. As I point out elsewhere, the year Fenno relocated to New York from Philadelphia, he would have encountered dozens of printers, booksellers, and bookbinders in the city, many of which resided in or near Hanover Square. See Smith, "A World the Printers Made," chap. 1. For discussion of Caritat, see especially Raddin, *Hocquet Caritat and the Early New York Literary Scene*.

15. See Caritat, *The Feast of Reason and the Flow of the Soul*.

16. Fenno, *Supplementary Catalogue, Consisting of Books, Imported from London, Per the Latest Arrivals*, 11–12, 23–24; 7; 20.

17. Fenno to Dickins, 21 February 1801, Loudon papers, Box 27, HSP.

18. For a brief biographical treatment of Madame de Genlis, see Shapiro, *French Women Poets*, 476–77. See also Schaneman, "Rewriting 'Adèle Et Théodore'"; Schroder, "Going Public against the Academy"; Trouille, "Toward a New Appreciation of Mme De Genlis"; Wahba, "Madame De Genlis in England"; and Walker, "Producing Feminine Virtue."

19. Maria Fenno's letters are in the Gratz Family Collection, Manuscript Collection No. 72, American Philosophical Society Philadelphia, PA.

20. Gilmartin, *Writing Against Revolution*, 119–21. See also Gilmartin, *Print Politics*. For the broader world of British literary and political print culture, see especially Barker, *Newspapers, Politics and English Society*; Harris, *Politics and the Rise of the Press*; Raymond, *News, Newspapers, and Society*; Raymond, *Pamphlets and Pamphleteering*; Thompson, *The Making of the English Working Class*; and Thompson, *Customs in Common*.

Anti-Jacobin Review, 1 (1798), 2; Gilmartin, *Writing Against Revolution*, 110, 98, 99, 105, 137, 141, 151, 171, 221.

The periodicals noted above are listed in the Estate Inventory of John Ward Fenno, John Ward Fenno Papers, NYHS.

21. For an overview of this transformation, see Green, "Rise of Book Publishing." For a general overview, see Gross's introduction ("An Extensive Republic") to the second volume of the *History of the Book in America* series. For an excellent discussion of the early book trade, see Davidson, *Revolution and the Word*, especially chapter 1. For the changes that affected print laborers, see Pretzer, "'Of the paper cap and inky aptron'"; and Rorabaugh, *The Craft Apprentice*, especially chapter 4. For an example of New York booksellers who remained in contact with the London book trade, see Joseph Johnson Letterbook, The Carl H. Pforzheimer Collection of Shelley and His Circle, A-RD 09, New York Public Library: Astor, Lenox and Tilden Foundations. For letter citations, see Fenno to Dickins, 15 June 1801, Loudoun Papers, Box 27, HSP.

22. Estate Inventory of John Ward Fenno, John Ward Fenno Papers, NYHS.

23. See Pasley, "'*The Tyranny of Printers*,'" 100, 101–3. For more on Cobbett's American career, see Daniel, "'Ribaldry and Billingsgate,'"and List, "The Role of Cobbett ."

24. Publishers would often store their texts either in rolls or flat, "in sheets," after they were received from the printer due to the spatial restraints of the shop. Only when ready to be bound did the publisher then send it to the local bindery for completion. Later on in the nineteenth century, as Michael Winship points out, larger publishers began warehousing excess stock at the bindery. The practice of warehousing unbound sheets at the bindery meant that publishers neither tied up capital in the cost of binding copies of a work for which there was no demand, nor risked loss on damage or wear to books stored in bound form. It was also an efficient way to manage printed sheets, since under normal circumstances, a single binder continued to bind each subsequent printing of a work using the final sheets from one printing to those of a new printing. If an accident or loss occurred at the bindery, this system made it easier and cheaper to make good on the damage by reprinting just those sheets that had been spoiled or that were short. See Winship, *American Literary Publishing*, 131.

25. For a discussion of commission accounts, see Remer, *Printers and Men of Capital*, 82; Estate Inventory of John Ward Fenno, John Ward Fenno Papers, NYHS.

26. See Remer, *Printers and Men of Capital*, 70–71. For a sampling of the texts published and distributed by the Conrad family, see *The Constitutions of the United States, According to the Latest Amendments to Which Are Prefixed, the Declaration of Independence; and the Federal Constitution, with the Amendments* (Philadelphia: Printed for Robert Campbell, no. 30, Chesnut-Street., 1800). A bookseller's catalog of John Conrad and Co., Philadelphia; M. and J. Conrad and Co., Baltimore; and Rapin, Conrad and Co., Washington, DC, is included at the end of the catalog.

27. Davis, *Travels*, 129; Fenno to Joseph Dennie, 17 January 1800, Meredith Papers, *Port Folio* Section, Historical Society of Pennsylvania, Philadelphia, PA; for Francis Asbury, see Wigger, *American Saint*; Parker, "Asbury Dickins," 465.

28. Fenno to Dickins, 19 October 1801, Loudoun Papers, Box 27, HSP.

29. Kaplan, *Men of Letters*, 141; See also Dowling, *Literary Federalism*; Fenno to Dickins, 13 August 1800, Loudoun Papers, 1696–1800, Box 27, HSP.

30. Fenno to Dickins, 21 February 1801, Loudoun Papers, Box 27, HSP.

31. Fenno to Dickins, 25 July 1800, Loudoun Papers, Box 27, HSP. For Hill's career as a bookseller, see a variety of advertisements in Baltimore newspapers; for example, the *Federal Gazette and Baltimore Daily Advertiser* noted that the "Clerical Candidates, a Poem," was available for sale at the "Bookstores of George Hill, Andrews & Butler, and Warner & Hanna"; *Federal Gazette and Baltimore Daily Advertiser*, 19 November 1801.

George Hill to Dickins, 18 June 1801, Loudoun Papers, Box 27, HSP; Hill to Dickins, 1 July 1801, Loudoun Papers, Box 27, HSP.

32. Fenno to Dickins, 23 January 1801, Loudoun Papers, Box 27, HSP; Fenno to Dickins, 10 February 1801, Loudoun Papers, Box 27, HSP; ibid. Fenno to Dickins, 19 February 1801, Loudoun Papers, Box 27, HSP; Fenno to Dickins, 20 July 1801, Loudoun Papers, Box 27, HSP;

Fenno to Dickins, 21 August 1801, Loudoun Papers, Box 27, HSP. See Kaplan, *Men of Letters*.

33. For recent work on periodicals and political culture in the early republic, see Haberman, "Magazines, Presentation Networks, and the Cultivation of Authorship," and Haberman, "Provincial Nationalism."

34. Fenno to Dickins, 13 October 1800, Loudoun Papers, Box 27, HSP. Ever the faithful protégé, Dickins went straightaway to the office of the *Gazette of the United States* to place the advertisement. It appeared on 25 October 1800, and seems to have not been a multiple run. See *Gazette of the United States*, 25 October 1800.

35. Fenno to Dickins, 15 July 1801, Loudoun Papers, Box 27, HSP; C. W. Hare to Dickins, 26 October 1801, Notice of Summons, Loudoun Papers, Box 27, HSP. For work on debt in early America, see Mann, *Republic of Debtors*. LeCarner's forthcoming dissertation, "The 'F' Word," examines the intersection of debt and literature in order to parse out the origins of financial "forgiveness"; LeCarner's work promises to be a tremendous new contribution.

Copy, dated 3 December 1803, of General Power of Attorney Executed by Asbury Dickins in Favor of Thomas W. Armat, 27 October 1801, Loudoun Papers, Box 27, HSP; Parker, "Asbury Dickins," 481; List of Debts and Assets, undated, endorsed "Dickins Estate," Loudoun Papers, Box 27, HSP.

36. John Ward Fenno to John Rodman, 8 January 1802, Loudon Papers, Box 27, HSP; Mr. Asbury Dickins in Account with the Estate of John Ward Fenno, as drawn up by John Rodman, 24 May 1802, Loudon Papers, Box 27, HSP.

37. Fenno to Dickins, 16 March 1801, Loudoun Papers, Box 27, HSP; Asbury Dickins to Thomas Armat, 22 February 1802, Loudoun Papers, Box 27, HSP; Thomas W. Armat to Asbury Dickins, no date, Loudoun Papers, Box 27, HSP. Armat was not exaggerating all that much in this particular letter, as Dickins left behind considerable debts and stock that would remain untouched until an estate sale in July 1805. According to the official list of debts and inventory that Armat drew up, Dickins had $6,420.17 in debt while his shop had more than 3,000 unsold volumes in 348 titles, of which 1,436 were bound and 1,600 were in sheets, in addition to a considerable inventory of stationery and blank books. See Agreement for Purchase between David Hogan and Thomas W. Armat, 25 July 1805, Loudoun Papers, Box 27, HSP.

38. See Parker, "Asbury Dickins," 482–483; see Pasley, *"The Tyranny of Printers,"* esp. chaps. 5–7; Pasley, "1800 as a Revolution."

BIBLIOGRAPHY

Banner, James M. *To the Hartford Convention: The Federalists and the Origins of Party Politics in Massachusetts, 1789–1815*. New York: Knopf, 1970.

Barker, Hannah. *Newspapers, Politics and English Society, 1695–1855*. New York: Longman, 2000.

Barnard, Philip, Mark Kamrath, and Stephen Shapiro. *Revising Charles Brockden Brown: Culture, Politics, and Sexuality in the Early Republic*. Knoxville: University of Tennessee Press, 2004.

Ben-Atar, Doron S., and Barbara Oberg. *Federalists Reconsidered*. Charlottesville: University Press of Virginia, 1998.

The Carl H. Pforzheimer Collection of Shelley and His Circle. New York Public Library.

Cunningham, Noble E. "John Beckley: An Early American Party Manager." *The William and Mary Quarterly* 13.1 (1956): 40–52.

Daniel, Marcus Leonard. "'Ribaldry and Billingstate': Popular Journalism, Political Culture and the Public Sphere in the Early Republic." PhD diss., Princeton University, 1998.

Davidson, Cathy N. *Revolution and the Word: The Rise of the Novel in America.* New York: Oxford University Press, 2004.

Davis, John. *Travels of Four Years and a Half in the United States of America during 1798, 1799, 1800, 1801, and 1802.* Edited by A. J. Morrison. New York: Holt, 1909.

Dowling, William C. *Literary Federalism in the Age of Jefferson: Joseph Dennie and the Port Folio, 1801–1812.* Columbia: University of South Carolina Press, 1999.

Elkins, Stanley M., and Eric L. McKitrick. *The Age of Federalism.* New York: Oxford University Press, 1993.

Ellis, Joseph J. *Founding Brothers: The Revolutionary Generation.* New York: Knopf, 2000.

Fenno, John Ward. Papers. The Library of the New-York Historical Society.

Fischer, David Hackett. *The Revolution of American Conservatism: The Federalist Party in the Era of Jeffersonian Democracy.* New York: Harper and Row, 1965.

Freeman, Joanne B. *Affairs of Honor: National Politics in the New Republic.* New Haven, CT: Yale University Press, 2001.

______. "Dueling as Politics: The Burr-Hamilton Duel." *New-York Journal of American History* 65.3 (2004): 40–49.

______. "Dueling as Politics: Reinterpreting the Burr-Hamilton Duel." *William and Mary Quarterly* 53.2 (1996): 289–318.

Gilmartin, Kevin. *Print Politics: The Press and Radical Opposition in Early Nineteenth-Century England.* New York: Cambridge University Press, 1996.

______. *Writing Against Revolution: Literary Conservatism in Britain, 1790–1832.* New York: Cambridge University Press, 2007.

Grasso, Christopher. *A Speaking Aristocracy: Transforming Public Discourse in Eighteenth-Century Connecticut.* Chapel Hill: University of North Carolina Press, 1999.

Gratz Family Collection. Manuscript Collection No. 72. American Philosophical Society, Philadelphia, PA.

Green, James N. "The Rise of Book Publishing." In Gross and Kelley, *An Extensive Republic*, 75–127.

Greenberg, Kenneth S. *Honor and Slavery: Lies, Duels, Noses, Masks, Dressing as a Woman, Gifts, Strangers, Humanitarianism, Death, Slave Rebellions, the Proslavery Argument, Baseball, Hunting, and Gambling in the Old South.* Princeton, NJ: Princeton University Press, 1996.

Gross, Robert A. "An Extensive Republic." In *An Extensive Republic: Print, Culture, and Society in the New Nation, 1790-1840*, edited by Robert A. Gross and Mary Kelley, 1–50. Chapel Hill: University of North Carolina Press, 2010.

Haberman, Robb K. "Magazines, Presentation Networks, and the Cultivation of Authorship in Post-Revolutionary America." *American Periodicals* 18.2 (2008): 141–62.

Harris, Bob. *Politics and the Rise of the Press: Britain and France, 1620–1800*. New York: Routledge, 1996.

Hench, John. "Letters of John Fenno and John Ward Fenno, 1779–1800." *Proceedings of the American Antiquarian Society* 89.2 (1979): 299–368.

______. "Letters of John Fenno and John Ward Fenno, 1779–1800." *Proceedings of the American Antiquarian Society* 90.1 (1980): 163–234.

Horn, James P. P., Jan Lewis, and Peter S. Onuf, eds. *The Revolution of 1800: Democracy, Race, and the New Republic*. Charlottesville: University of Virginia Press, 2002.

Kaplan, Catherine O'Donnell. *Men of Letters in the Early Republic: Cultivating Forums of Citizenship*. Chapel Hill: University of North Carolina Press, 2008.

Kelley, Mary. "'While Pen, Ink & Paper Can Be Had': Reading and Writing in a Time of Revolution." *Early American Studies* 10.3 (2012): 439–66.

Kerber, Linda K. *Federalists in Dissent: Imagery and Ideology in Jeffersonian America*. Ithaca, NY: Cornell University Press, 1970.

Lampi, Philip J. "The Federalist Party Resurgence, 1808–1816." *Journal of the Early Republic* 33.2 (2013): 255–81.

LeCarner, Thomas. "The 'F' Word: The Struggle over Forgiveness in Nineteenth-Century American Law, Literature, and Culture." PhD diss., University of Colorado, Boulder, forthcoming.

List, Karen K. "The Role of William Cobbett in Philadelphia's Party Press, 1794–1799." *Journalism Monographs* 82 (1983): 1–41.

Loudoun Papers. 1696–1939. Collection 1971. Historical Society of Pennsylvania, Philadelphia, PA.

Mangu-Ward, Katherine. "The Orphan Scholar." *Humanities: The Magazine of the National Endowment for the Humanities* 29.2 (2008): 36–37, http://www. neh. gov/humanities/2008/januaryfebruary/feature/the-orphan-scholar.

Mann, Bruce H. *Republic of Debtors: Bankruptcy in the Age of American Independence*. Cambridge, MA: Harvard University Press, 2002.

Marsh, Philip M. "John Beckley: Mystery Man of the Early Jeffersonians." *Pennsylvania Magazine of History and Biography* 72.1 (1948): 54–69.

Nerone, John C. *Violence against the Press: Policing the Public Sphere in U.S. History*. New York: Oxford University Press, 1994.

Parker, Peter J. "Asbury Dickins, Bookseller, 1798–1801, or, the Brief Career of a Careless Youth." *Pennsylvania Magazine of History and Biography* 94.4 (1970): 464–83.

Pasley, Jeffrey L. "1800 as a Revolution in Political Culture: Newspapers, Celebrations, Voting, and Democratization in the Early Republic." In *Revolution of 1800* Horn, et al., 121–52.

______. "'A Journeyman, Either in Law or Politics': John Beckley and the Social Origins of Political Campaigning." *Journal of the Early Republic* 16.4 (1996): 531–69.

______. "The Two National 'Gazettes': Newspapers and the Embodiment of American Political Parties." *Early American Literature* 35.1 (2000): 51–86.

______. *"The Tyranny of Printers": Newspaper Politics in the Early American Republic.* Charlottesville: University Press of Virginia, 2001.

Pasley, Jeffrey L., Andrew W. Robertson, and David Waldstreicher. *Beyond the Founders: New Approaches to the Political History of the Early American Republic.* Chapel Hill: University of North Carolina Press, 2004.

Pretzer, William S. "'Of the paper cap and inky apron': Journeymen Printers." In Gross and Kelley, *An Extensive Republic*, 160–71.

Raddin, George Gates. *Hocquet Caritat and the Early New York Literary Scene*. Dover, NJ: Dover Advance Press, 1953.

Radway, Janice. "Interpretive Communities and Variable Literacies: The Functions of Romance Reading." *Daedalus* 113.3 (1984): 49–73.

Raymond, Joad. *News, Newspapers, and Society in Early Modern Britain*. Portland, OR: F. Cass, 1999.

______. *Pamphlets and Pamphleteering in Early Modern Britain*. New York: Cambridge University Press, 2003.

Remer, Rosalind. *Printers and Men of Capital: Philadelphia Book Publishers in the New Republic*. Philadelphia: University of Pennsylvania Press, 1996.

Rorabaugh, W. J. *The Craft Apprentice: From Franklin to the Machine Age in America.* New York: Oxford University Press, 1986.

______. "The Political Duel in the Early Republic: Burr V. Hamilton." *Journal of the Early Republic* 15.1 (1995): 1–23.

Schaneman, Judith Clark. "Rewriting 'Adèle Et Théodore': Intertextual Connections between Madame De Genlis and Ann Radcliffe." *Comparative Literature Studies* 38.1 (2001): 31–45.

Schroder, Anne L. "Going Public against the Academy in 1784: Mme De Genlis Speaks out on Gender Bias." *Eighteenth-Century Studies* 32.3 (1999): 376–82.

Shapiro, Norman R. *French Women Poets of Nine Centuries: The Distaff and the Pen.* Baltimore: Johns Hopkins University Press, 2008.

Smith, Jeffery Alan. *Franklin and Bache: Envisioning the Enlightened Republic*. New York: Oxford University Press, 1990.

Smith, Steven Carl. "'Elements of Useful Knowledge': New York and the National Book Trade in the Early Republic." *Papers of the Bibliographical Society of America* 106.4 (2012): 487–538.

______. "A World the Printers Made: Print Culture in New York, 1783–1830." PhD diss., University of Missouri, 2013.

Stewart, Donald Henderson. *The Opposition Press of the Federalist Period.* Albany: State University of New York Press, 1969.

Tagg, James. *Benjamin Franklin Bache and the Philadelphia Aurora*. Philadelphia: University of Pennsylvania Press, 1991.

Thompson, E. P. *Customs in Common: Studies in Traditional Popular Culture*. New York: New Press, 1990.

______. *The Making of the English Working Class*. Harmondsworth, NY: Penguin Books, 1979.

Trouille, Mary. "Toward a New Appreciation of Mme De Genlis: The Influence of Les Battuécas on George Sand's Political and Social Thought." *French Review* 71.4 (1998): 565–76.

Wahba, Magdi. "Madame De Genlis in England." *Comparative Literature* 13.3 (1961): 221–38.

Waldstreicher, David. "Founders Chic as Culture War." *Radical History Review* 84 (2002): 185–94.

______. *In the Midst of Perpetual Fetes: The Making of American Nationalism, 1776–1820.* Chapel Hill: University of North Carolina Press, 1997.

Walker, Lesley H. "Producing Feminine Virtue: Strategies of Terror in Writings by Madame De Genlis." *Tulsa Studies in Women's Literature* 23.2 (2004): 213–36.

Waterman, Bryan. "The Bavarian Illuminati, the Early American Novel, and Histories of the Public Sphere." *William and Mary Quarterly* 62.1 (2005): 9–30.

______. "Charles Brockden Brown, Revised and Expanded." *Early American Literature* 40.1 (2005): 173–91.

______. *Republic of Intellect: The Friendly Club of New York City and the Making of American Literature.* Baltimore: Johns Hopkins University Press, 2007.

Watts, Steven. *The Romance of Real Life: Charles Brockden Brown and the Origins of American Culture.* Baltimore: Johns Hopkins University Press, 1994.

Wigger, John H. *American Saint: Francis Asbury and the Methodists.* New York: Oxford University Press, 2009.

Wilentz, Sean. *The Rise of American Democracy: Jefferson to Lincoln.* New York: Norton, 2008.

Winship, Michael. *American Literary Publishing in the Mid-Nineteenth Century: The Business of Ticknor and Fields.* New York: Cambridge University Press, 1995.

Wood, Gordon S. *The Creation of the American Republic, 1776–1787.* Chapel Hill: University of North Carolina Press, 1969.

______. *The Radicalism of the American Revolution.* New York: Knopf, 1992.

Maternal Fathers; or, The Power of Sympathy: Phillis Wheatley's Poem to and Correspondence with "His Excellency General Washington"

Jillmarie Murphy
Union College

WRITING to George Washington from Providence, Rhode Island, on 26 October 1775, Phillis Wheatley acknowledged the "freedom" she had taken by directly addressing him in a letter in which she also enclosed her poem "To His Excellency General Washington."[1] In her letter, Wheatley invoked the "fame" of Washington's "virtues" in the hope that his "generosity" would excuse the epistolary and lyrical "sensations" (*CW*, 185) his eminence had prompted in her. Extolling Washington's "valour" but his "virtues more" (l. 27), Wheatley's poem encourages the "great chief" to "Proceed" in the contest for the colonies' liberation "with virtue on thy side" (l. 39). Composed shortly after Congress appointed Washington "Generalissimo of the armies of North America" (*CW*, 185) in 1775, the poem has come to represent the mythic proportions to which his reputation would swell during the American Revolution and his canonization over the course of his presidency and after his death.

Wheatley's poem to Washington is drawn from her experience living in Boston just prior to and at the onset of the American Revolution. The increasing presence of British troops disrupted the everyday affairs of most Bostonians at the time, and outbreaks of violence over acts of British power became more frequent in the months leading up to the

Literature in the Early American Republic: Annual Studies on Cooper and His Contemporaries
Volume 6, 2014. Copyright © 2014 by AMS Press, Inc. All rights reserved.

Siege of Boston (April 1775–March 1776). However, by the time she wrote "To His Excellency General Washington," Wheatley had already fled to Providence, Rhode Island with John and Susannah Wheatley's daughter, Mary Wheatley Lathrop, and her family.[2] Thus, in spite of Wheatley's seeming diffidence in her letter to Washington, the poem may be taken as a clear directive to the Great Chief to liberate Boston without delay. Her Washington poem and others Wheatley wrote during and shortly after the Revolution are, according to John C. Shields, "straightforward and forceful political poems" that no doubt cast her as the "most ardent female poet of the Revolution."[3]

That said, much of the earliest commentary on the interaction between Wheatley and Washington emphasizes, instead, Washington's magnanimity and graciousness in his 1776 letter to her, in which he acknowledges her poem.[4] Nineteenth-century historians and critics who reference the poem idolized Washington as a founder and, ultimately, the savior of the New Republic. On the whole, they ignored Wheatley's poetic talents and, instead, emphasized Washington's letter to Wheatley as the more important of the two documents by reprinting it more often than the poem that had inspired it.[5] Although the poem remained largely invisible into the early twentieth century, several adjustments in scholarly perspective were forthcoming. At the outset of the Harlem Renaissance, James Weldon Johnson asserted in "Early American Negro Poets" (1921) that Wheatley had "never been given her rightful place in American literature" and called her omission from most American literary anthologies an outright "conspiracy." Although Johnson cites only a handful of lines from Wheatley's poem to Washington, pointing out that Wheatley was "the first person to apply to George Washington the phrase 'first in peace,'"[6] he clearly considers the poem itself more important than Washington's response to it.[7] The most noteworthy discussions of Wheatley and her poetry, however, are those written over the past twenty-five years by scholars engaged in influential critical debates concerning Wheatley's importance to the American literary canon. Indeed, one of the finest discussions of Wheatley's poem to Washington is included in John C. Shields's editorial essay in the definitive *Collected Works of Phillis Wheatley* (1988). Insisting that Wheatley's political poetry "had been ignored for too long," Shields maintains that Wheatley's verses to

Washington constitute "a paean to freedom," rather than "a eulogy to Washington."[8]

Surprisingly, though, what has been lacking in the critical studies of Wheatley's verse to Washington is the emphasis the poem places on Washington's virtue and its power to liberate the "land of freedom's heaven-defended race!" (1. 32). A panegyric on the young Republic's attitude toward Washington, whose reputation in the mid-1770s was based largely on his military prowess as a captain in the British Army during the French and Indian War, Wheatley's poem and accompanying letter, and Washington's response to each, reveal a paradoxical development between the paternal and the maternal aspects of Washington's virtue. Although the poem may be addressed to Washington, the father, more than half the lines are comprised of compellingly resilient maternal imagery, imagery emphasizing feminine virtue, forgiveness, and freedom and challenging many of the political, legal, and gender limitations prevalent in 1770s America. "To His Excellency General Washington" asserts that genuine freedom for all Americans and a triumphant conclusion to the war are possible only through the syncretization of both masculine and feminine, paternal and maternal virtues.

Opening with an appeal to the "Celestial choir!" (l. 1), Wheatley begins "To His Excellency General Washington" by merging religious and classical allusions. Traditionally, angels are depicted as an assembly of genderless beings who are closest to God; as such, they act as mediators between God and humanity, enlightening human beings by revealing that which is unseen. Although Wheatley opens a number of her poems written in the neoclassical tradition with direct addresses to figures such as the "Grim monarch!," "Ye martial pow'rs," the "heav'nly muse," "muse divine," "Indulgent muse!," and "Celestial muse!,"[9] in this poem, Wheatley solicits the celestial hierarchy of divine beings to emphasize an androgynous image of virtue "Enthron'd in realms of light" (l. 1) and to signify and ultimately produce a poetics of cooperation between the traditionally oppositional pairings of public/private, religious/secular, and masculine/feminine virtues.

As an aesthetic contribution, the poem sets in motion an alliance that is transformational in that it awakens the senses to an experience involving provocative nuances surrounding gender possibilities. The poem's opening plea to the celestial choir to see the pagan image of "mother earth" grieve over "her offspring's fate" and "heaven's revolving light / Involved in the sorrows" (ll. 5, 7–8) of humanity not only solicits the aid of God's closest allies but also establishes the necessity for collaborative measures to guarantee success in the fight for freedom.

Wheatley's poem, which was the first public statement to align Washington consistently with those standards of feminine virtue that offer physical and emotional comfort and nourishment to others, served as a nascent but nevertheless fitting depiction of Washington's maternal character, which is clearly reflected in the first twenty-three lines of the poem, which aggrandize powerful female images.

In the second stanza of her poem, Wheatley introduces and elaborates on an authoritative feminine force by summoning a classical image of the goddess Justice, who "moves divinely fair," wearing "Olive" (peace) and "laurel" (victory) in "her golden hair" (ll. 9–10). Her use of "fair" conveys a twofold meaning in its suggestion of the Anglos with whom Wheatley has had to contend throughout her life (many of whom were unjust in their perceptions of her race) and of a figure not unlike the traditional image of Washington: divinely inspired, reasonable, and just. Wheatley's most important theme in this stanza is that "Unnumber'd charms and recent graces rise" (l. 12) "[w]herever shines" this fair deity "of the skies" (1. 11). Should Washington prove to be as fair as the goddess Justice, he will be victorious in his crusade.

The third stanza establishes for the reader the historical context of Washington's status in both past and present conflicts. As the stanza opens, Wheatley summons the "Muse! [to] bow propitious" (l. 13) while the poet recounts her own recent experience of witnessing the British army pouring "through a thousand gates, / As when Eolus heaven's fair face deforms" (ll. 14–15). This is the first time in the poem that Wheatley entertains the notion of a masculine image, but this *god of the winds* is clearly associated with the British army, "Enwrapp'd in tempest and a night of storm" (1. 16). Here, as she introduces a potentially destructive masculine force into the poem to illustrate the Moloch of the British forces "beat[ing America's] . . . sounding shore" (l. 18), Wheatley narrates an experience that must have been frightening to any Bostonian who witnessed the movement of "the warrior's train, / In bright array" (ll. 20–21) marching into the city at the conclusion of the Battle of Bunker Hill in June 1775.

Surely, at this point in the poem, it is not a parapraxis on Wheatley's part that Washington is contrasted with the pernicious power of Eolus, a power with which he is already familiar, having fought "in the fields of fight" (l. 24) in the British army during the French and Indian War (1754–63). But unlike "Britannia," whose "thirst of boundless power" (l. 38) "increase[s] the rising hills of dead" (1. 36), Washington is surrounded here by the splendor and magnificence of the Continental forces. As Britannia's menacing authority intensifies along with the loss of life, "Fix'd are the eyes of nations on the scales, / For in their hopes Columbia's arm prevails" (ll. 33–34). The protective, life-sustaining virtues of Washington and his army thus give hope to other nations for eventual success in their own struggles against oppression. As the nurturer and leader of the promised Republic, Washington assumes the role of benevolent parent on a near-global scale as the poem challenges the ruthless tyranny demonstrated by the parental pairing of Mother Country and King and inaugurates a new, and decidedly virtuous, filial union of Liberty and Justice.

As the third stanza continues, Wheatley focuses on the subject of her verse when she asks, "Shall I to Washington their praise recite?" (l. 23). Although Washington has been routinely referred to as a "Founding Father," an architect of a national identity and an originator of peace, independence, and prosperity for an emerging nation, he is also credited as protecting, nurturing, and sustaining the people of the United States and their freedom. As evidenced in the following lines, Wheatley acknowledges Washington's paternal capacity to enact "fury / [on] whoever dares disgrace / The land of freedom's heaven-defended race" (ll. 30–32), as he heroically assumes guardianship of the American people; however, she also recognizes the necessity for Washington's maternal virtues to solidify and harmonize the new nation: "Thee, first in peace and honours,—we demand / The grace and glory of thy martial band. / Fam'd for thy valour, for thy virtue more, / Hear every tongue thy guardian aid implore!" (ll. 25–28).

Concluding "To His Excellency General Washington," Wheatley imaginatively anticipates the national character her subject will enjoy forever: "A crown, a mansion, and a throne that shine, / With gold unfading, WASHINGTON! be thine" (ll. 41–42). As she issues her final verdict on the personal and military course Washington should take, she emphasizes the necessity for him to move forward in the fight "with virtue on [his] side"; however, he must let every battle, every conflict, and every act "the goddess guide" (l. 40), for only through uniting the masculine and the feminine spirit of his virtues will he succeed in the quest to create in the "land of freedom's heaven-defended race" (ll. 32) a fusion of both maternal and paternal classical, religious, and earthly virtues.

1. Classical Republican Virtue

> "Man's business is *virtue*, not *words*"
> —Seneca, "Epistle III"

Historically, within the classical republican tradition, virtue and liberty worked in concert, obligating leading citizens, in particular, to possess sufficient virtue to place the public good over private gain. Beginning with Aristotle's *zoon politikon*, or, political man, political activity has been considered an essential part of human behavior. The Aristotelian concept that man was, by nature, a citizen was vigorously revived during the eighteenth century in response to Enlightenment claims regarding civic humanist ethos. Joseph Addison's *Cato, A Tragedy* (1712), which extols the concepts of virtue, liberty, individualism, and republicanism, was a favorite among many American patriots, including Washington, and is credited by some historians as inspiring the framework for the colonies' rebellion against British tyranny. Indeed, Jeffry H. Morrison identifies Washington as the "most classically republican American of his generation"[10] and closely aligns him with Cincinnatus and Cicero, two crucial political figures of the Roman Republic.

It has been well documented, however, that the concept of virtue at the time of the American Revolution was also nurtured by several feminizing influences during the emergence of eighteenth-century Anglo-American sentimental culture. While the etymology of virtue, a term derived from the Latin *virtūs*, literally means virility or manliness, Enlightenment attitudes created a transatlantic culture of civility, compassion, and congeniality that effectively softened the classical definition of virtue and facilitated the creation of a prosperous and, especially, harmonious Republic in the post-Revolution United States. As Wai Chee Dimock has argued, "[T]he feminization of virtue registered in the broadest sense a cognitive revolution, a revolution in the way institutional domains were conceptualized, organized, and differentiated."[11]

The integration of public and private spheres in 1770s America allowed numerous middle-class women to contribute to, and thus further influence, middle-class cultural standards of virtue. As leading participants in various religious movements, women, according to Ruth H. Bloch, "recommended that men become more graceful, emotive, and gentle—more like women—in order to improve themselves and save the world from commercial decadence." Women such as Abigail Adams and Mercy Otis Warren adopted leadership roles that had previously been denied them and became, in effect, formidable architects of contemporary constructions of virtue. Wheatley's poem to Washington effectively illustrates and promotes the necessity of including authoritative feminine virtue in the struggle for independence. Contemporary gender theorists, in fact, offer informative arguments related to the conception of women's sphere during the American Revolution, arguments that ought to bear on our reception of Wheatley's poem to Washington. Rosemarie Zagarri holds that the Scottish Enlightenment encouraged critical links between European and American gender constructions in eighteenth-century America, citing a "broad, long-term, transatlantic reformulation of the role and status of women."[12] Reasoning from the work of several Scottish civil jurisprudential thinkers who believed that women assuaged the savage hearts of men and were necessary conduits toward defining virtue in practice, Zagarri suggests that the woman's role as keeper of the family formed the foundation of social structures in the eighteenth century. Bloch considers a tripartite tradition incorporating classical republican theory, natural law theories (one inherited from Locke, the other from the Scottish Enlightenment), and the historical implications of dissenter Protestantism in evaluating characteristics of the public and the private.

Although Puritan laws of submission regarding both the public sphere and the private sphere were outdated by the end of the seventeenth century, American Protestant thinking, according to Bloch, "continued to straddle the line between public and private that had been drawn by both the classical republican and the natural rights traditions." Claire A. Lyons references the feminization of religion as offering "credence to women's positive moral character" and credibility to their function during the Revolution when she states that "women were granted the custodianship of the nation's civic virtue." As an African American woman and slave, Wheatley recognized the manner in which religious and Republican virtue coalesced in the struggle for independence. Specifically, as Carla Mulford affirms, Wheatley and other learned Africans of the period used Christianity to further problematize gender spheres by bringing racial oppression to the forefront of the American struggle for freedom and democracy.[13] Writing on 11 February 1774 to the Mohegan preacher Samson Occom, who had attacked Christian preachers who held slaves, Wheatley acknowledges the contradictoriness of the popular notion of liberty: "I . . . am greatly satisfied with your Reasons respecting the Negroes, and think highly reasonable what you offer in vindication of their natural Rights" (*CW*, 176). In recognition of both Occom's and her own Christian awareness, Wheatley insists that "the glorious Dispensation of civil and religious Liberty . . . are so inseparably united, that there is little or no Enjoyment of one without the other" (*CW*, 176).

Lyons, however, also draws attention to the "deeply gendered" language of the mid- to late eighteenth century, when political relationships were routinely allegorized in terms of rape and seduction as "Americans were warned to guard against the rape of liberty and to be aware of the seduction of British corruption." Thus, according to Bloch, during the 1770s, the image of a mother "passively donating her sons" to the war effort was one of the few feminine images of Revolutionary virtue available at the time, and it encouraged an idealized vision of women as fonts of both domestic and civic virtue. As Linda K. Kerber notes, during the Revolutionary period, mothers were commonly thought to play the "crucial role" of raising children and shaping their moral character, but, in fact, mothering was more typically regarded as a "fourth branch of government," involving a type of parenting that "ensured social control in the gentlest possible way."[14]

Wheatley's relationship with her own mistress reflects the strong mother-child bond she felt toward Susannah Wheatley. In a letter she wrote to John Thornton in 1774, her last extant letter written before she sent her poem and letter to Washington, Wheatley expressed the great loss she had sustained on the death of Susannah, her "best friend," stating that she felt "like One forsaken by her parent in a desolate wilderness, for such the world appears to me, wandring thus without my friendly guide" (*CW*, 183). Unquestionably, Susannah was the one woman who was in all respects the only mother Wheatley entirely remembered, the one whose "uncommon tenderness" (*CW*, 183) supplied her with a sense of direction and stability in the world.

Fig. 1. John Norman, *Instruction of American Youth*, Library of Congress, Rare Book & Special Collections Division, LC-USZ62-45279

By highlighting the puissance associated with feminine virtue, Wheatley's poem to Washington offers a variety of potent maternal images that reach far beyond that of a submissive mother relinquishing her sons to the war effort. The poem is explicit on this point: should Washington refuse to allow an authoritative maternal force to guide him through the war, he will be less likely to succeed in "freedom's cause" (l. 3).

The engraving, *Instruction of American Youth*, by John Norman (1783) sums up the importance the new Republic placed on feminine authority by the end of the war; however, it also reaffirms the compelling message Wheatley inscribes to George Washington as the nation embarked on war. The illustration depicts the Goddess of Peace turning a young child away from a pyramid that lists famous battles of the American Revolution and, instead, turning the youth toward three other goddesses who represent Religion, Liberty, and Commerce, thus underscoring Wheatley's guiding message to Washington regarding the importance of powerful maternal virtue.

2. Maternal Fathers

As a result of his virtuous character, Washington has typically been portrayed as a leader filled with compassion and empathy, whose self-effacing influence extended far beyond the borders of the early American Republic. Paul Carrese historicizes the perception of Washington as the epitome of Aristotle's "great-souled man," one who is "at once worthy of great honors" and yet spurns "both populism and abuse of power." From the moment he was named General of the Continental Army, Washington's contemporaries emphasized his virtuous character. On 19 June 1775, the first Continental Congress of the United Colonies, "reposing special trust and confidence in [his] patriotism, conduct, and fidelity,"[15] commissioned Washington to serve as General and Commander-in-Chief of the Army of the United Colonies. Writing to Washington on 1 July 1775, General Philip Schuyler explicitly foregrounded "the Wish of every honest American" that "Success and Happiness *equal to* the Merit & Virtue of my General may crown all his Operations." Two weeks later, Jonathan Trumbull told Washington, "Virtue ought always to be made the Object of Government," effectively highlighting the association between Washington's private sensibility and his public conduct. And then on 17 July 1775, H. Wentworth, a chairman from the committee of Portsmouth, New Hampshire, wrote to Washington that he was "filled with the deepest sense of Gratitude" when he considered "the Alacrity with which [Washington has] as it were flown to our relief, to protect us from the relentless ravages of a Merciless Enemy," and he added that Washington's "Great Military Skills, together with [his] many Virtues," distinguish him as "an accomplish'd gentleman." Thomas Paine's introductory letter to Washington in *The Rights of Man* (1791) acknowledges Washington's "exemplary virtue" and "benevolence"; Paine states that, in order to be a *true* American, to obtain the *true* "character of man," one must be compassionate. After Washington's death, Mason Locke (Parson) Weems declared that the war was won and the nation founded as the direct result of Washington's many virtues. He identifies Washington as "the Hero, and the Demigod— . . . the sun-beam in council, or the storm in war," and reminds readers, "It is the private virtues that lay the foundation of all human excellence—since it was these that exalted Washington to be '*Columbia's first and greatest Son*,' be it our first care to present these, in all their lustre, before the admiring eyes of our children. To *them* his private character is *every thing*; his public hardly *any thing*."[16]

The resulting historiography of the Revolutionary generation typically provided a "heroic" interpretation of the founding fathers' virtue, yet the principles of masculinity underwent an androgynous transformation shortly before the Revolution, a transformation that momentarily harmonized public and private conceptions of virtue, sentimentality, and individual integrity. While self-discipline, acts of charity, diligence, and discretion were virtues expected of both men and women, women were also viewed as protectors of virtue as they aided and supported their fathers, husbands, and sons who went off in the 1770s and early 1780s to fight in the war and, later, as they gave birth to the first generation of free Americans and instructed those children in the ways of virtue. By the mid-eighteenth century, the patriarchal authority system of the colonial period had already begun to surrender to what Jay Fliegelman describes as a "new parental ideal characterized by a more affectionate and equalitarian relationship with children." The decline of patriarchal authority, which was prompted in America by doubts raised in England over sovereign rule, weakened notions of traditional fatherhood on both sides of the Atlantic.[17] As a result, the critical tensions between monarchical control and self-governing independence throughout the 1760s and early 1770s were often described in familial terms. Anticipating a diplomatic resolution during the initial conflicts between England and America, American patriots took a more conciliatory tone toward England by describing the British monarchy as a tender mother; as hostilities intensified, however, descriptions of England were transformed from a compassionate and benevolent mother to a cruel and insensitive matriarch. Consequently, because this latter image, according to Bloch, "represented a violation of the feminine maternal principle [and] . . . [p]ower itself was typically symbolized as aggressively masculine," by the end of the 1770s, negative filial characterizations of George III as a "heartless father emerged with a vengeance."[18]

Attempts to clarify perceptions of gender at this time were further complicated by the fact that, during the mid-1770s, precisely during the period in which Wheatley composed her poem and letter to Washington, the "physical courage and valiant self-sacrifice of male citizen-soldiers" were at the "height of the military vogue" while women were expelled from this "militant conception of citizenship" and were oftentimes associated with representations of "laziness, cowardliness, and corruption."[19] Betsy Erkkila extends this image by highlighting the violence associated with the gendered iconography of the period in which female figures—as alternate representations of Britannia or America—are depicted "naked . . . , enchained, [and] amputated." For example, Erkkila considers the popular engraving "The Able Doctor, or America Swallowing the Bitter Draught" (1774), in which a partially clothed Indian woman, America, is "violated by a number of male figures who force her to submit to the 'bitter draught' of the Boston Port Bill and other British policies while Britannia," the only other female figure in the engraving, "turns away in distress."[20]

Fig. 2 *America in Flames,* Library of Congress, Prints & Photographs *Division, LC-USZC4-5288*

The above image shows a woman, representing America, seated in flames with her legs spread apart. Two men in the clouds above her are fanning the flames as each brandishes copies of British measures against the colonies. Four British men, representing the British opposition, stand around her halfheartedly dousing the flames. The teapot, lying on the steps beneath her open legs, represents the aborted birth of the new nation.

In spite of the violence that should naturally be associated with these images, Erkkila maintains that their inherent emotionality persuaded women to "imagine and act on a revolutionary vision of themselves as historical actors on the stage of the world."[21] And Wheatley's poem to Washington does just that. Since poetry performs a variety of discourse that may simultaneously question and support the physicality of war, Wheatley places her poem to Washington at the center of gendered eighteenth-century spheres of private and public action. Although it was considered acceptable for a woman to write out her thoughts (but certainly not to act on them), the epistolary and poetic genres in which Wheatley addresses Washington situate her, as a woman and a recently freed black, in the untenable position of uttering a political mandate to a man, a general, an acknowledged war hero, and a slaveholder to "Proceed" (l. 39) forward, "Thy ev'ry action" escorted by "the goddess" (l. 40). The poem euphemistically offers a challenge to the "great chief" (l. 39) to perform bloody deeds "in . . . fields of fight" (l. 24) that promote masculine virility, violence, and death; yet, consistent with the spirit of gender unity in her poem, Wheatley's language also aligns him with virtuous feminine images that celebrate Washington as a warrior whose ultimate goal is peace.

To be sure, representations of Washington written around the same time as Wheatley's poem cultivate images of Washington that exclusively promote his public persona—his masculinity, physical strength, paternalism, and military prowess—rather than advance his private virtues. For example, Charles Henry Wharton's "A Poetical Epistle to His Excellency George Washington" (1779) concentrates on Washington's "Herculean labors" (l. 85), his resemblance to classic Greek and Roman heroes, and the "embattled field[s]" (l. 87) and "rattling storms that war around his head" (l. 90). While a powerful, autonomous portrait of the goddess Liberty, who embodies "Unnumber'd charms" (l. 12) and "moves divinely fair" (l. 9), is united to

Washington's virtue in Wheatley's poem, a paradoxical image of Liberty is portrayed in Wharton's, in which "Fair Liberty" obediently serves as man's "noblest claim," as she meekly bears "these rhymes smiling to her fav'rite chief" (ll. 21, 26). In an earlier sketch of Washington, George Mercer describes the twenty-eight-year-old Washington's imposing stature, "measuring six feet 2 inches in his stockings," his frame "padded with well-developed muscles, indicating great strength," and his "commanding countenance." Similarly, underscoring Washington's masculine persona, Richard Howell's sonata, "Sung by a Number of young Girls, dressed in white and decked with Wreaths and Chaplets of Flowers, holding Baskets of Flowers in their Hands, as General Washington passed under the Triumphal Arch raised on the Bridge at Trenton, April 21, 1789," draws attention to Washington's bravery in protecting those who were perceived as delicate and defenseless, as his "conquering arms did save" (l. 7) the "Virgins fair and matrons grave" (l. 6).[22]

Weems's mythographical *Life of Washington* (1800), written shortly after Washington's death in 1799, emphasizes the nuances of Washington's virtue in both his public and his private life. Weems created a public persona for Washington, the "paternal figure whose life," as Elizabeth Barnes reads it, is made to represent the "renunciation of English history and the inauguration of a new American epic." Yet Weems also constructed a private life that worked in tandem with Washington's national character. While Washington's public service is surely enmeshed with his paternal nature, Weems's characterization of Washington as "[l]oving his soldiers as his children" appears as much, if not more, maternal than paternal. Though Washington is "the friend of justice and father of his army," and his soldiers looked with "reverence and love" upon "their honoured chief, to whom they had ever looked as to a father," his men had also frequently "marked his tears, as, visiting their encampments, he beheld them suffering and sinking under fevers and fluxes, for want of clothes and provisions."[23] This emotion-laden image of Washington weeping over the illness and deprivation of his soldiers is comparable to the image Wheatley establishes in her poem of "mother earth" (l. 5) "flash[ing] dreadful in refulgent arms" (l. 4), lamenting "her offspring's fate" (l. 5).

Without doubt, this maternal representation of Washington is likewise evocative of William Carlos Williams's depiction of Abraham Lincoln in *In the American Grain* (1956) in which Lincoln is cast in the same maternal mold from which both Wheatley and Weems ostensibly cast Washington. In Lincoln, the lowliest soldier would find "a woman to caress him," a pardoner of the "fellow who slept on sentry duty," and a "woman in an old shawl—with a great bearded face and a towering black hat." Yet, in his characterization of George Washington in the same collection, Williams acknowledges the Great Chief's divided self, the more passionate aspect of which Washington refused to unshackle for fear it would expose a side of him that might dismantle his public reputation. For a man such as Washington, "[b]attle," according to Williams, was the "expression of that something in [him] which [he] fear[ed]," and Washington's "calmness of demeanor and characteristics as a military leader" reflect that fear. It is understandable that Washington was at odds with his public and private persona and conscious of the need, as Williams put it, to "resist, be prudent, be calm—with a mad hell inside that might rise, might one day perhaps do something brilliant, perhaps joyously abandoned—but not to be thought of."[24] Yet this is precisely the divided nature that Wheatley encourages Washington to conflate for the good of the country. Although Washington's treatment of his soldiers was seen as commanding and compassionate, it is his gentle concern for their welfare—as a traditional maternal figure who is protector, nurturer, and sustainer—that will lead the country to victory.

As illustrated by Wheatley's verse, Washington, by discharging his military duties in a gender-neutral manner and surrendering his patriarchal privilege—the *patria potestas* of Roman law—to a more rational management of society, will enact a type of benign national paternalism that is free from the social interference of bloodlines, thoughtless obedience to mob mentality, or narrow institutional authority such as that represented by religion.

Furthermore, although an elite and exclusionary adaptation of republicanism romanticizes patrician rights and titles, Wheatley consciously encodes a set of political standards in her poem that includes both women and non-Anglos. Writing this poem, Wheatley is, herself, acting as a channel toward social progress, particularly when she urges Washington to unite his virtues—paternal virility and maternal compassion—and reminds him that the masculine attention to "freedom's cause" fills America's "anxious breast" with fear (l. 3). As evidenced by a letter Washington wrote to John Hancock, President of the Continental Congress, on 23 December 1776, the maternal images of America's fears for her people that Wheatley embedded in her poem are ultimately confirmed by Washington's humane, parental concern for his soldiers. For example, filled with anxiety over the campaign for liberty and the lack of provisions available to his soldiers at Valley Forge, many of whom were left unfit for duty owing to the "hardships and exposures they have undergone," Washington raises a complaint against those members of Congress who believe "the Soldiery were made of Stocks or Stones, and equally insensible of Frost and Snow." Continuing his appeal, Washington states that, although those men in power "seem to have little feeling for the naked and distressed Soldier," he, as the primary caretaker of soldiers under his command, must himself "feel superabundantly for them, and from [his] soul pity those miseries" that, he fears, he has neither "the power to releive [*sic*] or prevent."[25]

The maternal metaphor developed in Wheatley's poem is thus borne out in three specific ways: America is depicted as a "dreadful" (l. 4) mother, shining radiantly in the midst of war and poised to protect her children; Washington, whom Wheatley consistently aligns with the poem's maternal images, is portrayed as a "guardian aid" who will answer "every tongue" (l. 28) that implores his assistance; and Wheatley, as poet, ultimately becomes a mother for a literally enslaved people by communicating, according to Antonio T. Bly, a "strong sense of black pride to her fellow slaves."[26]

3. The Letters

The androgynous imagery that exists in Wheatley's "To His Excellency . . ." is also manifested in her correspondence to Washington. When sending her letter to Washington in October 1775, Wheatley expressed her faith in his virtues to obtain "all possible success in the great cause [he is] so generously engaged in" (*CW*, 185). Washington's responses to Wheatley's verse affirm her notion of citizenship and appear to allocate shares in an American patrimony in a more equitable gender and racial manner than existed under British rule.

In the letter he wrote back to Wheatley on 28 February 1776, in which he belatedly acknowledged his receipt of her poem, Washington "apologize[d] for the delay" in replying to her letter and its enclosure and "plead [his] excuse for the seeming, but not real, neglect" by offering a "tribute justly due to [her]." He referred to Wheatley's poem as "her favors" and hoped she would understand that the "variety of important occurrences" with which he had had to contend—driving the British out of Boston, raising troops, entreating Congress for funds to raise pay for enlisted soldiers, and negotiating peace—prevented him from making a more timely acknowledgement to her. Washington's considerate reaction to her poem thus represents his consciousness of a conflict between his imposing public persona and the responsibilities associated with it and his maternal side, which is grateful, apologetic, and humble in its compliment to Wheatley's "poetical talents," even as he considered himself "undeserving . . . of such encomium and panegyrick." He concluded the letter by inviting her to visit him at his headquarters in Cambridge, and then he again paid tribute to her as one "so favoured by the Muses, and to whom Nature has been so liberal and beneficent in her dispensations."[27]

Much more than his military heroism, Washington's maternal act of nurturing, feeding, and cultivating the hearts and minds of the people of the newly formed United States of America is precisely what David M. Ramsay, mayor of Alexandria, Virginia, invoked in a letter to him dated April 1789, shortly after Washington accepted nomination to the presidency. Ramsay emphasized Washington's selfless, nurturing qualities: "Again your country commands your care. Obedient to its wishes, unmindful of your ease, we see you again relinquishing the bliss of retirement." However, it was not Washington's "glory as a soldier," his "unexampled honour," or his "patriotism" that prompted Ramsay's letter to "the best of men"; rather, it was Washington's private virtues, those "themes less splendid, but more endearing" that provoked the sadness felt by Ramsay and those "neighbors and friends" who would be bereaved of their "ornament," "model," "improver," "friend," "protector," "benefactor," "institutor and promoter," and the "first and best of citizens."[28] The fusion of paternal and maternal virtues in Ramsay's letter underscores the motivation that no doubt prompted Phillis Wheatley to inscribe her poetic tribute to a man whose powerful sympathies might eventually lead the United States to peace and liberty, but it also encouraged others after his death to cite similar observations.

4. Washington's Reputation and the Early Republic

> TRUE, my friends, no children of his loins lifted their little arms and raised their suffused eyes around his dying bed, to catch a father's last blessing; but WASHINGTON was not childless; he was the father of his country, the parent of millions; and who is there so mean among you, that is not of the happy number?
>
> —Royall Tyler, "An Oration on the Death of George Washington"[29]

In spite of Wheatley's confidence in Washington's virtues to lead the country to victory—and the nineteenth-century's very deliberate glorification, preservation, and advancement of Washington's reputation—Washington's unique qualities portrayed in Wheatley's verse some fourteen years prior to his assuming the presidency were not entirely validated during his term in office. When Washington embarked on a presidency that was in effect forced upon him, hostile responses against him began almost immediately. The public opposed his Proclamation of Neutrality (1793) in the war between France and Great Britain, and he encountered both public and private opposition, particularly around the crucial issue of executive authority, when he signed the Jay Treaty with Great Britain in 1794. An article appearing in the *Philadelphia Aurora* on 4 March 1797, the day Washington left office, elaborates on the future judgments the anonymous writer assumed would be taken of Washington's administration, stating, "it is the subject of the greatest astonishment that a single individual should have cankered the principles of Republicanism in an enlightened people, just emerged from the gulf of despotism, and should have carried his designs against the public liberty so far as to have put in jeopardy its very existence."[30]

But this manner of criticism did not persist in any remarkable way after Washington's death in December 1799. In fact, though they do not emphasize Washington's maternalism, obituaries of, and early poetic tributes to, Washington applauded his virtues with a vengeance and sought a return to Washington's unblemished character such as is celebrated in Wheatley's pre-presidency poem.

For instance, in a eulogy printed in *The Monthly Magazine, and American Review*, Washington is described as an "illustrious man" whose death "will long occupy the attention of his fellow citizens." Furthermore, the eulogy states that Washington "anticipated his approaching dissolution with every proof of that equanimity for which his whole life has been so uniformly evident"; however, in much the same way that a child might react to the death of a beloved parent with fear, the article expressed anxiety that "[w]ords cannot fully describe the solemn and awful sensations which these tidings universally diffused." Two poems directly followed this eulogy, "imparting to the world at large . . . faithful pictures of the sentiments which the memory of WASHINGTON excited in the hearts of his contemporaries."[31] While neither poem conveys sentiments about Washington identical to those evoked in Wheatley's "To His Excellency," vestiges of Washington's many maternal virtues are illustrated in both poems. "On the Death of Gen. George Washington" remembers Washington, "Our FRIEND, our GUIDE, our FATHER" (l. 26), as a "protecting form" (1. 37) and recalls the "mighty hand" that lead the country "Thro' Faction's rough and overwhelming tide" (ll. 39–40). However, rather than anticipating the peace and victory Washington's virtues will bring to America as does Wheatley's verse, "On the Death of Gen. George Washington" expresses dread that "Washington [is] no more" (l. 41). His death, as the poem implies, leaves the fledgling country prey to the "deadliest mischief" (l. 45) of our enemies, whose "fears all vanish'd when his spirit fled" (l. 50). The second poem, "Monody on the Death of George Washington," delivered at the New-York Theatre, 30 December 1799, similarly presents Washington as "our parent, guardian, guide, and friend" (1. 18), but rather than succumb to the fears surrounding his loss, the poet reminds readers that, because Washington "liv'd to give us liberty and life" (1. 94), "Each future age, through wide-extended earth, / Like us, may triumph in his hour of birth" (ll. 23–24).

Other eulogies and poetic tributes that appeared within two years of Washington's passing also bring to mind Wheatley's emphasis on his maternal virtues. Anthony Pasquin's "A National Dirge" begins by distinguishing Washington as "the Councillor, the Mighty Man, the Man of War"; however, in much the same way that Wheatley combines Washington's masculine and feminine virtues in classical and religious imagery, Pasquin tells us that Washington also "temper'd the energies of Roman Virtue with the forbearance of the Christian Spirit": his paternal (Roman) virtue "broke the fetters of the land," but his maternal (Christian) virtues "taught us to be free."[32]

In John B. Johnson's *Eulogy on General George Washington, A Sermon*, delivered 22 February 1800, Washington is clearly identified with his military prowess, as "the leader of our armies—the founder of our infant republic—the guide of our councils—the patriot, who united and swayed all hearts"; however, although he is the "hero, friend, father" to his country, he is memorialized in the sermon for "his large and consummate knowledge of the human heart, in silencing murmurs, in allaying fears, in rekindling hope, in communicating to a small, destitute, defeated army, a portion of that greatness which upheld, and that patriotism that inflamed his soul."[33] To be sure, calmly quieting the fears of his soldiers and inspiring hope are maternal gestures, traits, and virtues that Johnson underscores in his eulogy.

Thus, as the new nation moved into a new century in which fresh hostilities, such as the War of 1812, drew Americans further away from the enthusiasm and spirit of the Age of Revolution, Washington's reputation, like that of other American presidents to come, exploded into mythic proportion. Perhaps one of the most striking nineteenth-century illustrations of Washington's maternal nature, and possibly the closest iconographic parallel to Wheatley's verse, is depicted in an image of Washington encircled by classical feminine authority in Constantino Brumidi's *Apotheosis of Washington* (1865), which was painted on the 4,664-square-foot canopy over the eye of the dome above the Rotunda in the Capitol.

In this immense fresco the "Great Chief" is flanked by the goddesses Liberty and Victory and surrounded by maidens as he faces eastward toward Great Britain. Venus, who is positioned below him and to the right, lays the transatlantic cable while directly below the figure of Washington the goddess Freedom, armed with a sword and aided by a menacing eagle, crushes the figures of Tyranny and Monarchy. To the right of Freedom is Minerva, goddess of wisdom and the arts, pointing to a generator and surrounded by the American inventors Benjamin Franklin, Robert Fulton, and Samuel F. B. Morse.

Fig. 3 Detail of *The Apotheosis of Washington,* Library of Congress, Prints & Photographs Division, Detroit Publishing Company Collection, LC-DIG-det-4a26376

This is the image Wheatley effectively conjectured almost one hundred years earlier in her poem "To His Excellency, General Washington" and one that, like Wheatley's verse, encapsulates the spirit of unanimity that is indispensable in a successful fight for liberty and justice for all.

NOTES

I would like to thank Ronald A. Bosco, April R. Selley, Mark Kamrath, and *LEAR*'s anonymous readers for their insightful comments and invaluable suggestions throughout the various stages of my work on this essay.

1. Wheatley's poems and letters are quoted from *The Collected Works of Phillis Wheatley*, hereafter labeled *CW* with subsequent paginal references cited parenthetically in the text.

2. In 1761, when Phillis was nine years old, John Wheatley purchased her as a

servant for his wife Susannah. Their daughter Mary taught Phillis to read and write.

3. Shields, "Wheatley's Struggle," 240.

4. A partial exception to this generalization occurs in Jared Sparks's edition of *The Writings of George Washington*, where in a note to Washington's response to Wheatley's poem and letter, Sparks comments that Wheatley "was a whig in politics after the American way of thinking; and it might be curious to see in what manner she would eulogize liberty and the rights of man, while herself, nominally at least, in bondage" (3:299n). However, other than to comment on her poetry in general as "the most favorable evidence on record, of the capacity of the African intellect for improvement" (3:298n), Sparks does not remark on the specific content of the poem; rather, he claims that he "had not been able to find, among Washington's papers, the letter and poem addressed to him" (3:299n). Moreover, he does not consider why Wheatley would have taken what might have appeared to some as a significant risk in writing to the most politically revered and militarily renowned man in the country.

5. Sarah Josepha Hale, for example, remarks in *Women's Record, or, Sketches of All Distinguished Women* (1855) that Wheatley's poem to Washington "gives her a more enduring fame than all her printed pieces," yet she ultimately deflates this assertion by declaring that "Phillis Wheatley's poems have little literary merit: their worth arises from the extraordinary circumstances that they are the production of an *African woman*; the sentiment is always true, but never new" (552). W. H. Jackson's "Memoirs" is representative of contemporaneous Anglo perceptions of Wheatley's life and treatment as a slave. Although Jackson appears sympathetic to Wheatley's being "kidnapped and sold" to a captain of a slave ship on its way to Boston and the "shameful condition" under which "she awaited the coming of a purchaser" (118–19), he, like other critics of the period, reminds readers that the Wheatleys, particularly Susannah, "loved her as one of [their] own children" (120). The concept of slave ownership and the psychological and emotional barriers it creates, regardless of how a slave is treated, had yet to be considered during the early nineteenth century. Jackson also reminds his readers that while in England, Wheatley's "color was overlooked" (121). For comparable examples, see *The Anti-Slavery Record*, 2:55–56; *Slavery and the Internal Slave Trade*, 220; Child, *Freedmen's Book*, 91; G. W. Williams, *History of the Negro Race*, 1:201–2; and Slattery, "Phillis Wheatley."

6. J. W. Johnson, "Early American Negro Poets," 240, 240-41.

7. An anonymous article titled "Expressional Power of the Colored Race" (1901) describes Wheatley's poem to Washington as "[o]ne of her best known" (459) but does not reprint it. The poem is also absent from Emily Foster Happer's "The First Negro Poet of America" (1904), an otherwise complimentary treatment of Wheatley in which Happer includes both Wheatley's and Washington's mutual correspondence. Happer does not make overtly flattering remarks about Washington, but her comments about Wheatley—"When we measure what Phillis Wheatley accomplished we must measure her by the slaves of her day[;] . . . even the white women of educated families were not expected to know the classics" (74)—reflect an increasing awareness of Wheatley's importance in the American canon.

8. Shields, "Wheatley's Struggle," 232, 237.

9. In *CW* see, respectively, "To a Lady on the Death of her Husband," 29; "Goliath of Gath," 31; "Isaiah LXIII. 1-8," 60; "To Captain H—D, of the 65th Regiment," 72; "To a Lady on her Coming to North America with Her Son, for the Recovery of Her Health," 78; and "To a Gentleman of the Navy" and "The Answer [By the Gentleman of the Navy]," 140–43.

10. See McCullough, *1776*, 47, 53, and *John Adams*, 91; Lantzer, "Washington as Cincinnatus," 34; and Morrison, *Political Philosophy of George Washington*, 62–106, 63.

11. See, e.g., Bloch, "Gendered Meanings of Virtue," 136–53, which concentrates on the moral theories of the Scottish Enlightenment and doctrinal arguments; Barnes, *State of Sympathy*, which investigates the emergence in American fiction of a sympathetic identity; Norton, *Liberty's Daughters*, which emphasizes the notion that piety was closely allied with feminine virtue and women's equality; Wood, *Radicalism of the American Revolution*, which discusses the shifts that occur between classical and Enlightenment notions of virtue; and Juster, *Disorderly Women*, which explores the religious and political dimensions of androgyny in eighteenth-century New England. Dimock, *Residues of Justice*, 49.

12. Bloch, *Gender and Morality*, 53; in fact, according to Harris, "America's Evangelical Women," New England black women participated in "religious traditions where women were often priests and ritual leaders" (448), and Mays, *Women in Early America*, notes that "the religion practiced by black women in early America was an amalgamation of African spirituality and Christianity," which allowed many black women in America to partake in the leadership roles expected of them in Africa (14). See also Wood, *Empire and Liberty*, 341–42 and 598, and Westerkamp, *Women and Religion*, 104–30, for discussions of Anglo-American women and leadership roles; Zagarri, "Morals, Manners, and the Republican Mother," 193.

13. Bloch, *Gender and Morality*, 158; Lyons, *Sex among the Rabble*, 290; Mulford, "Print and Manuscript Culture," 339.

14. Lyons, 297; Bloch, "Gendered Meanings of Virtue," 143; Kerber, *Women of the Republic*, 200.

15. See also Shogan, "George Washington" for further discussion of Washington as "the great-souled man"; Carrese, "Washington's Greatness," 147; Eliot, *History of the United States*, 192.

16. Washington and Bayard, *Specimens*, 10, 32, 42–43; Paine, *Rights of Man*, 3; Weems, *Life of Washington*, 3.

17. Fliegelman, *Prodigals and Pilgrims*, 1; for an extended discussion of early American patriarchal politics, see Kann, *Republic of Men*.

18. Bloch, "Construction of Gender," 606.

19. Ibid., 607.

20. Erkkila, "Phillis Wheatley," 162.

21. Ibid.

22. Wharton, "Poetical Epistle"; Mercer, "Letter 1776," 14; Howell, "Sung by a Number of Girls."

23. Barnes, *State of Sympathy*, 43; Weems, *Life of Washington*, 94, 96, 95.

24. W. C. Williams, *In the American Grain*, 234, 142.

25. Washington, *Papers, Revolutionary*, 12:685.

26. Bly, "Wheatley's 'To the University,'" 205–6.
27. Washington, *Papers, Revolutionary*, 3:387.
28. Ramsay, *Life of Washington*, 172.
29. Tyler, *Prose*, 273.
30. *American Historical Review*, 100.
31. "Death of Washington," 476, 477.
32. Pasquin, "A National Dirge."
33. J. B. Johnson, *Eulogy*, 6, 12.

BIBLIOGRAPHY

American Historical Review. Vol. 9. New York: Macmillan, 1904.

The Anti-Slavery Record. 2 vols. New York: R. G. Williams, for the American Anti-Slavery Society, 1835–36.

Barnes, Elizabeth. *States of Sympathy: Seduction and Democracy in the American Novel*. New York: Columbia University Press, 1997.

Bloch, Ruth H. "The Construction of Gender in a Republican World." In *A Companion to the American Revolution*, edited by Jack P. Greene and J. R. Pole, 605–09. Malden, MA: Blackwell, 2004.

———. *Gender and Morality in Anglo-American Culture*, 1650–1800. Berkeley: University of California Press, 2003.

———. "The Gendered Meanings of Virtue." In Bloch, *Gender and Morality*, 136-53.

Bly, Antonio T. "Wheatley's 'To the University of Cambridge in New England.'" *Explicator* 55.4 (1997): 205–08.

Carrese, Paul. "George Washington's Greatness and Aristotelian Virtue: Enduring Lessons for Constitutional Democracy." In *Magnanimity and Statesmanship*, edited by Carson Holloway, 145–70. Lanham, MD: Lexington, 2008.

Child, Lydia Maria. *The Freedmen's Book*. Boston: Ticknor and Fields, 1865.

"Death of General George Washington." *Monthly Magazine, and American Review* 1 (Apr.–Dec. 1799): 475–479.

Dimock, Wai Chee. *Residues of Justice: Literature, Law, Philosophy*. Berkley: University of California Press, 1996.

Eliot, Samuel. *History of the United States*. Boston: Brewer and Tileston, 1876.

Erkkila, Betsy. "Phillis Wheatley and the Black American Revolution." In *Feminist Interventions in Early American Studies*, edited by Mary C. Carruth, 161–82. Tuscaloosa: University of Alabama Press, 2006.

"Expressional Power of the Colored Race." *Werner's Magazine* 26 (Feb. 1901): 459–78.

Fliegelman, Jay. *Prodigals and Pilgrims: The American Revolution against Patriarchal Authority, 1750-1800*. Cambridge: Cambridge University Press, 1982.

Hale, Sarah Josepha. *Women's Record, or, Sketches of All Distinguished Women*. New York: Harper, 1855.

Happer, Emily Foster. "The First Negro Poet of America." *Literary Collector* 3 (May–Oct. 1904): 73–76.

Harris, Jane. "America's Evangelical Women: More than Wives and Mothers—Reformers, Minister, and Leaders." In *Encyclopedia of Women and Religion in*

North America, edited by Rosemary Skinner Keller and Rosemary Radford Ruether, 447–57. Bloomington: Indiana University Press, 2006.

Howells, Richard. "Sung by a Number of young Girls, dressed in white and decked with Wreaths and Chaplets of Flowers, holding Baskets of Flowers in their Hands, as General Washington passed under the Triumphal Arch raised on the Bridge at Trenton, April 21, 1789." *Report on the Star-Spangled Banner, Hail Columbia, America, Yankee Doodle.* Compiled by Oscar George Theodore Sonneck (1909). Rpt. in *Report on the Star-Spangled Banner, Hail Columbia, America, Yankee Doodle*, 63. Honolulu: University Press of the Pacific, 2001.

Jackson, W. H. "Memoirs." In *Poems on Various Subjects, Religious and Moral.* Denver: W. H. Lawrence, 1887.

Jefferson, Thomas. *Notes on the State of Virginia.* Richmond: J. W. Randolph, 1853.

Johnson, James Weldon. "Early American Negro Poets." *The Standard* 3 (July 1921): 240-41.

Johnson, John B. *Eulogy on General George Washington, A Sermon*, 5–22. Albany: L. Andrews, 1800.

Juster, Susan. *Disorderly Women: Sexual Politics and Evangelicalism in Revolutionary New England.* Ithaca, NY: Cornell University Press, 1994.

Kann, Mark E. *A Republic of Men: The American Founders, Gendered Language, and Patriarchal Politics.* New York: New York University Press, 1998.

Kerber, Linda K. *Women of the Republic: Intellect and Ideology in Revolutionary America.* Chapel Hill: University of North Carolina Press, 1980.

Lantzer, Jason S. "Washington as Cincinnatus: A Model of Leadership." In *George Washington: Foundation of Presidential Leadership and Character*, edited by Ethan M. Fishman, William D. Pederson, and Mark J. Rozell, 33–52. Westport, CT: Praeger, 2001.

Lewis, Jan. "The Republican Wife: Virtue and Seduction in the Early Republic." *William and Mary Quarterly* 44 (1987): 689–721.

Lyons, Clare A. *Sex among the Rabble: An Intimate History of Gender and Power in the Age of Revolution, Philadelphia, 1730–1830.* Chapel Hill: University of North Carolina Press, 2006.

Mays, Dorothy A. *Women in Early America: Struggle, Survival and Freedom in a New World.* Santa Barbara: ABC-CLIO, 2004.

McCullough, David. *1776.* New York: Simon and Schuster, 2005.

———. *John Adams.* New York: Simon and Schuster, 2008.

Mercer, George. "Letter 1760." In *Early Sketches of George Washington*, edited by William S. Baker, 13–14. Philadelphia: Lippincott, 1893.

Morrison, Jeffrey H. *The Political Philosophy of George Washington.* Baltimore: Johns Hopkins UP, 2009.

Mulford, Carla. "Print and Manuscript Culture." In *The Oxford Handbook of Early American Literature*, edited by Kevin J. Hayes, 321–44. Oxford: Oxford University Press, 2008.

Norton, Mary Beth. *Liberty's Daughters: The Revolutionary Experience of American Women, 1750–1800.* Ithaca, NY: Cornell University Press, 1996.

Paine, Thomas. *The Rights of Man.* Edited by Ronald Herder. Mineola, NY: Dover, 1999.

Pasquin, Anthony. "A National Dirge." *Columbian Phenix and Boston Review* 1 (1800): 178–79.

Proceedings of the Massachusetts Historical Society. Boston: Wiggin and Lunt, 1864–65.

Ramsay, David M. *Life of George Washington*. 3rd ed. Baltimore: Joseph Cushing, 1814.

Shields, John C. "Phillis Wheatley's Struggle for Freedom." In *The Collected Works of Phillis Wheatley*, edited by John C. Shields, 229–70. New York: Oxford University Press, 1988.

Shogan, Colleen J. "George Washington: Can Aristotle Recapture What His Countrymen Have Forgotten?" In *George Washington: Foundation of Presidential Leadership and Character*, edited by Ethan M. Fishman, William D. Pederson, and Mark J. Rozell, 53–70. Westport, CT: Praeger, 2001.

Slattery, John R. "Phillis Wheatley, the Negro Poetess." *Catholic World* 39 (Apr. 1884–Sept. 1884): 497–98.

Slavery and the Internal Slave Trade in the United States of North America. Executive Committee of the American Anti-Slavery Society. London: Thomas Ward, 1841.

Sparks, Jared. *The Life of George Washington*. Boston: Little, Brown, 1857.

Tyler, Royall. *The Prose of Royall Tyler*. Montpelier: Vermont Historical Society, 1972.

Washington, George. *The Papers of George Washington, Confederation Series*. 6 vols. Edited by W. W. Abbott, Dorothy Twohig, et al. Charlottesville: University of Virginia Press, 1992–97.

———. *The Papers of George Washington, Revolutionary War Series*. 18 vols. to date. Edited by W. W. Abbott, Theodore J. Crackel, et al. Charlottesville: University of Virginia Press, 1987–.

———. *The Writings of George Washington*. Edited by Jared Sparks. 12 vols. Boston: American Stationers' Company, 1834–37.

Washington, George, and Thomas Francis Bayard. *Specimen Pages of a Proposed Publication of the Papers of Washington, Franklin, etc., 1775*. [Original from University of Michigan].

Weems, Mason Locke. *The Life of Washington*. Armonk, NY: M. E. Sharpe, 1996.

Westerkamp, Marilyn J. *Women and Religion in Early America, 1600–1850: The Puritan and Evangelical Traditions*. New York: Routledge, 1999.

Wharton, Charles Henry. "A Poetical Epistle to His Excellency General Washington." *Monthly Review; or, Literary Journal* 62 (Jan.–June 1780): 390.

Wheatley, Phillis. *The Collected Works of Phillis Wheatley*. Edited by John C. Shields. New York: Oxford University Press, 1988.

Williams, George Washington. *History of the Negro Race in America from 1619–1880*. 2 vols. New York: Putnam's, 1883.

Williams, William Carlos. *In the American Grain*. New York: New Directions, 1956.

Wood, Gordon S. *Empire and Liberty: A History of the Early Republic, 1789–1815*. Oxford: Oxford University Press, 2009.

———. *The Radicalism of the American Revolution*. New York: Knopf, 1992.

Zagarri, Rosemarie. "Morals, Manners, and the Republican Mother." *American Quarterly* 44.2 (1992): 192–215.

Disturbing Hunting Grounds: Negotiating Geocultural Change in the Western Narratives of George Catlin and Washington Irving

Matthew J. C. Cella
Shippensburg University

WHEN the speaker of William Cullen Bryant's "The Prairies" (1834) comes upon the midwestern "gardens of the Desert," he imagines the landscape as both a canvas and a palimpsest. The poem is framed by an acknowledgment of the speaker's status as an American Adam who beholds the "glorious work" of "the hand that built the firmament" and who is transformed by the experience. This original experience with the "unshorn fields" of the prairies, however, also evokes a dream about the ghosts in landscape. While he claims in the first section that "man hath no power in all this," his dream illustrates otherwise.[1] Features like the "mighty mounds" (127) and the "ancient footsteps" (128) of the hunted bison that dot the landscape are physical manifestations of how the prairies have also been fashioned by a series of cultural arrivals and removals. What on his first beholding appears as a pristine wilderness transforms into sacred ground, rich in the history of those who have come before: the ancient mound builders and the "roaming hunter tribes" (127).

As the forerunner of the next phase of prairie occupation, the speaker visualizes the removal of the "red man" to the "wilder hunting-ground" of the west. Into the void created by this removal reverberates

Literature in the Early American Republic: Annual Studies on Cooper and His Contemporaries
Volume 6, 2014. Copyright © 2014 by AMS Press, Inc. All rights reserved.

the auditory evidence of advancing European American colonists: the "domestic hum" of the bee, harbinger of civilization; the "laugh of children;" the "hymn / Of Sabbath worshippers;" and the "low of herds" and "rustling of the heavy grain" (128–29). The series of oscillations between blanking and filling the prairie canvas in the poem reflects a general ambivalence toward the prospect of settling the vast interior of North America. This ambivalence, or double-sightedness, about the future of the prairie region registers the more general doubts concerning the prospect of developing and maintaining roots in the arid West. Although Bryant's poem moves imaginatively across the more fertile prairies east of the 100th meridian, it illustrates the schizophrenia that characterizes early American assessments concerning the value of the western grasslands. In contending with *and admiring* the supposed uninhabitability of the arid West—that is, its seeming uselessness from an agrarian perspective—writers such as Bryant began the process of negotiating the status of the Great Plains as a marginal but potentially cultivatable space, a landscape that required *imaginative* domestication in advance of any attempts to physically develop and improve it. While many antebellum writers viewed the impending appropriation of the Indian wilderness by European American settler culture as tragic, even those most skeptical of American progress saw the erasure of the great bison hunting-grounds as inevitable and irreversible.

George Catlin and Washington Irving—who published popular accounts of their travels through the West in the 1830s—provide a representative spectrum of antebellum perceptions concerning the upshot of this presumably inevitable transformation of the western wilderness.[2] On the one hand, as romancers of the plains, these two authors recognize the aesthetic value of the Native hunting-grounds and must reconcile this value with their prophecies concerning its future erasure at the hands of frontier advancement; on the other hand, their approaches to western space reveal subtle differences in each writer's final assessment of what the Great Plains mean, or should mean, to the American project. While working backward chronologically from Catlin's *Letters and Notes* (1841) to Irving's *A Tour on the Prairies* (1835), I trace a thematic arc occurring in these narratives that moves from Catlin's protopreservationist stance to Irving's romantic domestication of Great Plains space. Ultimately, the arid environment prompted two primary responses from an antebellum society defined by agricultural and industrial pursuits: either the arid land of the West should be left to the Indians or it should be converted, through labor and imagination, into an agrarian paradise. The former response is articulated best through Catlin's overtly romantic construction of Plains Indian culture, a description that clearly manifests the aesthetic power of the Indian wilderness in the antebellum imagination. Irving, too, articulates the *aesthetic* value of the Indian wilderness, but his appreciation is tempered by images that prophetically prefigure the conversion of this wilderness into more recognizable and permanent Euro-American settlements. Although the actual transformation of the Great Plains was only in its nascent stages during the antebellum period, Irving's writing represents an important step in the process of making the region inhabitable by agrarian standards. That is, Irving more self-consciously mediates the conflicting impulses of westward expansion: he acknowledges, as Catlin does, that the Native hunting-grounds are a dynamic and environmentally appropriate land-use system at the same time that he views the plains as a blank canvas awaiting the masterful strokes of the European American imagination and its concomitant paradigm of agricultural development. As two writers from the east who travel through a western landscape on the verge of what they perceive as a forthcoming geocultural upheaval, Catlin and Irving represent the intellectual front line of America's westward movement because their narratives begin the process of negotiating the consequences of frontier progress and manifest destiny.

1. The Agrarian Dream Meets the Bad Lands

In the decades before the plow became a more permanent feature of the Great Plains, the largest question surrounding the future of the region within the European American imagination was, could the American Desert be inhabited? The earliest surveys of the region suggested that the answer to this question was a resounding "no!" Thanks to the documents and descriptions provided by surveyors and travelers such as Zebulon Pike, Stephen Long, and Henry Brackenridge, the reputation of the plains as the Great American Desert was well entrenched in the European American imagination.[3]

Such a characterization ran well against the grain, so to speak, of the agrarian principles of the American republic; nonagricultural land was useless land, or land accorded to the lowest ranks of human society on the evolutionary scale. To move west into the Indian wilderness was to move backward in time to a more primitive era during which hunter and gatherer cultures reigned. Once the Indians were removed from the wilderness, the land could be developed and reclaimed as part of the agrarian dream. When the advancing guard of civilization came in contact with the arid region past the 100th meridian, however, the yeoman—Jefferson's chosen ones of the North American continent—and the whole agrarian myth they embodied hit a major obstacle. In the first half of the nineteenth century, frontier expansion leapfrogged over the Great Plains and pushed on toward the Far West. In the second half of the century, when the populations of the United States and Canada were expanding, the governments on both sides of the 49th parallel began to look differently at the arid West: what was deemed a savage wasteland was now viewed as a territory to be settled and cultivated.

Chronicles of first encounters with the Great Plains frontier, such as those penned by Catlin and Irving, provide an overarching narrative design for ways of assessing the present and future value of the Indian wilderness. As Thomas Hallock's study of eighteenth- and nineteenth-century trans-Appalachian frontier narratives demonstrates, authors of frontier narratives look to negotiate "their position on already claimed country."[4] Frontier writers operate from the premise that "a new empire should take root," not in a *virgin* land, but "in the humus left by a vanished people."[5] Such was the pattern inherent in the social-evolutionary design: once the Indian presence was erased from the scene, the so-called Indian wilderness would give way to the progress of the European American empire. Because the quality of the soil in the Great Plains was suspect, hopes for an agrarian empire taking root in the humus of the arid grasslands were dim and slow to ignite. Thus, early accounts of the plains frontier essentially proscribe two strategies for managing the wilderness beyond the isohyetal perimeter, where rainfall is not sufficient to support conventional agricultural practices: leave it alone or conquer it and transform it into something viable.

Ultimately, these two approaches overlap as they both branch out from a characterization of the grasslands as a marginalized and exotic Other—with its Otherness fortified by its "savage" occupants. The plains are distinguishable strictly as an antithesis to more recognizable landscapes east of the 100th meridian. Whether demonized and dismissed as a wasteland or romanticized as the last haunts of the wild Indians, the driving ethic behind this process of Othering relies on the notion that the best thing for European Americans to do with the arid lands is to leave them alone. Unable to meet the needs of a progressive, agrarian nation, the Great Plains were destined to remain, for the immediate future at least, the homeland of those societies presumably stuck in the first or second stage of social development. The wilderness of wide open spaces belonged, for better or worse, to the savage nomads, and it is in this linkage, in this imagined symbiosis, that the chief value of the Great Plains adheres. This is true not only for the nineteenth-century European American authors who documented this symbiotic relationship in journals, travel narratives, and sketchbooks but also for their largely Eastern audiences who consumed expressions of this romantic aesthetic at an impressive rate.

The inescapable fact that the western grasslands would *not* be left alone—that even the West was destined to be settled and developed—served only to heighten the power of this romantic aesthetic. Within the social-evolutionary imagination, the course of empire must necessarily carve a path through the Great Plains, and cultures tending toward rootedness and settlement must win out. While writers such as Catlin and Irving lamented the passing of the Indian wilderness and treated the inevitability of westward expansion with ambivalence, the projected triumph of "progress" over "wildness" required the erasure of the Indian presence from the Great Plains landscape. The depiction of the arid grasslands as a blank canvas upon which to write anew the agrarian dream suggested that the promise of the Great Plains lay in its future; the already-occupied American grasslands thus presented a challenge to be met, an obstacle to overcome with technology, innovation, and imagination. While the settlement of the arid West would take the better part of the century to complete, the process was in its early stages when Catlin and Irving traveled through the region in the 1830s. Signs of change were already present in the region, for example, in the form of the whisky and fur trades that were already altering the indigenous cultures and their ways of inhabiting the unique landscape of the arid West. In forecasting further geocultural upheaval, Catlin and Irving begin the process of negotiating the inevitable outcome of frontier progress: the loss of wildness. While they both lament this loss, their narratives are ripe with images and descriptions that reveal a different perspective concerning frontier progress: one that moves beyond the concept of terminal change to instead embrace the certainty of unremitting geocultural change.

2. The Protopreservationist Fantasy of George Catlin

For George Catlin, the Native hunting-grounds of the western prairies represented a geocultural ideal, an aesthetically powerful commingling of Native culture and nonhuman nature that provided an exhilarating contrast to life in the more populated and built up environs of the East. For this Pennsylvania lawyer-turned-artist who traveled extensively throughout the region between 1830 and 1836, the nomadic tribes of the Great Plains and the expansive open country of the western prairies formed a perfect fit that should go undisturbed. Indeed, it was his mission as an artist to capture this perfect fit on canvas in a large catalog of ethnographic paintings that formed "Catlin's Indian Gallery," which opened in 1837.[6] Dismayed by the conditions of the eastern and frontier Indians, whose "habits have been changed—whose pride has been cut down—whose country has been ransacked," Catlin went west to feverishly record the Great Plains Indians in their wild and native state, for he sensed that they would soon meet the same fate as their eastern counterparts.[7]

In addition to his sketches and paintings of his western subjects, Catlin documents the symbiotic relationship between the Plains Indians and their physical environment in his *North American Indians*, published in two volumes in 1841. It is in letter 31, "Mouth of Teton River, *Upper Missouri*," that the artist most fully articulates his vision for the future of the Great Plains, wherein he situates the Indian wilderness, or the "buffalo Plains," as an ideal model of inhabitation. In this letter, Catlin describes in great detail the habits, domain, and ecological niche of the American bison, as well as the customs and practices of those tribes that rely upon the buffalo for subsistence. Catlin depicts the buffalo, the grasslands, and the nomadic Indians as a harmonious system, divinely sanctioned and nearly perfect in its existence. He notes how the numerous herds of buffalo seem to "have been spread over the plains of this vast country, by the Great Spirit, for the use and subsistence of the red men, who live almost exclusively on their flesh, and clothe themselves with their skins" (1:247). In his call later in this letter to preserve the plains in its wild state, Catlin again emphasizes how it is on the "plain of grass," where the "buffaloes dwell," that "the tribes of Indians [live and flourish], whom God made for the enjoyment of that fair land and its luxuries" (1:261).

The romantic union between environment and Native inhabitants is illustrated through the sublime aspect of the buffalo hunt, which throws Catlin himself into a transcendental reverie. The sublimity of the buffalo hunt emerges from what Catlin imagines to be a wholly natural dynamic between Native hunter and beast: the fluid motion of bison, horse, hunter, and weapon, coupled with the overarching mingling of danger, beauty, and power of the scene endow the hunt with a magical and spiritual quality (1:252–53).

Threatening this natural dynamic, Catlin warns, is the ever-increasing infringement of more advanced modes of subsistence. Beside the looming threat posed by the encroachment of European American civilization—with their weapons, whiskey, disease, and plows—the idealized model of the Plains Indian wilderness is already being torn asunder by the American market economy. The subsistence-oriented hunt, where the relationship between the hunter, the hunted, and the environment is in balance, is now replaced by wide-scale slaughter, as the goal of the hunt shifts toward profiteering. Catlin acknowledges with a note of disappointment the initiation of winter buffalo hunts, a dramatic change in the pattern of Native hunting practices: "The Indians generally kill and dry meat enough in the fall, when it is fat and juicy, to last them through the winter; so that they have little other object for this unlimited slaughter, amid the drifts of snow, than that of procuring their robes for traffic with their Traders" (1:254). The fur trade and the increasing demand for bison skins disrupt what he imagines is the wild and natural harmony already established in the region. Catlin goes on to list other examples of the "profligate waste of the lives of these noble and useful animals" (1:256), a pattern of abuse enacted by whites and Indians alike, which will ultimately erase the "last abode" (1:260) of the Indian wilderness from the face of the earth.

In the face of this "profligate waste," Catlin makes a plea for the preservation of the Great Plains in all its "primitive rudeness" (1:260). At the end of the letter, which marks the end of the first volume of *North American Indians*, he speculates:

> And what a splendid contemplation too, when one . . . imagines [the plains] as they *might* in future be seen, (by some great protecting policy of government) preserved in their pristine beauty and wildness in a *magnificent park*, where the world could see for ages to come, the native Indian in his classic attire, galloping his wild horse, with sinewy bow, and shield and lance, amid the fleeting herds of elks and buffaloes. What a beautiful and thrilling specimen for America to preserve and hold up to the view of her refined citizens and the world, in future ages! A *nation's Park*, containing man and beast, in all the wild and freshness of their nature's beauty! (1:261–62)

This call for preservation establishes the Plains Indian wilderness as a spectacle, a model of emplacement not to be emulated but instead to be frozen in time for the pleasure of the more advanced (though nostalgic-minded) citizens of America.[8] As David Spence notes in *Dispossessing the Wilderness*, on the basis of this call for a "nation's Park," Catlin is often regarded as the intellectual father of the national park movement and part of a "genealogy that includes Henry David Thoreau, John Muir, Aldo Leopold, and the environmental movement of the past three decades." However, what separates Catlin from his intellectual successors is the "fact that Catlin's conception of a wilderness preserve included the presence of the Indians."[9] Through partitioning off the Great Plains from the refinery of American civilization, Catlin hopes to preserve the natural dynamic he admires as being implicit in Native land-use practices. It is on the Great Plains, after all, that the "finest specimens of the Indian race are to be seen," where the Indian is "stimulated by ideas of honour and virtue, in which the God of Nature has certainly not curtailed him" (1:262).

The "nation's Park" proposal is predicated on an evolutionary paradigm wedded to a biological imperative: America as an advanced nation of farmers and industrialists can afford to let the Great Plains remain as Indian Territory because only the Indians can subsist in the arid region. Catlin proclaims that the western grasslands may be easily preserved "without detriment to the country or its borders" because "the tracts of country on which the buffaloes have assembled, are uniformly sterile, and of no available use to cultivating man" (1:262). Again, the nomadic Indian and the "sterile" landscape of the Great Plains belong together; they merge to form a symbiotic and harmonious unity that would be disrupted only by the arrival of the plow and the "desolating hands of cultivating man" (1:260).

The Plains Indian wilderness ultimately intrigues Catlin because it presents an exotic mode of inhabitation, a land-community distinct from the cultivated prairies and forests east of the Mississippi. Catlin's idealization of the Plains Indian wilderness thus issues forth from a tendency to essentialize the cultures of the western American Indians. That is, Catlin's wilderness aesthetic spawns from a desire to imbue the wild tribes of the Plains with a kind of cultural purity and static immutability, bolstered through their primitive and primal engagement with the Plains environment. To preserve this environment is to guarantee the continuation *ad infinitum* of the Indian mode of cohabitating with the wilderness. This geocultural ideal offers one standard of measuring the value of the bad lands of the Plains, as Catlin recognizes the aesthetic worth of the Native hunting-grounds from the European American perspective. It can retain this value only by being left alone, which Catlin knew was unlikely; its future value therefore could not extend beyond its status as a source for nostalgia.

3. Fettering Unfamiliar Terrain: Washington Irving's A Tour on the Prairies

While Catlin proposes a let-it-alone strategy for the Indian wilderness as a way to prevent its dissolution by "desolating hands of cultivating man," his approach reflects an exception to the standard romantic ambivalence implicit in the social-evolutionary paradigm. For those such as James Fenimore Cooper and Irving, the beautiful harmony embodied in the Indian wilderness is necessarily ephemeral as it must give way, for better or worse, to European American order. The ambivalence evoked by the prospect of inevitable geocultural change is ultimately heightened by the fact that these authors are often complicit in the transformation as they make the Great Plains hospitable through language. As his *A Tour on the Prairies* (1835) manifests, Irving's relationship with the arid West is tenuous at best. As the title of his narrative suggests, he is a mere tourist, an interloper in a region whose trails are fresh and whose future as a site for permanent European American settlement was undefined, though coming into focus. Writing against a backdrop of westward progress, Irving attempts to reconcile his desire to celebrate and romanticize the exotic character of the wilderness with a foreboding sense that this exoticism is something that will, and perhaps must, be domesticated as European American civilization advances. Irving's narrative is particularly valuable for the way that he mediates between mimetic and romantic evaluations of Great Plains space, between his desire to chronicle his experience of the foreign, arid West and his impetus to subordinate this experience to accepted conventions.

Irving first establishes a link between Indianness and wildness in a highly romanticized and stylized description of a Cree on horseback. Upon his departure from Fort Gibson, the stepping-off point for his tour, he notices the young Cree across the river looking down on them: "He had paused to reconnoiter us from the brow of a rock, and formed a picturesque object, in unison with the wild scenery around him."[10] Irving's gaze positions his Cree subject at the center of an idealized geocultural landscape: environment and inhabitant form an aesthetically pleasing and unified vision that embodies the allure of the Indian wilderness. This image of Cree, horse, and "scenery" encapsulates the romance of the Great Plains. Irving imaginatively frames his subject in such a way as to emphasize the symbiosis of man, beast, and landscape. His use of "reconnoiter" suggests that the Cree has some business he is attending to and thus occupies the scenery with purpose. Irving is drawn to the scene, in part, because he recognizes that *he* is the intruder, the foreign presence in the West who must be monitored by the original inhabitants. Therefore, Irving both disturbs (through his physical presence) and creates (through his imagination) a harmonious system of Native cohabitation as he chronicles his entrance into the Indian wilderness.

Although they are more hostile than the Cree and Osages, the Pawnees also represent the association between savage landscape and savage inhabitants. Occupying the buffalo ranges of the high plains, the Pawnees, Irving explains, embody Native America in its most savage state:

> There is always some wild untamed tribe of Indians, who form, for a time, the terror of a frontier, and about whom all kinds of fearful terrors are told. Such, at present, was the case with the Pawnees who rove the regions between the Arkansas and Red River, and the prairies of Texas. . . . [They are] sometimes engaged in hunting the deer and the buffalo, sometimes in warlike and predatory expeditions; for, like their counterparts, the sons of Ishmael, their hand is against every one, and every one's hand is against them. Some of them have no fixed habitation but dwell in tents of skin, easily packed up and transported, so that they are here to-day, and away, no one know where, to-morrow. (75–76)

As wanderers in the Great American Desert, with no "fixed habitation," the Pawnees lend to the grassland wilderness a sense of danger and unpredictability. The ominous threat that accompanies Irving's entrance into Pawnee territory bolsters the aesthetic of savagery that defines Irving's "region of adventure" (84).

The Pawnee "hunting region" is thus a dialectical space where the human and nonhuman communities each impart wildness to its counterpart. For Irving, however, this howling wilderness is not something to be condemned, but rather something to take pleasure in as a tourist. The aesthetics of fear and wildness draw Irving deeper into the West and invigorate him: "There is something exciting to the imagination and stirring to the feelings, while traversing these hostile plains, in seeing a horseman prowling along the horizon. It is like descrying a sail at sea in time of war, when it may be either a privateer or a pirate" (84). Again, the unpredictability of the environment and its inhabitants lend an air of exoticism and excitement to the region, imbuing it with a value that only an outsider might enjoy.

Irving's view might have been different, of course, had he and his party actually encountered the Pawnees; it is their general absence that allows Irving to maintain his romantic perspective concerning the Indian wilderness as a playground for the European American imagination.[11] The threat that the Pawnees pose, however, represents an aspect of the wilderness aesthetic that is jeopardized by the encroachment of European American civilization. While the physical environment might be preserved—and its lack of cultivability suggests, as Catlin fervently argued, that it might be kept unsullied by the work of the plow—Irving has a sense that the element of terror implicit in the Indian wilderness will soon be tamed by advancing white civilization. This gives Irving a sense of urgency, a call to capture the essence of the Indian wilderness before it presumably disappears.

Irving most explicitly manifests his critical stance toward this transformation on the Great Plains through repeated references to wild horses. For Irving, wild horses epitomize the exotic character of the Indian wilderness, its alluring Otherness as opposed to the stale familiarity of the cities and towns of the east. Once he enters the high plains, he describes no less than seven encounters with wild horses, mostly alluding to their capture by various members of his party (see 114, 117–22, 137, 147–50, 155, 182, 195–96). Irving's description of his first contact with a wild horse establishes a dichotomy of wildness and domestication that underscores his wilderness aesthetic: "It was the first time I had ever seen a horse scouring his native wilderness in all the pride and freedom of his nature. How different from the poor, mutilated, harnessed, checked, reined-up victim of luxury, caprice, and avarice, in our cities!" (114). Horses represent a feature of the landscape that are at once familiar and exotic. On the one hand, unlike the bison or wolf, the horse is a common enough animal east of the Missouri and Irving travels on horseback throughout his western journey; on the other hand, the wild prairie environment affords Irving the opportunity to view the animal from a new perspective in its "native wilderness," thus exoticizing the experience. For Irving, the horse nicely images a point of comparison between the proud and free cultures of the West and the "harnessed" and "reined-up" cultures of the East, the latter being a corruption of the former. The wild horse of the high plains represents the ideal of unfettered freedom and motion that lends to the region its romantic and aesthetic cache, a potent fusion of wildness and purity that is threatened by the westward crawl of the capricious and avaricious cities.

For the most part, Irving witnesses wild horses in the process of their being captured by members of his party, thus forcing him to engage with the prospect of their domestication. He is generally ambivalent on the subject, as the captured horse simultaneously represents the Native land-use practices and the European American economy that threatens to consume that wilderness. He notes how the capture of wild horses is one of the characteristic "achievements of the prairie tribes" (117) and a manifestation of the classic Great Plains culture in action. He speculates on the origins of the horses, tracing their roots back to Spain, Africa, and Arabia, and he offers some ethnographic commentary upon the deep kinship between the Plains Indian and the wild horse, who are both "rover[s] of the plain" (117). While the Eurasian roots of the horse tell a more complicated story, which I address in the concluding section, what draws Irving's attention is their status as a symbol for unfettered wildness. Together, the prairie tribes and wild horses contribute to a region of "rapid motion" and form an idyllic "sunshiny life" (117) that rejuvenates Irving and his eastern companions.

The participation of outsiders in the capture of wild horses, however, is not so idyllic and prophesies the forthcoming domestication of the western wilderness by European American settlers. The ambivalence Irving feels toward the enterprise of horse capture is revealed in "The Camp of the Wild Horse," which focuses on Beatte, the half-blood hunter, who is the first of the group to capture a wild horse. When Beatte first enters the camp with his prize, Irving notes how "the whole scene was singularly wild" with the "wild huntsman and his wild horse" (118). The appeal of the scene thus resides in its wildness, as with the Cree on horseback near Fort Gibson. However, as a man who straddles savagery and civilization, Beatte ultimately represents both the ideal of wildness and the ill effects of taming that wildness.

While Irving is drawn to the "singularly wild" scene, he also closes the chapter by reflecting on the tragedy implicit in the image of the captured horse:

> I could not but look with compassion upon this fine young animal, whose whole course of existence had been so suddenly reversed. From being a denizen of these vast pastures, ranging at will from plain to plain and mead to mead . . . he was suddenly reduced to perpetual and painful servitude, to pass his life under the harness and the curb, amid, perhaps, the din and dust and drudgery of the cities. The transition in his lot was such as sometimes takes place in human affairs: . . . one day, a prince of the prairies—the next day, a pack horse. (122)

The domestication of the wild horse symbolizes the taming of the wild land and the eventual passing away of the Indian wilderness. While Beatte's triumph over the denizen of the high plains echoes the grandeur of the prairie tribes' hunting practices, his victory foreshadows the transformation of the Great Plains from a wild to a domesticated space. Indeed, Beatte's success creates quite a buzz in the camp, as "nothing was talked of but the capture of wild horses" (120), and throughout the rest of the narrative, the wild horses are pursued with reckless abandon by Irving's traveling companions. The half-blood hunter's achievement thus ushers in a process of taming and subduing the West; like the honey bees, Beatte introduces European American enterprise into the wild landscape.

Irving's ambivalence toward European American frontier advancement ultimately runs quite deep, in large part because Irving is a forerunner of this advancement. As much as Irving might wish to subvert the "westering myth," as William Bedford Clark suggests, he ultimately participates in the process of *imaginatively* domesticating the West through his narrative.[12] Many critics find *A Tour on the Prairies* to be deeply flawed as a result; they read it as an awkward attempt by Irving to impose romantic conventions on a landscape that was relatively incomprehensible to him.[13]

Irving's Europeanization of the landscape, so well documented by John Joseph, exhibits only one level of his domestication of Great Plains space.[14] More striking are the pastoral and agrarian images he grafts onto the prairie landscape. His ambivalent response to the uncultivated prairies is most explicitly revealed in "The Grand Prairie" chapter as his traveling party engages in a buffalo hunt on an open plain. The barren quality of the landscape once again evokes an aesthetic and emotional response from Irving, as he articulates the feelings that the desert wilderness inspires:

> To one unaccustomed to it, there is something inexpressibly lonely in the solitude of a prairie. The loneliness of the forest seems nothing to it. . . . Here we have an immense extent of landscape without a sign of human existence. We have the consciousness of being far, far beyond the bounds of human habitation; we feel as if moving in the midst of a desert world. (176–77)

Here, Irving documents the emotional power and exotic Otherness of the "desert world" of the western prairies. Such a world provides the occasion to experience a unique kind of solitude, an experience unavailable in the cities—or even forest wilds—of the East. What strikes Irving is that the prairies lack landmarks that indicate the presence of "human habitation." This comment at once reveals the exotic appeal of the empty prairies and suggests Irving's bias toward static and rooted forms of inhabitation. That he is in the midst of the buffalo ranges means that he is on land already occupied and used by the nomadic Indians, whose absence from the region is only temporary. Whereas he elsewhere celebrates the Native cultures of the prairie, he seems to erase them here, as he fails to acknowledge their cultural life-ways as a viable form of "human habitation."

Shortly after noting the absence of "human existence" on the prairie blank canvas, Irving imagines the buffalo ranges as a site of "human"—that is, agricultural and European American—industry. Upon spotting a herd of grazing buffalo, Irving explains: "It required but little stretch of fancy to picture them so many cattle grazing on the edge of a common, and that the grove might shelter some lowly farm-house" (176). Again, Irving filters the image through his pastoral imagination, converting the Pawnees' hunting region into a middle landscape; the "wild" scene becomes domesticated and Irving's imagination provides the "human habitation" that the open plain lacked. His "fancy" shapes the literary landscape so that it reflects an image that is familiar rather than exotic and controllable rather than incomprehensible. His imaginative feat had such broad contemporary appeal, Joseph suggests, because Irving's writing—his mythification and, as I would argue, domestication—helps to make the Great Plains inhabitable from a European American perspective.[15]

The shift from an image of an open plain devoid of "human" settlements (and thus unoccupied) to an image of agrarian domesticity illustrates Irving's conflicted engagement with the western landscape. *A Tour on the Prairies* presents a conventionally romantic portrait of the Indian wilderness as a haven of freedom and primitive wildness; Irving celebrates the idea of a landscape unsullied by European American culture even as he recognizes that this wild state cannot last. Even though the repeated contrast of wild and captured horses underscores the tragic tone of Irving's frontier aesthetic, it is important to recognize that Irving himself participates in the domestication of the Great Plains landscape. His imaginative cultivation of the Indian wilderness furrows the grasslands and achieves through "fancy" what the fence, lasso, and plow will accomplish in fact in succeeding generations. While Irving was no booster of western agriculture, *A Tour on the Prairies* documents an attempt to reconcile competing valuations of Great Plains space. Irving's book thus provides a template for the debate over land-use practices in the arid region, as his work both directly and indirectly engages with two visions of the prairie landscape: the arid, uncultivated, and wild grasslands and the cultivated and viable fields of pasturage and grain. Ultimately, as an outsider to the region, Irving cannot resist the impetus toward transforming the "realm of adventure"—the great Pawnee hunting-grounds—into familiar images of the built environments of the East. In this way, Irving's narrative serves as an imaginative front line of the European American pursuit of its manifest destiny, as his descriptions of the West mediate forthcoming geocultural change by foreshadowing the domestication and cultivation of the western wilderness.

4. Embracing a Region of Flux

Both Irving's wild horse lament and Catlin's "nation's park" proposal register an early American sentiment concerning the terminal nature of frontier-based geocultural change. Even as both writers resist and resent the *forthcoming* upheaval of the Indian wilderness and reconcile such change in their own ways, the most prominent images in their narratives ironically undercut the alpha/omega paradigm of geocultural change, one that presumes that the face of the North American landscape will be progressively altered by a series of permanent land-use transitions that move up a social-evolutionary scale from hunting and gathering to agricultural and then industrial development. Read in another way, Catlin's and Irving's narratives reveal an ironic counterforce to this alpha/omega paradigm in that they reflect how change in the West is ongoing and one of the defining features of the place.

In this light, the wild horse serves as a powerful symbol for the dynamic interplay between nature and culture in the region. Irving himself acknowledges the European origins of the horse, how the North American herds are descended from formerly domesticated ancestors. The wild horse therefore reflects a more complex reality than Irving's wild/tame dichotomy admits: it troubles the very notion that such a dichotomy exists. Furthermore, the appropriation of horses by the bison-hunting tribes of the West, which both Irving and Catlin read as integral to the romantic aesthetic of the "wild" Indian, is more properly read as one point in a cycle of geocultural exchange. Likewise, Irving's portrait of the Cree on horseback, more than simply an image of the untamed lord of the grasslands, actually reveals a process of ongoing interaction between indigenous and invading cultures; that is, the bison-hunting cultures of the West that Irving and Catlin celebrate are themselves the product of geocultural evolution, one generated by the introduction of the horse. While bison hunting had long been a component of indigenous land-use practices in the West, the introduction of the horse to the region by the Spanish revolutionized the bison hunt and created what James Wilson refers to as the "classic" plains culture. Because of this "equestrian revolution," Wilson explains, "a previously almost uninhabitable area suddenly offered an accessible, dependable, and—with an estimated total of sixty million or so bison—apparently boundless food supply."[16] Many of the tribes who inhabited the region abandoned farming along the river basins to follow the bison herds; they adapted their life-ways to fit this new economic potential. The bison-hunting grounds that Catlin and Irving are so eager to experience in their pure state are thus a geocultural phenomenon formed in the crucible of the very same frontier that they project will be the source of its inevitable undoing.

Read through this lens, Catlin's "nation's park" proposal is problematic. On the surface, the proposal presents a benevolent alternative to cultural and physical genocide, but in failing to account for the extensive record of change that is an integral part of the heritage of the bison-hunting cultures, Catlin overlooks the value of cultural adaptability in the face of change. That is, Catlin's proposal ultimately prescribes the complete negation of Native sovereignty, as it denies bison-hunting communities the ability to determine the best way to mitigate forthcoming change. Instead, Caitlin proposes that the fate of these communities be managed and maintained by the US government, so that the Indians are preserved in a state of museum-like sterility for future European American tourists to enjoy.[17] The only way for Indians to truly remain Indians is for them to remain sequestered off from outside contact. The alternative is outright erasure. This linear, either/or paradigm denies the potential for a middle ground, for intermediate categories such as those represented by the wild horse and the Cree on horseback.

Like the speaker of Bryant's "The Prairies," who spends so much time admiring the past occupants of the prairie landscape, Catlin and Irving view geocultural change as a series of abrupt and distinct phases of progress with one community of inhabitants giving way to the next. Thus, both of these writers cannot move beyond thinking about the postfrontier western landscape in terms of loss: vanishing Indians and diminishing wildness. What ultimately unifies these two authors' prognostications about the future of the Great American Desert is that they are both based on an underlying assumption that the frontier represents an either/or line of demarcation: *either* there is wilderness *or* there is civilization; there is *either* the Indian *or* the European American. When the bad lands of the arid West were deemed reclaimable and fit for agricultural development, the bison-hunting indigenous communities were doomed to be wiped off the face of the continent. Frontier-based change was considered terminal, which is why Catlin felt so compelled to capture and preserve on canvas the indigenous cultures and the untouched wilderness they inhabited, and why Irving and his traveling companions felt equally compelled to visit the region before it was irrevocably altered. Their narratives therefore offer interesting attempts to reconcile conflicting attitudes toward the conquest of the arid West. While romantic nostalgia for a fleeting geocultural landscape obviously motivates their responses to their western experiences, their narratives ironically reveal a much more complicated picture of change in the region, one more in tune with the nature of the place. As the record of human inhabitation of the Great Plains over the past few centuries suggests, change is one of the region's defining characteristics, as true now—especially in the wake of the Great Plow-Up and the subsequent Dust Bowl—as it was when Catlin and Irving encountered it.

NOTES

1. Bryant, "The Prairies," 126. Subsequent references to this edition will be cited parenthetically in the text.

2. Although Catlin's *Letters and Notes* was not published until 1841, his diaries upon which this publication is based were written during his travels throughout the plains between 1832 and 1839. He even references Irving's book to offer a point of comparison about attitudes toward the plains.

3. See Smith's *Virgin Land* for a concise examination of the American desert construction.

4. Hallock, *From the Fallen Tree*, 23.

5. Ibid., 9.

6. Robert Thacker notes how Catlin "best serves as historian of the prairie environment, documenting the land and its people, seeing them as existing in a kind of symbiotic relationship" (*Great Prairie Fact*, 57).

7. See Caitlin, *North American Indians*, 1:7. All references to this text will henceforth be cited parenthetically.

8. For a concise and intelligent analysis of the imperialist implications behind Catlin's "nation's Park" proposal, see Mazel's "Death of Wilderness."

9. Spence, *Dispossessing the Wilderness*, 10.

10. Irving, *Tour on the Prairies*, 20. Subsequent references to this edition will be cited parenthetically in the text.

11. His actual exposure to the Pawnees is indirect: a false alarm about an approaching Pawnee war party ends up being a complete fabrication; the stories of Tonish, the half-blood hunter, are largely tall tales meant to inspire fear in the audience; and while a found pair of "Pawnee moccasons [*sic*]" provide a reminder that he is in Pawnee territory, no actual Pawnees ever materialize during the course of Irving's journey. For more on the significant disconnect between what Irving expected to encounter with regard to the Indians and the prairie landscape and what he actually experienced, see Burns, who argues in "'Ineffectual Chase'" that this disconnect reveals how *A Tour on the Prairies* troubles the notion of an "authentic" American West.

12. See Clark, "How the West Was Won." Clark notes how Irving depicts a number of scenarios where the eastern "greenback" and the European American civilization he represents are overwhelmed by the southern plains environment, which Clark reads as a concerted effort on Irving's part to posit the western landscape as the stronger force. Clark, however, overstates the West's victory in *A Tour on the Prairies.* It is relatively clear through the narrative that European American civilization will soon hold dominion over the western Indian wilderness. In the chapter titled "A Bee Hunt,"

Irving notes the profusion of honey bees throughout the Far West, which he reads as a sign of the coming of the whites and the erasure of the Indians: "[I]n proportion as the bee advances, the Indian and buffalo retire" (50). Irving thus openly expresses the process of transformation that is already at work on the high plains, as the "industry" of European American civilization will slowly but surely cultivate the arid wilderness as the bees convert the forests of the West into groves of honey trees.

13. See Thacker, *Great Prairie Fact*, 70 and 242.

14. See Joseph, "The Romantic Lie." Joseph points out how Irving repeatedly draws associations between the geocultural landscape of the West and European cultural artifacts, including a comparison made between Osages and Romans (Irving, *Tour on the Prairies*, 21–22); a grove of trees and a Gothic cathedral (41); and a "crest of broken rocks" to a "Moorish Castle" (106). This attempt to familiarize an unfamiliar landscape is something of a commonplace in writings about the plains environment; this point is developed in Thacker's *The Great Prairie Fact*, Harrison's *Unnamed Country*, and Ricou's *Vertical Man/Horizontal World.*

15. Joseph, "The Romantic Lie," 133–35.

16. Wilson, *The Earth Shall Weep*, 252.

17. The paternalistic and ethnocentric dimensions of Catlin's proposal have long been recognized, even by those who celebrate Catlin's contribution to the preservation movement. See Hausdoerffer, "The 'Nature' of Environmental Disaster," who offers a compelling argument about how Catlin's consistent diatribes against the destructive force of progress actually contributed to the exploitation of the Indians by positing them as passive objects of an inevitable catastrophe.

BIBLIOGRAPHY

Bryant, William Cullen. "The Prairies." 1834. In vol. B of *The Norton Anthology of American Literature, 1820–1865*, Edited by Nina Baym, et al., 8th ed., 126–29. New York: Norton, 2012.

Burns, Mark K. "'Ineffectual Chase': Indians, Prairies, Buffalo, and the Quest for the Authentic West in Washington Irving's *A Tour on the Prairies*." *Western American Literature* 42.1 (2007): 55–79.

Catlin, George. *North American Indians: Being Letters and Notes on their Manners and Customs, and Conditions, Written During Eight Years' Travel Among the Wildest Tribes in North America, 1832–39.* 1841. 2 vols. Philadelphia: Leary, Stuart, 1913.

Clark, William Bedford. "How the West Was Won: Irving's Comic Inversion of the Westering Myth in *A Tour on the Prairies*." *American Literature* 50.3 (1978): 335–47.

Hallock, Thomas. *From the Fallen Tree: Frontier Narratives, Environmental Politics, and the Roots of a National Pastoral, 1749–1826.* Chapel Hill: University of North Carolina Press, 2003.

Harrison, Dick. *Unnamed Country: The Struggle for a Canadian Prairie Fiction.* Edmonton: University of Alberta Press, 1977.

Hausdoerffer, John. "The 'Nature' of Environmental Disaster: George Catlin's Lament as Eco-Genocide." *Tamkang Review* 37.1 (2006): 141–57.

Irving, Washington. *A Tour on the Prairies.* 1835. Edited by John Francis McDermott. Norman: University of Oklahoma Press, 1956.

Joseph, John. "The Romantic Lie: Irving's 'A Tour on the Prairies' and Stendahl's 'Promenade dans Rome.'" In *The Old and New World Romanticism of Washington Irving*, edited by Stanley Brown, 127–37. Westport, CT: Greenwood, 1986.

Mazel, David. "'A beautiful and thrilling specimen': George Catlin, the Death of Wilderness, and the Birth of the National Subject." In *Reading the Earth: New Directions in the Study of Literature and Environment*, edited by Michael Branch, 129–43. Moscow, ID: Idaho University Press, 1998.

Ricou, Laurence. *Vertical Man/Horizontal World: Man and Landscape in Canadian Prairie Fiction.* Vancouver: University of British Colombia Press, 1973.

Smith, Henry Nash. *Virgin Land: The American West as Myth and Symbol.* Cambridge, MA: Harvard University Press, 1950.

Spence, David. *Dispossessing the Wilderness: Indian Removal and the Making of the National Parks.* New York: Oxford University Press, 1999.

Thacker, Robert. *The Great Prairie Fact and Literary Imagination.* Albuquerque: University of New Mexico Press, 1989.

Wilson, James. *The Earth Shall Weep: A History of Native America.* New York: Atlantic Monthly Press, 1999.

Agrarian Gothic: Carwin, Class Transgression, and Spatial Horrors in Charles Brockden Brown's Wieland

Tyler Roeger
Pennsylvania State University

IN describing American visions of agrarianism, several adjectives have been used by early American authors and contemporary scholars. "Horrifying" is not often one of those adjectives. Charles Brockden Brown's *Wieland; or the Transformation. An American Tale* (1798), however, is a work that depicts an agrarian nightmare. Thomas Jefferson's agrarian vision takes a gothic turn in one of the first novels to be written in the United States. While the agrarian farmer, tending to his humble property, seems a curious suspect for images of horror, Brown's novel imagines transitioning practices of agriculture in a way that is quite gothic for early American farm owners and for the fictional Wieland family.

What engenders the horrors that befall the Wieland family has been a topic of debate among critics of Brown's first fully published novel, one of the inaugural American novels as well as one of the seminal pieces of the American gothic. That the Wieland family meets a horrific end is unequivocal, but articulating precisely what facilitates the novel's mania, the unraveling of Mettingen and Theodore Wieland's murder, has often been a point of contention. Scholars have considered the breakdown of the Wieland family through such angles as focusing on the inevitable downfall of an aristocratic-leisure class, the dilemma

Literature in the Early American Republic: Annual Studies on Cooper and His Contemporaries
Volume 6, 2014. Copyright © 2014 by AMS Press, Inc. All rights reserved.

created by Clara's dual position as female and aristocrat, and the way radical religion haunts the family, to name just a few arguments from a range of significant scholarship on the novel.[1] While such readings elucidate the text's historical and gothic contexts, many interpretations forsake one of the most crucial catalysts to the hysteria that falls on Mettingen: Carwin and the agrarian-class implications that his ambiguous identity conjures for the Wielands. By focusing on Carwin's social and intellectual transgressions in the text, I would like to offer a reading of *Wieland*, not as a tale about the American past haunting the family's present, but as a progression to agrarian labor that threatens to bury the separation between property management and manual work. As such, the novel is not so much a gothic tale about an American past rising from the grave as it is the fear of a yeoman republic spreading the dirt over rural aristocratic living. In considering the subversive threat of agrarianism, I seek to merge two of the leading strands of criticism of *Wieland* (strands that often apply to Brown's other novels as well) that seldom come together satisfactorily in scholarship about Brown's work: historical context and gothic conventions.

Placing Carwin, and the effects rendered by his presence, at the center of the Wieland family's downfall connects the spatial and class transgressions that permeate the novel. The centralization of Carwin's presence within the novel's mania affects both readings of labor in the novel and considerations of the need to contextualize the gothic: First, Carwin's infiltration of the Wieland circle destabilizes and implodes social and economic hierarchies when Carwin reveals that class status in rural America, specifically aristocracy, is a posture.[2] Second, by centralizing Carwin's narrative role and his context within the threat that early American agrarianism posed to class distinctions, we can observe that the gothic (a genre that Brown helped to situate in America, thus paving the way for later authors such as Edgar Allan Poe and George Lippard) does not exist in a vacuum. In other words, it is imperative to read the gothic as an expression of cultural and psychological paradoxes that negotiate history in imaginatively unreal terms but still find a basis in their real, contemporary milieu. Genre criticism often runs the risk of isolating form and aesthetic from cultural context and forsaking the way in which context dictates and relies on genre to navigate considerations of contemporary reactions and ideologies. My discussion of the American contexts for Brown's gothic is in consideration of Leslie Fiedler's claims in *Love and Death in the American Novel* that the gothic has "projected certain obsessive concerns of our national life" such as America's history of troubling and disturbing relationships with nature and with indigenous peoples as well as slaves, relationships that have never been reconciled and that the gothic continues to forefront through texts that depict undeniable psychological and social tensions.[3] Contextualizing the use of gothic tropes as they represent and respond to cultural tensions contributes to explanations of what has made the gothic so pervasive throughout American literary history as a method that combines aesthetic and political responses.

This essay will proceed, first, by considering theories of horror and the gothic from Noël Carroll and Eve Kosofsky Sedgwick that provide a language for the gothic that will allow for more nuance in understanding why both the physicality and the ambiguous class status of Carwin is seen as threatening to Mettingen. Establishing, next, a context of early American conceptions of agrarianism will help to contextualize these fears of Carwin's ability to transgress boundaries and perform multiple identities. The essay will then explore how these destabilizations affect the space of Mettingen and how this gothic reimagining of space within the novel draws on agrarian preoccupation with space and property.

By penetrating the Wieland family's social circle and the spaces of Mettingen, the figure of Carwin destabilizes class boundaries in that it illustrates upper-class living as a pose rather than a privilege. Carwin's combination of lower-class vagrancy with elocution and intelligence unsettles the Wieland household. The striking descriptions within *Wieland* in which Clara describes Carwin as an "evil genius" come to illustrate, as I will describe later in the essay, an uneasiness toward laboring farmers that is exacerbated by early American agrarianism: as laboring farmers gain property, they gain new political power and demonstrate a social progression that implodes previous boundaries. Considering the relationships among class, land, and gothic transgression within the novel allows for a reading of *Wieland* that recognizes the affective horror faced by the Wieland family while also considering the way Brown's gothic novel offers a disturbing, yet potentially liberating, depiction of class divisions within rural early America.

1. The Horrors of Failed Taxonomy and Frightening Transitions in Early America

The gothic is often characterized by a threatening transgression of boundaries, a horrific destabilization of corporeal and ontological divisions. Monstrous figures blur perceived normative boundaries between human and animal, living and dead, disrupting taxonomy and dominance.[4] The threat of interstitial beings consists of the destabilization of identity divisions created by understood scientific, economic, and gender differences that rely on classification as a method of control.[5] Such indeterminacy poses a significant threat to early American understandings of the environment and animals, such as the travels of William Bartram and Thomas Jefferson's *Notes on the State of Virginia* (composed in 1781–82 and first published in America in 1787), that often use tedious classification to manage the unknown in America.

The fear of interstitial beings and their breakdown of clear identities, however, not only is an assault on the senses or an affront to taxonomy but also can shock perceived ontological formulations, as it disrupts conceptual limits of reality. Beyond only repulsing and confusing the onlooker, horrific transgressions of interstitiality also disrupt a cogent understanding of the "real" and the self. In the gothic, what is both threatening and frightening is not the mere existence of monsters and interstitial beings; rather, it is what happens to preconceived knowledge and ontological barriers when these monsters make a sudden emergence into perceptions of reality.[6] Discovering that what once existed as reality can never be reconstructed and accepted is the ultimate threat that the gothic poses. Such a breakdown unravels ontological constructions that enable both social interactions and a stable understanding of the self.

The intersection of categorical impurities with the deconstruction of reality foregrounds the gothic threat posed within early America by some of the prominent tenants of early agrarianism and the reception of its evolving practice and ideology. While the rhetoric of "change" was rekindled in American politics during recent years, America's current mutability pales in comparison to what has been described as the "hothouse atmosphere" of transformation that made up the early Republic during Brown's upbringing in Philadelphia.[7] The fact that the developing nation was often envisioned as up for grabs and open for business (so long as the presence of native populations was displaced) engendered an outpouring of new ideas and contentions regarding "geographic mobility, challenges to social deference, the search for profit in the marketplace, and popular political participation."[8] The division of land and the role of agriculture were often at the forefront of debates as these subjects had major implications for the economic prosperity and growth of the now-independent colonies. Discourses imagining a yeoman nation rose to prominence in America during the late eighteenth century, near the time of Brown's composition of *Wieland*.[9] In query 19, "Manufactures," of Thomas Jefferson's widely read *Notes on the State of Virginia*, after describing "those who labour in the earth" as "the chosen people of God," Jefferson claims that widespread cultivation of the land will prevent the moral decay found in industrialized urban living.[10] Grasping on to the emerging agrarian ideal in America, Timothy Dwight uses the language of a heavenly destiny to depict an agrarian future for America in his 1794 poem "Greenfield Hill," as Dwight envisions "the state, by Heaven design'd" as a "realm in equal shares possess'd."[11] Beyond only the georgic ideals regarding the positive impact on one's virtue that came from a relationship with the land, proponents of agrarianism believed that laboring on the land demonstrated a form of ownership, thereby granting the property to those who actually farmed the soil rather than wealthy owners who did not get down on their hands and knees to sow seeds and till the fields.[12]

Although Jefferson's specific yeoman vision did not quite imagine the agrarian farmer as a new emerging class, the yeoman can be considered as a step toward leveling a previous class hierarchy primarily based on property ownership. As Timothy Sweet has argued, Jefferson's agrarian ideology laid out in *Notes on the State of Virginia*, along with much agrarian writing of the time, "tends to obscure the realities of the rural class structure" by setting up a dichotomy based on the divide between rural and urban without considering the evident divisions that already existed in the countryside.[13] More attuned to the divisions of class within rural agrarianism was Benjamin Rush's 1798 essay "An Account of the Progress of Population, Agriculture, Manners, and Government in Pennsylvania," which categorized agrarian workers in Brown's own Pennsylvania within three distinct categories. However, while the generalized discourse of agrarianism taken up by Jefferson and others does not make explicit class formations as does Rush, Jefferson's ideas for reconstructing land boundaries based on property create strong implications for how such reconstruction would affect wealth and, in turn, political agency. Jefferson's theory of agrarianism relied on reified land boundaries, distinguishing one farmer's land from another's. As the construction of property lines (along with the cultivation of that land) defined ownership, these boundaries reconfigured political power structures by granting more agency to working farmers as they became (at least in theory) property owners and self-employed capitalists. Potentially, these new boundaries could wrest political power away from those who owned property and business but did little day-to-day work and thus create a more approachable political landscape for the laboring classes. The construction of land boundaries for the yeoman farmer, paradoxically, deconstructed economic and political walls and thus created a threatening loss of security for the rural upper class in such a place as Brown's Pennsylvania. Amidst this backdrop of agricultural development and the reimagining of class in early America, the conceptual loss of security and the fear of an intrusive laborer torments the Wieland family. Brown's novel emerges within this threatening gothic context of agrarian interstitiality.[14]

The conception of the new American agrarian farmer is notably gothic because the yeoman is characterized by the conflation of what were thought to be contradictory categories. The idealized yeoman farmer blurs class boundaries and thus threatens previous divisions that allowed for property ownership divorced from labor and for static wealth to be consistently passed down through heredity. Through the yeoman's dual role as owner and laborer, his (the term "his" is appropriate as the agrarian farmer was largely conceived as a male patriarch) interstitial position deconstructs the class boundary between farm worker and farm owner that is needed to isolate the landowner in a space of monetary and political power.[15] Though inequalities clearly existed in late eighteenth-century America, the idealized discourse of agrarianism imagines class ambiguity and the deflation of economic difference among white men.[16] While Jefferson may not have desired to change the class structure of America (after all, Jefferson relied on the primarily forced labor of others to enable him to retain Monticello and have to time for his myriad studies), to property owners that relied solely on the labor of others, the early yeoman vision in America can be viewed as a legitimate fear.[17] The construction of a class of property owners/laborers imagines an alternative class system that would prove horrific for an isolated bourgeoisie. Charles Brockden Brown, as an author of fiction and as a well-documented Godwinian activist, was engulfed in this zeitgeist of transition, excitement, and anxiety in early America, "swept up in a strong current of challenges to traditional authority."[18]

Written amidst this volatile atmosphere just before the turn of the century, Brown's *Wieland* shows a consideration of radical agricultural change similar to Jefferson's yeoman vision, a vision that Brown would counter just a few years later. While it may not come as a surprise that Brown contested one of Jefferson's ideals, Brown's 1805 vision for a prosperous system of agriculture differs from the agrarian aspects that shape *Wieland*, which will be discussed later in the essay. In 1805, Brown published a piece titled "A Specimen of Agricultural Improvement. *Extracted from the correspondence of a traveller in Scotland.*" The text tells the story of a man who inherits, through marriage, a large quantity of land that he finds in great disorder due to several crooked landlords. In order to turn the farm around, the new owner takes on the position of a feudal overseer, giving executive orders to large numbers of workers and creating a top-down system of order. Through the landlord's agricultural and economic ingenuity and "the invariable equity with which the great power of the landlord was exercised," the property becomes exceedingly successful, and this economic success, in turn, benefits the surrounding town, for the landlord is able to provide money that helps to build schools and improve defenses. While the basis of such a top-down system would not differ notably from typical farming practices of an owner having hired-hands to aid in the work, the owner in Brown's story manages over 10,000 acres of farmland and oversees 3,000 workers.[19] His role is to direct the labor, to calculate uses for the land and determine the best tools without ever getting his own hands dirty in the fields. This system of "agricultural improvement" envisioned by Brown returns power to a few who, in theory, will rule efficiently and humanely, thus leading to the greater good of society. While his essay clearly demonstrates the antagonism Brown felt toward Jefferson's agrarianism as the superior way to provide for a family and a community, the earlier, gothic *Wieland* tells a different story.

In 1798, Brown's first complete novel imagines the possibilities of agrarianism to destabilize class hierarchies. Pervading discourses of agrarian labor and gothic transgression come through in full force in Brown's cultural interjection to the tense milieu of the developing republic; America's first gothic novel draws on the prospects and anxieties of reconfiguring agricultural roles and property. Ed White has pointed out that "Brown carefully located his novel [*Wieland*] at the moment of the Paxton Riots."[20] Conscious of social upheaval and the prominent revolts of the time, such as the Whiskey Rebellion, Brown crafts his narrative in such a way as to draw on the rural unrest, so that the owners of Mettingen are made anxious by yeoman discourses during a time of localized uprising. As a gothic transgression of class and property, agrarianism creates a surprisingly violent threat in Brown's *Wieland.*

2. Carwin and the Fear of an Articulate Farmer

Throughout much of the scholarship on *Wieland*, critics have offered myriad reasons to elucidate what causes such vast turmoil and mania to fall on Mettingen. The agrarian context and (more surprisingly) Carwin often do not play a significant part in this conversation. Prominent readings have viewed *Wieland* as a critique of aristocracy in that they explore the way the characters' isolation creates boredom and mania, as well as the irreconcilable tensions that pervade the novel as a result of Clara's position as both female and aristocrat. Scholars looking at the problem of inheritance within the novel have focused on the broad sense of history that haunts the family, rather than on the inheritance of biological gender and commercial wealth that informs readings in the previous vein. These readings are important in that they present convincing points about historicized gothic tropes and the problems of class difference in Brown's novel; however, they come at the expense of isolating a significant figure of the text from the primary dilemma. Jane Tompkins's argument about Brown's overt federalist intentions in the novel reads Carwin as a "symptom" of the problems that already exist at Mettingen; Tompkins cites Carwin's lack of "markers that define and fix the self" as emblematic of an already-pronounced "emptiness" in which the Wielands exist.[21] To claim that there is nothing off-kilter and troubling about the Wieland family before Carwin arrives certainly would be to give too much credit to the group. Yet, to forsake Carwin's role as intruder, the fears conjured by his explicit intrusion into Clara's bedroom and his ventriloquil interruptions in the otherwise-steady conversations of Mettingen, is to overlook the crucial role that the threat of ambiguous class identities and the transformation of space plays in the transformation within *Wieland*.[22] I would like to consider the previous, beneficial focus on class within the text and argue that a discussion of class is inseparable from the agrarian transgression Carwin enacts as the lowly laborer enters the land of aesthetic pleasures.

While Clara and Theodore's father enacts the agrarian ideal of engaging in the physical labor of cultivating the land before acquiring enough wealth to "dispense with personal labour, and direct attention to his own concerns," his children are exempt from ever having to manually keep up the property.[23] Clara writes that Theodore's profession was "determined" to be agriculture but that "his fortune exempted him from the necessity of personal labour" (21). Clara even goes on to downplay the amount of work that is required in Theodore's role as superintendent. She writes that "the skill that was demanded by this was merely theoretical, and was furnished by casual inspection, or by closet study," and that "the attention that was paid to this subject did not seclude him for any long time from us. . . . Our tasks, our walks, our music, were seldom performed but in each other's company" (21). Rather than continuing on in the somewhat agrarian footsteps of their family, prior to Carwin's arrival, Clara, Theodore, Pleyel, and Catherine spend much of their time in a rather patrician way. They have spirited discussions about Cicero, philosophize, and pass the time with such activities as knitting.[24] While knitting was often a form of domestic labor for women in the agrarian economy, there is nothing in these early moments of *Wieland* to suggest that Clara's and Catherine's knitting is done for reasons of necessity rather than leisure. Some tensions certainly exist in these opening scenes, owing no small part to Clara and Theodore's father having spontaneously combusted when the two were children. It is difficult to imagine such an event not being rather significant in a child's life. As a result, Clara lives in a continual tension of desiring to be content as an Enlightenment thinker (at times epitomizing Brown's vision of a strong, self-reliant woman), valuing reason and subtlety over sentiment and passion, while recognizing the significance of religious enthusiasm in her family's history and within her brother, Theodore's perspective. The patriarchal explosion at the narrative's beginning certainly looms over the text and the Wieland family. Problems unequivocally exist at Mettingen as Clara and Theodore struggle over their identities and their family's past. However, until Carwin's entrance, both Wielands remain content to pass their time in a situation that exempts them of notable labor, the manual work done on Mettingen being performed by hired servants who are curiously invisible for much of the novel.[25]

When Carwin first appears, Clara is puzzled by his clownish accoutrements, yet Carwin is able to seamlessly insert himself into their social circle. While Clara marks a distinction in Carwin's elocution and his appearance, she is content to accept his speech as the true signifier of his character. Clara describes Carwin's voice as "not only mellifluent and clear, but the emphasis was so just, and the modulation so impassioned, that it seemed as if an heart of stone could not fail of being moved by it. It imparted to me an emotion altogether involuntary and incontroulable" (47). From the beginning, Clara is preoccupied with Carwin's ability to control his voice as she focuses on the precision of his "emphasis" and his "modulation." Control and presentation are believed to signify respectability. Since Carwin can control his voice, providing a controlled rhetoric, Clara assumes his character must also exhibit such self-control.[26] Thus far in the novel, Clara has prided herself on her ability to control her emotions, for she recognizes the line between reason and affect and believes the latter should be contained and considered reckless. While Clara appreciates the control within Carwin's voice, her reaction betrays a slight anxiety regarding this voice's ability to rouse her own sentiment. It poses a challenge to the sense of self-control that shapes Clara as Brown's intelligent, capable protagonist.

Carwin's ability to captivate Clara's interest and the ease in which he situates himself in Mettingen speak to the performative nature of the aristocratic lifestyle into which the Wieland family often dips. As Mettingen's new visitor becomes more accustomed to the lands and to the group, the Wielands and Pleyel appreciate Carwin's presence, yet their reverence remains a surprisingly shallow admiration of what seems to be hollow discourse. Clara describes the wonders of Carwin's speech, and proclaims the impressive depth it reveals in Carwin, yet she never goes beyond describing the mere presentation. In claiming, "whatever he said was pregnant with meaning, and uttered with rectitude of articulation, and force of emphasis" (61), Clara fails to provide any specifics of what Carwin *actually* says. During such moments, Clara seems taken in more by Carwin's presentation than by the content of any of his pontifications, which fail to receive the same level of attention. This becomes more evident as Clara realizes, as time passes, that she knows nothing about Carwin but still regards him "as an inestimable addition to our society" (64). As her view of Carwin begins to deflate later in the narrative, Clara struggles to reconcile the knowledge of his malicious ruses with his earlier self-presentation. "Was not this the man whom we had treated with unwearied kindness? Whose society was endeared to us by his intellectual elevation and accomplishments? Who had a thousand times expatiated on the usefulness and beauty of virtue? Why should such a one be dreaded?" (75), asks Clara. As she learns more about Carwin's ventriloquism, it is not simply the process of his ventriloquist performance (the physical ability) that is threatening to Clara.[27] That he was able to infiltrate her social circle through mere elocution reveals a far more unsettling notion: the leisured-class mode is not merely generic to the point of being easily reproduced, but such reproductions can apparently be performed by anyone, even a vagrant. If Carwin is able to pontificate on subjects such as Cicero and "the usefulness and beauty of virtue" with his sole intention being to pass in the group, how does the knowledge of that transgression affect Clara's seemingly stable identity as a rational thinker at the well-off Mettingen? Clara's Enlightenment ideals, privileging the ability to form a rational response separated from affect, are challenged by Carwin's speech: his "rectitude of articulation" causes her to confuse sentimental admiration for rational respect. While, during this time, it may have been easy to enter into the upper class of a developing urban space such as Philadelphia, the rural setting of Mettingen is explicitly set apart from the city and thus retains a much clearer history of inherited wealth.[28] Yet, as a consequence of Carwin's seamless entry, the Enlightened philosopher of Mettingen is deconstructed as simply a role to play in a now seemingly frivolous social circle.

Carwin's ability to perform a more elite position shows an agrarian movement among class identities that goes beyond the anachronistic structures of class hierarchy that are necessary for the Wielands' survival.[29] By exhibiting multiple identities of laboring vagrant, sophisticated orator, and "evil genius," Carwin inhabits identity categories perceived to be impossible by stable class distinction. In other words, the Wielands cannot understand how a person can be both abject and eloquent. During Carwin's initial appearance at Mettingen, Clara struggles to reconcile his place in the pastoral landscape:

> His pace was a careless and lingering one, and had none of that gracefulness and ease which distinguish a person with certain advantages of education from a clown. His gait was rustic and aukward. His form was ungainly and disproportioned. Shoulders broad and square, breast sunken, his head drooping, his body of uniform breadth, supported by long and lank legs, were the ingredients of his frame. His garb was not ill adapted to such a figure. A slouched hat, tarnished by the weather, a coat of thick grey cloth, cut and wrought, as it seemed, by a country tailor, blue worsted stockings, and shoes fastened by thongs, and deeply discoloured by dust, which brush had never disturbed, constituted his dress. (45)

Clara immediately recognizes Carwin as a lower-class worker and connects him to farm labor through the "garb not ill adapted to such a figure." Carwin wears soiled clothes that seem tailored for labor rather than aesthetic, as is evidenced by their never having seen a brush and their dusty, tarnished condition. Yet, while his clothes are consistent with a farm laborer, there is something ill fitting about his appearance.

His face is "aukward" and his form "disproportioned." Clara then explains that Carwin seems out of place along the banks of Mettingen. Even though Carwin has the "careless and lingering" pace of a clown, Clara finds him walking in the lawn that "was only traversed by men whose views were directed to the pleasures of the walk, or the grandeur of the scenery" (46). Carwin's clothes and figure signal an identity that is accustomed only to labor and production, yet his movement is casual, and he walks through a space that is traveled only for aesthetic appreciation and consumption. In this initial encounter, Carwin presents a contradiction that both troubles and fascinates Clara.

When he first speaks, Clara experiences the same problem of misrecognition and identity confusion, a problem that troubles her belief in the security of deductive reasoning. She first hears Carwin's voice as he asks for a cup of buttermilk. Clara is astonished by his elocution, yet she struggles to reconcile this voice with the clownish figure she previously saw walking on the lawn. She writes, "My fancy had conjured up a very different image. A form, and attitude, and garb, were instantly created worthy to accompany such elocution; but this person was, in all visible respects, the reverse of this phantom" (47). The simple misrecognition of class identity categories is, in itself, an unsettling experience for an Enlightenment rationality that prides itself on clear empiricism. When the voice (evidence) does not match Clara's assumption (controlled elocution signifies upper-class refinement), her logic is threatened by what could be described as class interstitiality.[30]

Specifically, Carwin's agrarian status signals a transgression of the divide between lower-class labor and the upper-class ownership of land. This interstitiality is most potent within Brown's novel when it resonates with the discourses of agrarianism.[31] Carwin's threat is that he is both laboring vagrant and philosophical speaker, a dichotomy that results in the formulation of the "evil genius" for the Wielands. Upon first seeing Carwin walking on the grounds, Clara imagines a hopeful agrarianism in a way that would bring a smile to Jefferson's face. After being captivated by Carwin's appearance, Clara writes that she "reflected on the alliance which commonly subsists between ignorance and the practice of agriculture, and indulged myself in airy speculations as to the influence of progressive knowledge in dissolving this alliance, and embodying the dreams of the poets" (46). She then draws more explicitly on Jeffersonian sentiments in pondering "why the plough and the hoe might not become the trade of every human being, and how this trade might be made conducive to, or, at least, consistent with the acquisition of wisdom and eloquence" (46). Clara's vision of combining the physical laboring of the land with "wisdom and eloquence," presumably tied with the knowledge of philosophy and practice of rationalism that Clara professes throughout the novel, looks to Jeffersonian ideals as well as anticipates later developments and tensions in American agrarianism that Benjamin R. Cohen describes as "book farming." Cohen writes of "book farming," a topic of agricultural discussion and conflict that can be traced to works such as John Spurrier's 1793 *The Practical Farmer* but rose to greater prominence in the 1830s, that "the contrast worth examining . . . is between the farming class and the philosopher class." Cohen further writes that, "despite the many differences in class status, education, and social power of the antebellum American populace[,] . . . the majority of the agrarian society shared the position of the nonphilosophical citizen wrestling with issues of new knowledge and advice from outside their community."[32] Through the combination of his posturing as a member of the philosophizing class within the Wieland circle and his apparent tie to working the land in his soiled clothing, Carwin, at first, is a hopeful vision of agrarianism for Clara, a vision that bridges the perceived divisions of philosophy and physical labor that continued into mid-nineteenth-century agrarian practices and discourse. Yet, while she approaches reverence for a possible yeoman ideology, Clara's transition away from these thoughts is striking, as it eschews the role of philosophy in agrarianism for a greater focus on property and wealth. She grows "weary" from "these reflections" and goes "to the kitchen to perform some household office" (46) while making a distinct note about her servant's presence as well. The reemergence of a servant in the house returns Clara to a world of class distinctions, removed from the agrarian possibility that has caused her to become "weary." Although agrarian property ownership at this time would have been unheard of for a woman, Clara recognizes the problems Carwin's social liminality causes for her own monetarily privileged, though socially self-reliant, position in the household. The next scene,

Carwin's previously mentioned request for a cup of buttermilk, puts the agrarian threat of ambiguous class distinctions back at the forefront of Clara's mind. Clara's seeming laud of agrarianism proves to be not only a fleeting sentiment but also a frightening idea when Carwin literally enters the private spaces of Mettingen (Clara's bedchamber), and the "progressive knowledge" of agrarianism is reinterpreted as Carwin's "evil genius."

After fear has been building in the pastoral Mettingen, Clara discovers Carwin in her bedroom, and the nature of Carwin's intellect is put into question as the group shifts their reading of this curious stranger and is no longer able to look past his laboring roots. This illicit intrusion (combined with Carwin's presumed inability to read the group's new German book) prompts the end of Carwin's pleasantries in Pleyel and the Wieland's social circle. After the discovery of Carwin in the bedroom, Clara and Pleyel still hold that Carwin demonstrates intelligence, yet his mental propensities are now regarded as an evil cunning. As the group researches the background of the once "inestimable addition" to their society, Pleyel tells of the information he has recently heard about Carwin's past in Europe, now painting him as a sadistic mastermind that "wages a perpetual war against the happiness of mankind, and sets his engines of destruction at work against every object that presents itself" (104). The tides have changed for Carwin as he is not merely an imposter, but a *scheming, lower class* imposter. Pleyel goes on to say that "bloodshed is the trade, and horror is the element of this man. . . . As to an alliance with evil geniuses, the power and the malice of daemons have been a thousand times exemplified in human beings. There are no devils but those which are begotten upon selfishness, and reared by cunning" (104–5). Describing Carwin as an "evil genius" brings into question Clara's earlier ruminations on agriculture and ignorance. As the Wieland circle recognizes Carwin's malicious intent, Clara's new conclusion revises her speculations about a possible marriage between "wisdom" and "the plough." Carwin's supposed genius is now inseparable from his malevolent purposes. The vagrant Carwin can speak as a member of an upper class, but his laborious roots prevent him from attaining the moral superiority of a Clara or a Pleyel.[33] Intelligence and agricultural labor, in the example the Wieland family reads in Carwin, cannot coexist in a benevolent figure. When they do commingle, they produce a dubious clown who throws his voice all about their home simply for the hell of it.

Clara's conception of the farmer is finally restored to safety when his labor and genius are again separated and Clara believes Carwin has returned to his rural agrarian roots, far removed from upper-class living. During Carwin's confession to Clara near the end of the novel, he explains his relationship with the land as one of leisure, denoting upper-class sensibilities. Carwin says, "My principal haunts were the lawns and gardens of Mettingen. In this delightful region the luxuriances of nature had been chastened by judicious art, and each successive contemplation unfolded new enchantments" (151). Clara does not rest, then, until the last chapter when she envisions Carwin returning to a position of laboring the land rather than appreciating its aesthetic, pastoral value. In the final, baffling, chapter of Brown's novel, Clara writes of Carwin, "He is now probably engaged in the harmless pursuits of agriculture, and may come to think, without insupportable remorse, on the evils to which his fatal talents have given birth. The innocence and usefulness of his future life may, in some degree, atone for the miseries so rashly or so thoughtlessly inflicted" (179). Clara finds security in Carwin's life being "useful" rather than full of contemplating "judicious art" and "new enchantments." When the agrarian Carwin is part of Mettingen's social circle, he contains "engines of destruction" and his trade is "bloodshed." However, back as a laborer on the farm, his work is "harmless" and his life is both "innocent and useful."

Carwin is safe only so long as he does not ventriloquize and does not move beyond a place of physical labor, both of which have the threatening potential to transgress the class boundaries that allow for the leisure at Mettingen.[34] The narrative illuminates the fearful implications of agrarianism, the prospects of combining agriculture and knowledge in the same figure, to a family that relies on the stability of a lower class of laborers who will perform manual labor and not consider the possession of their own property. For Clara's position, Carwin's only secure place becomes back on the farms, relegated to "a remote district of Pennsylvania" far from social circles where both his voice and his interstitial position hold unwanted potential.

3. Vainly Seeking Safety in "Doors and Bars": Spatial Fears

Through Carwin's infiltration of the society and grounds of Mettingen, the narrative draws on agrarianism's threat to the physical isolation of a rural upper class, with the intrusive vagrant proving a threat, not to bodies, but to borders. One of the primary sources of fear for the Wielands, leaving Clara to express (or perhaps feign) security only when she is across the Atlantic in Europe and Carwin is contained in the backwoods, is the transformation of space. As well as imploding ontological divisions between lower and upper class, worker and owner, agrarianism significantly changes land boundaries and the division of property. Jeffersonian agrarianism imagined natural land structures functioning as divisions between property, delineating ownership among the families within their naturally sectioned-off land. Boundaries were imagined, though actual walls rarely went up. This transformation of space into property, erecting conceptual land boundaries, paradoxically deconstructs divisions of class. With property being one of the central markers of wealth and political power (property being the prerequisite for voting rights), the creation of land-as-property for laboring workers and every one "picking up the plough" symbolically dissembles the political and economic walls between workers and property owners. Written in this context, spatial fears pervade Brown's novel as the text navigates and depicts the ramifications of deconstructed domestic boundaries.

While the physical space of Mettingen does not change until near the end of the novel, when the house burns down, the home's secure atmosphere is greatly transformed over the course of the narrative. Positing that the characters in Wieland consistently react to and interpret events in relation to the places in which the events occur, Lisa West Norwood argues that "the landscape of Mettingen cannot be reduced to a consistent symbolic meaning" and that "there is no thinking that is not tied to the places in the novel."[35] While it is certainly fruitless to reduce Mettingen to one static symbol, I would argue that Clara does, indeed, consistently map her abstract fears of Carwin's social and economic penetration and transgressions onto Mettingen. She, herself, reads the space as a symbol that is capable of changing from an isolated pastoral home into an open and vulnerable political and economic landscape.

As Clara's anxiety builds throughout the narrative, she persists to tell the reader that Mettingen has changed; she articulates a fear of an attack on her home more than a fear of an attack on her body. After first hearing voices in her closet, voices that debate killing an unnamed woman (whom Clara perceives to be herself), she ruminates, "How had my ancient security vanished! That dwelling, which had hitherto been an inviolate asylum, was now beset with danger to my life. That solitude, formerly so dear to me, could no longer be endured" (53). Clara's remarks make a curious turn when she mentions that her "solitude . . . could no longer be endured." The "ancient security" is not mentioned in reference to bodily well-being; rather, her concern is on how her "dwelling" no longer allows for her isolation. Clara fears the penetration of space more than the threat of violence that such penetration enables. This fear of the entry rather than an accompanying violence manifests later when Clara understands Carwin to be the invader of her home and believes he has been using her father's "temple" as the site from which to plot her family's destruction. Clara mourns the transformation of the temple that used to be the place of religious devotion followed by aristocratic debates on Cicero:

> The spirit which haunted it formerly was pure and rapturous. It was a fane sacred to the memory of infantile days, and to blissful imaginations of the future! What a gloomy reverse had succeeded since the ominous arrival of this stranger! Now, perhaps, it is the scene of his meditations. Purposes fraught with horror, that shun the light, and contemplate the pollution of innocence, are here engendered, and fostered, and reared to maturity. (78)

What's striking about this description is that Clara's focus is on the location and not on the scheme. It seems likely that Clara would contemplate what horrors Carwin might be plotting, but instead her thoughts highlight that the intrusion of their "pure and rapturous" space has been committed by a "stranger!" Clara's fear focuses on the removal, not of mortality, but of isolated leisure and this transformation's social and political implications regarding power.[36] Agrarian interstitiality transgresses the walls of Mettingen (a space of leisure) and Clara's home (her space of independence). "I had vainly thought that my safety could be sufficiently secured by doors and bars, but this is a foe from whose grasp no power of divinity can save me" (89), writes Clara. The focus on social transgression rather than on physical threat coheres as Clara feels this loss of structural security before she even identifies Carwin as a threat to her body. After the initial penetration into her room, Clara has a mystifying dream that conjures up the vulnerability rendered by both the previous spatial intrusion and Carwin's initial entrance into their social circle.

Clara's nightmare is a manifestation of her newfound vulnerability as a result of her now-destabilized class identity. After Clara hears threatening voices in her closet, the next chapter opens with her depiction of a frightening dream that she had several weeks after this previous incident. Clara recounts her dream: "After various incoherences had taken their turn to occupy my fancy, I at length imagined myself walking, in the evening twilight, to my brother's habitation. A pit, methought, had been dug in the path I had taken, of which I was not aware" (54). She continues, "As I carelessly pursued my walk, I thought I saw my brother, standing at some distance before me, beckoning and calling me to make haste. He stood on the opposite edge of the gulph" (54). If not for a voice that commands her to "Hold!" Clara fears, she would have fallen into the ominous pit. One of the most significant aspects of this puzzling dream that contrasts with Clara's previous episode of terror is that, rather than a claustrophobic fear of being trapped in her bedroom with murderous thieves in the closet, the dream projects the vulnerability that exists from the absence of such retaining walls. Clara's dream is the only place in the novel that she feels threatened outside of the home. After the walls of her home have been infiltrated, Clara's anxiety manifests itself through a dream in which there is no longer a division to protect her from the encroaching outside world. Her dream marks an anxiety of ruptured isolation that takes its fear from the threat of no longer having her own walled-in space.[37] Clara, then, carries this fear of vulnerability back into reality when she wakes. She writes that she found herself "at the next moment . . . surrounded by the deepest darkness. Images so terrific and forcible disabled [her], for a time, from distinguishing between sleep and wakefulness" (55). She explains that her "first panics were succeeded by the perturbations of surprize, to find myself alone in the open air, and immersed in so deep a gloom" (55). Clara is struck by her solitude "in the open air" and her vulnerability to the "surrounding of deepest darkness." She wakes to discover that divisions have been ruptured between the real and the unreal, between space and class structures. Clara's anxiety culminates in this dream in a way that resonates with Sedgwick's claim that, "to wake from a dream and *find it true*—that is the particular terror at which these [gothic] episodes aim, and the content of the dream is subordinate to that particular terror."[38] As ontological fears emerge in the spaces of the home and the "open air," Clara's dream shatters differentiated concepts of inside/outside within both the American home and American political power.

4. Gothic Transitions

Though Carwin is finally removed from the grounds of Mettingen, Clara's final chapter provides little solace to the damage that has already been done. Her brother and his family are dead, and her former home has been burnt to the ground. While Theodore Wieland performs the most unequivocally brutal acts of violence in the text, Carwin's role in destabilizing the family's position of isolation is no less significant in determining the course of the novel and disrupting Clara's security. In this way, Carwin's gothic agrarianism proves an ontological threat to conceptions of a clear and pure class identity in the novel. While critics have often read Carwin's role as dwarfed by Theodore's multiple murder, calling Carwin a "most shabby" villain who "merely set the action in motion" and referring to him as "just a mischievous wanderer," writing off Carwin in this way risks placing too much emphasis on physicality within a novel that is obsessed with attacks on sentiment and reason.[39] Despite explicit focus on sensory perception, Clara is more threatened by the way material voices deconstruct paradigms than by how they allow for an attack on her body.[40] Clara not only is threatened by Carwin's ventriloquism and physical trespassing but also feels the pressure of what he represents: movement away from the possibility of an isolated leisure-class existence. That is not to say that Carwin is to be read simply as an allegory within the text; such a reading deflates both the novel's complexity and affective resonance (a character is never as frightening if he or she is simply a vehicle). Part of Clara's inability to classify Carwin and control him stems from the interstitiality of his being both a threatening corporeal presence and a referent to a future mode of labor and property ownership.[41]

Carwin's disruption of stable class identities in the already-unstable space of Mettingen is a surprising precursor, and strong contrast, to Brown's later writing on agrarianism, which is found in works that voice a belief in the greater prospects of agricultural systems in line more with feudalism than with idealized, georgic agrarianism.[42] Just seven years before such pronouncements, amid growing discourses on American agrarianism from the likes of Jefferson, and Crèvecouer, Rush, the gothic configurations of *Wieland* depict the localization of labor and property ownership as a prospect that is both unsettling and full of possibility. Through reading the way that *Wieland* challenges the notion of a static rural class position, we can recognize how the novel opens a space for prospects of future configurations of agricultural production, and we can appreciate how gothic fictions, in their particular transgressions, create room for such imaginative prospects. As such, the haunting atmosphere of *Wieland* echoes the immediate threat *and* potential of American agriculture changes. Through illustrating class as a precarious position and through dismantling boundaries of labor and ownership, the novel depicts agrarianism as an encroaching ideal that further destabilizes an early republic already on shaky ground.

NOTES

I would like to thank Carla Mulford, Mark Sturges, Robert Volpicelli, and the anonymous *LEAR* readers for providing helpful feedback on this essay.

1. For the former arguments, see Elizabeth Jane Wall Hinds's significant work *Private Property*. For the latter, see Eric Savoy's "Rise of American Gothic."

2. I specify "Carwin's presence" to emphasize that the effects Carwin has on the other characters throughout the narrative owe much of their impact to how he is interpreted by Clara and Theodore rather than to Carwin's own intent and volition. Regardless of how much Carwin wills the events that take place at Mettingen, and regardless of how centrally focused he is in the novel, his presence (and its class implications), as I will argue, shapes a majority of Brown's novel. In this way, while Carwin may not be the mastermind villain of the narrative (although Pleyel characterizes him as such), his role in the novel, and in this essay's consideration of the agrarian turns in the text, are crucial for the significant role that class transgression does play.

3. Fiedler, *Love and Death*, 27.

4. In his formative work *The Philosophy of Horror,* Carroll claims that, in order to meet a definition of "art-horror," a being must be both threatening and repulsive. Carroll's study offers a definition of "art-horror" and does not refer explicitly to "the gothic." I will apply his work to the gothic, for horror is a central feature of gothic works. I would argue that all gothic works function through horror but that not all subjects of horror are depicted through the gothic, which has often been defined within historical periods and cultural contexts as opposed to the purely affective definitions at the root of "horror."

5. However, for Carroll, the horror of categorical transgression is not as much a removal of power as a disgust by a subject's categorical impurity. In Carroll's configuration, repulsion is elicited when an entity is "categorically interstitial, categorically contradictory, incomplete, or formless." Carroll makes a distinction between figures of "fusion" and figures of "fission," a distinction that extends the threat posed by interstitial beings. In instances of "fission," the being contains contradictory identities; however, the identities never exist in the same body during the same temporal moments. For example, the werewolf is both man and wolf, but the two identities, arguably, never exist during the same time; the person turns into the wolf and reverts back to human at a later time. More important for a discussion of Carwin is the notion of the transgressions created by a figure of "fusion." Fusion characters are defined by "the compounding of ordinarily disjoint or conflicting categories in an integral, spatio-temporally unified individual" (*Philosophy of Horror*, 32, 46, 44).

6. Looking beyond affective disgust, Sedgwick argues in *Conventions* that the threat of the gothic has little to do with the specific experience that transgresses boundaries. In her formulation, "no nightmare is ever as terrifying as is waking up from even some innocuous dream *to find it true*" (13).

7. Watts, *Romance*, 3.

8. Ibid., 3.

9. The popular early image of the agrarian farmer in America comes primarily from J. Hector St. John Crèvecoeur's romantic imagining of the farmer in the 1770s and Thomas Jefferson's valorization of the American farmer in *Notes on the State of Virginia* in the 1780s. See Kulikoff, *Agrarian*, 129.

10. Jefferson, *Notes*, 217.

11. Dwight, *Greenfield Hill*, 153, ll. 127, 125.

12. This idea of cultivation as a form of ownership can be traced back to John Locke. For more, see "Of Property" in Locke's *Second Treatise of Civil Government* (1690), in which he considers how a person's changing the land implies a form of property.

13. Sweet, *Georgics,* 102.

14. Interestingly enough, Brown sent then-vice president of the United States, Thomas Jefferson, a copy of *Wieland.* See Barnard and Shapiro, "Introduction," x.

15. Benjamin R. Cohen, in *Notes from the Ground*, explores the role of physical labor in early American agrarianism and centralizes the Georgic experience as a crucial part of the agrarian farmer's interaction with the land.

16. Kulikoff, *Agrarian*, 35.

17. An example of the argument that claims that Jefferson, in his formulation of

agrarianism, did not desire to change his contemporary class structures can be found in Sweet's "American Pastoralism and the Marketplace."

18. Watts makes the point in *Romance* that the form of Brown's primary literary endeavors, the novel, "undermined older, more elitist genres in the realm of belles letters" (51).

19. Brown, "A Specimen," 93, 88–90.

20. White argues that Brown situates *Wieland* in a rural Pennsylvania that is divided between the backwoods folk such as Carwin and the middle ground "German Crescent" area of Mettingen. Considering Carwin as a figure of the baser rural class, White writes in "Carwin the Peasant Rebel" that "Brown's interest was not emancipatory—as a student of Proud [Robert Proud], he sought to decipher the backcountry in order to control and correct it—but he sought, nonetheless, a fairly sophisticated engagement with the rural subaltern that has tremendous heuristic value for contemporary criticism." I would argue that Carwin's primary threat to Mettingen is his ability to perform a deflation of the two rural categories White defines. As opposed to Carwin as "less a Subject marking a social type (e.g. 'the alien' or 'the farmer') than a baffling nexus of geography, voice, and project" (43, 44, 50–51), Carwin-as-yeoman-farmer is a nexus in itself: the intersection of labor and property ownership.

21. Hinds makes a compelling argument for readings about aristocracy and isolation; see *Property*, 99. Pondering who the protagonist of the text actually is, Savoy questions if the "agent might be the shadow of history itself, whether that shadow is understood as an inherited state of mind or the emergence of a ghostly phantom from the depths of the historical psyche?"; see "Rise," 174. Tompkins, *Sensational*, 52.

22. More recent work, such as that by Anthony Galluzzo in "Charles Brockden Brown's Wieland and the Aesthetics of Terror," has sought to place Carwin back at the crux of the horror that befalls Mettingen. Galluzzo argues that Carwin disrupts the primary mode of aesthetic appreciation at Mettingen. Carwin resembles the sublime, for Galluzzo, as he disallows the Wielands from appreciating aesthetics from a safe distance. While I share Galluzzo's focus on the centralization of Carwin and the terror he brings to the Wieland family, I find not only that Carwin destabilizes aesthetics but also that his influence has more far-reaching effects on configurations of property and class as well.

23. Brown, *Wieland*, 12. Subsequent references will appear parenthetically in the text.

24. Hsuan L. Hsu, in his chapter on Brown in *Geography and the Production of Space in Nineteenth-Century American Literature*, writes that *Wieland* begins by "thematizing the agrarian idea" with "an independent yeoman farm epitomized by Jefferson's ideal of self-sufficient private life at Monticello" (31–32). Tompkins also describes the Wieland family as appearing to live out the agrarian ideal and characterizes them as "Crèvecoeur's picture of sturdy yeomen living in rural decency" (*Sensational*, 49). While the opening scenes of Mettingen certainly establish Jefferson's ideals of smal-scale property ownership, Jefferson's professed value in one's directly laboring the land (an idea made more prominent, arguably, by Crèvecoeur's Farmer James) is notably absent from these descriptions. Indeed, Clara writes that her brother's profession

was agriculture but, as previously mentioned, "his fortune exempted him from the necessity of personal labour" (21).

25. Interestingly enough, the servants tend to be most visible during their interactions with Carwin, as Carwin uses the servant Judith to aid in infiltrating Clara's home.

26. In contrast to this introduction, Gale Temple's essay "Carwin the Onanist?" makes the fascinating case that the text constructs Carwin as a figure who utterly lacks sexual and bodily self-control.

27. Much has been made about the role of ventriloquism in the novel, and there have been many compelling arguments about ventriloquism's function in early America. Eric A. Wolfe, in "Ventriloquizing Nation," provides a nuanced reading of Carwin's ventriloquism in relation to early Federal desires to fashion a national voice.

28. Mark Decker writes that in late eighteenth-century Philadelphia, "relative to other cities" such as New York and Boston, it was "easier for newcomers to penetrate the city's upper social ranks" ("Class Anxiety," 475).

29. Lisa West Norwood, in her essay "'I May Be a Stranger to the Grounds of Your Belief,'" argues that Carwin's ventriloquism actually emphasizes him as a stationary character because the movement of his voice places a greater focus on the stillness of his body. While voice certainly demonstrates a greater movement than body for Carwin (though he does travel throughout Europe and walk the American countryside), I would argue for class identity as the largest category of movement within the text.

30. Carroll makes the point that the monster does not fit the "conceptual schemes" of the characters and of the readers; see *Horror*, 33. Indeed, the trouble of perception in the face of interstitiality continues to horrify the Wielands as Theodore Wieland, shortly before committing suicide, asks of Carwin, "What art thou?" (165).

31. Carroll claims that the biological interstitiality often present in horror can signal larger cultural struggles: "In the most fundamental sense of fusion and fission, these structures are meant to apply to the organization of opposed cultural categories, generally of a deep biological or ontological sort: human/reptile, living/dead, etc. But it is also true that in much horror, especially that which is considered to be classic, the opposition of such cultural categories in the biology of the horrific creatures portend further oppositions, oppositions that might be thought of in terms of thematic conflicts or antimonies which, in turn, are generally deep-seated in the culture in which the fiction has been produced" (*Horror*, 48).

32. Cohen, *Notes from the Ground*, 57, 57–58.

33. Clara's servant, Judith, shares in this connection between monetary and moral poverty as Carwin explains that, before being taken to Mettingen, Judith was in a family "where hypocrisy, as well as licentiousness, was wrought into a system" (152).

34. There is quite a bit of irony in this security, since Brown's prequel *Memoirs of Carwin the Biloquist* (published 1803–05) depicts Carwin honing his deceitful craft while laboring in Europe, a far cry from a content and remorseful tilling of fields.

35. Norwood, "Place," 90.

36. Norwood emphasizes this from a different angle to establish the connection between the place of events and characters' interpretations of them. She writes, "The link between belief and grounds seems to be a logical consequence of the connection

between politics and property in the early American republic. Since only property owners could vote, there was an implied yet very real connection between one's grounds and one's ability to express political opinions." Ibid., 91.

37. Critics have often focused on the incestuous nature of Clara's dream, reading the nightmare as either Clara's projecting a desire onto her beckoning brother or of her brother desiring her. Such readings provide compelling considerations of the problems inherent in the Wieland family, often using Freudian preoccupation with the gothic to point to the inevitability of Wieland's fall based on ruinous predispositions. What I find most interesting about the reading of the dream as incestuous fear and fantasy (both of which I agree are certainly evident in the text) is that it can still be seen as a desire for an aristocratic isolation. Incest actually provides a perverse security in that it prevents impurity from those outside of the family bloodline; this frightening isolation is later taken up by Poe, an admirer of Brown, in "The Fall of the House of Usher." In this way, incestuous desire still functions to retain the Wieland's social division from the encroachment of threats such as Carwin.

38. Sedgwick, *Conventions*, 28.

39. Grabo, *Coincidental*, 10; Hinds, *Property*, 110; Kafer, *Revolution*, 129.

40. I do not claim that corporeality has no significance in the novel. Indeed, during both the discovery of Catherine's body and during Wieland's suicide, the text emphasizes visual materiality and creates a sense of the grave consequences of actual physical attacks.

41. Such containment of a larger, more abstract fear is enabled by the genre, as the gothic so often materializes abstractions such as evil and otherworldly ideas into its figures. Pointing to the way gothic figures often open up to larger cultural anxieties, Savoy writes of the American Gothic: "[I]t manifests itself often in the strangest of tropes . . . a figure for which there exists no precise literal referent, a 'something' that can appear verbally in no other way." He, however, goes on to read *Wieland* as focusing primarily on the "repression of past historical gloom." While the novel's beginning certainly creates a foreboding atmosphere for the later events, setting up the Wieland's doom from the beginning, I want to suggest that it is not the past history that unravels the Wieland's present happiness; instead, it is the urgent and insistent future as modes of agriculture change in ways that cannot be reconciled with the current modes of living at Mettingen. See Savoy, "Rise," 171, 173.

42. Hinds argues that *Wieland* differs from Brown's other novels by creating "a resounding critique of an aristocratic class enabled by an overtly material and private set of values" (*Property*, 101).

BIBLIOGRAPHY

Barnard, Philip, and Stephen Shapiro. "Introduction." In Brown, *Wieland*, ix–xlvi.

Brown, Charles Brockden. *Memoirs of Carwin the Biloquist*. In Brown, *Wieland*, 230–78.

———. "A Specimen of Agricultural Improvement. *Extracted from the correspondence of a traveller in Scotland*." *Literary Magazine and American Register* 17.3 (1805): 86–93.

———. *Wieland; Or, the Transformation. An American Tale, with Related Texts.*

Edited with an introduction and notes by Philip Barnard and Stephen Shapiro. Indianapolis: Hackett, 2009.

Carroll, Noël. *The Philosophy of Horror: or, Paradoxes of the Heart*. New York: Routledge, 1990.

Cohen, Benjamin R. *Notes from the Ground: Science, Soil, and Society in the American Countryside*. New Haven, CT: Yale University Press, 2009.

Decker, Mark. "A Bumpkin before the Bar: Charles Brockden Brown's *Arthur Mervyn* and Class Anxiety in Postrevolutionary Philadelphia." *Pennsylvania Magazine of History and Biography* 124.4 (2000): 469–87.

Dwight, Timothy. *Greenfield Hill: A Poem in Seven Parts*. New York: Childs and Swain, 1794.

Fiedler, Leslie. *Love and Death in the American Novel*. Rev. ed. New York: Anchor Books, 1992.

Galluzzo, Anthony. "Charles Brockden Brown's *Wieland* and the Aesthetics of Terror: Revolution, Reaction, and the Radical Enlightenment in Early American Letters." *Eighteenth-Century Studies* 42.2 (2009): 255–71.

Grabo, Norman S. *The Coincidental Art of Charles Brockden Brown*. Chapel Hill: University of North Carolina Press, 1981.

Hinds, Elizabeth Jane Wall. *Private Property: Charles Brockden Brown's Gendered Economics of Virtue*. Newark: University of Delaware Press, 1997.

Hsu, Hsuan L. *Geography and the Production of Space in Nineteenth-Century American Literature*. Cambridge, UK: Cambridge University Press, 2010.

Jefferson, Thomas. *Notes on the State of Virginia*. In *The Portable Thomas Jefferson*, edited by Merrill D. Peterson, 23–232. New York: Penguin, 1975.

Kafer, Peter. *Charles Brockden Brown's Revolution and the Birth of American Gothic*. Philadelphia: University of Pennsylvania Press, 2004.

Kulikoff, Allan. *The Agrarian Origins of American Capitalism*. Charlottesville: University Press of Virginia, 1992.

Locke, John. *Of Civil Government, Second Treatise*. 6th printing. Chicago: Henry Regenry, 1955.

Norwood, Lisa West. "'I May Be a Stranger to the Grounds of Your Belief': Constructing Sense of Place in *Wieland*." *Early American Literature* 38.1 (2003): 89–122.

Rush, Benjamin. "An Account of the Progress of Population, Agriculture, Manners, and Government, in Pennsylvania." In *Essays, Literary, Moral and Philosophical*, 2nd ed., 213–25. Philadelphia: Thomas and William Bradford, 1806.

Savoy, Eric. "The Rise of American Gothic." In *The Cambridge Companion to Gothic Fiction*, edited by Jerrold E. Hogle, 167–88. Cambridge, UK: Cambridge University Press, 2002.

Sedgwick, Eve Kosofsky. *The Coherence of Gothic Conventions*. New York: Methuen, 1986.

Sweet, Timothy. *American Georgics: Economy and Environment in Early American Literature*. Philadelphia: University of Pennsylvania Press, 2002.

———. "American Pastoralism and the Marketplace: Eighteenth-Century Ideologies of Farming." *Early American Literature* 29.1 (1994): 59–80.

Temple, Gale. "Carwin the Onanist?" *Arizona Quarterly* 65.1 (2009): 1–32.

Tompkins, Jane. *Sensational Designs: The Cultural Work of American Fiction 1790–1860.* New York: Oxford University Press, 1995.

Watts, Steven. *The Romance of Real Life: Charles Brockden Brown and the Origins of American Culture.* Baltimore: John Hopkins University Press, 1994.

White, Ed. "Carwin the Peasant Rebel." In *Revising Charles Brockden Brown: Culture, Politics, and Sexuality in the Early Republic*, edited by Philip Barnard, Mark L. Kamrath, and Stephen Shapiro, 41–59. Knoxville: University of Tennessee Press, 2004.

Wolfe, Eric A. "Ventriloquizing Nation: Voice, Identity, and Radical Democracy in Charles Brockden Brown's *Wieland*." *American Literature* 78.3 (2006): 431–57.

Wieland, *Illustrated: Word and Image in the Early American Novel*

MEGAN WALSH
St. Bonaventure University

CHARLES Brockden Brown liked to draw. In his youth, he sketched out designs for towers, stairs, doors, windows, courtyards, rooms, closets, walkways, halls, multistoried buildings, single-story buildings, campus plans, and gardens, and he embellished them with an assortment of arches, domes, pediments, cornices, modillions, lunettes, and tympana. He drew with tools and, less often, freehand. He experimented with black ink and with watercolor paints. As Brown's first biographer, William Dunlap, notes Brown "would for hours be absorbed in architectural studies, measuring proportions with his compasses, and drawing plans of Grecian temples or Gothic cathedrals, monasteries or castles." Brown's interest in visual composition is echoed in his self-identification as American novelist in the opening "Advertisement" published with *Wieland*; or, The Transformation: An American Tale (1798). Explaining that the "incidents related" in the following pages "are extraordinary and rare," Brown admits that readers' probable skepticism is natural and warranted. Having elected to write about extreme characters and events, Brown forcefully asserts his justifications: "[I]t is the business of moral painters to exhibit their subject in its most instructive and memorable forms." Because the author of such a tale "aims at the illustration of some important branches of the moral constitution of man," he must consider himself an artist who embellishes past events into new fictional ones.[1]

Literature in the Early American Republic: Annual Studies on Cooper and His Contemporaries
Volume 6, 2014. Copyright © 2014 by AMS Press, Inc. All rights reserved.

Brown's choice to label himself a "moral painter" reveals the exceptionally close, even constitutive, relationship between his experiments with the visual arts and those with the verbal arts. Significant examples of Brown's early and varied interests, the sketches appear in the same notebooks in which he wrote, including the one in which he mapped plans for *Wieland*. Yet while many accounts have established Brown's occupation as a novelist, short fiction writer, essayist, and editor in order to articulate his significant role in a capacious republican print culture, much less has been done to assess the images in Brown's manuscripts.[2] The drawings in his (still mostly unpublished) letters, journals, and other early writings remain almost wholly unrecognized as significant imagistic texts within a larger early American literary culture.[3] These now-fragmentary and scattered drawings present especially promising examples of what Sandra M. Gustafson calls "new opportunities . . . for interpreting and representing the textual regimes of eras past."[4] The sketches Brown made on the verge of his career as eighteenth-century America's most prolific novelist constitute a vital, but understudied, part of his various "textual regimes." Taken seriously, Brown's drawings suggest new readings of *Wieland*'s familiar moments and new directions for analyzing his novelistic strategies.

Well known to scholars and teachers of early America, *Wieland* is set in the rural Delaware Valley just outside Philadelphia and offers readers a group of characters whose suspicions, zealotry, fears, devotions, and desires lead to a horrific quintuple homicide, an attempted murder, and a suicide. Clara Wieland, the narrator; her friend and lover, Pleyel; and her brother Theodore Wieland succumb to the ventriloquial tricks played on them by the mysterious stranger, Carwin, who has been lurking around their estate, hiding behind foliage, under windows, and within bedroom closets. Under the influence of Carwin's thrown voices and the conjurations of his own mentally disturbed mind, Theodore Wieland believes he is commanded by God to violently murder his family. Clara escapes unharmed only when Carwin uses his ventriloquism to intervene at the last minute, an act that saves her from possible rape and sure death at the hands of her murderous and deranged brother.[5] In the end, Wieland realizes his error and commits suicide; Clara and Pleyel eventually marry.

Critical accounts of *Wieland* have read the problems of the novel as emanating from the tightly knit Wieland family themselves, and not from the mysterious outsider Carwin. Carwin's arrival on the scene is a threat only because his ventrioloquial talents reveal the problems that are already present. Focused on the oral communication culture of the early republic, critical accounts have long treated Carwin's ventriloquism as a means to identify Brown's attitudes toward contemporary debates about nationhood, citizenship, gender, and race.[6] Such readings hinge on Brown's distrust of appearances, his arguments that everything from personal sincerity to political affiliation potentially masks true feelings and commitments. Sentimental and physiognomic reading practices were regular subjects of criticism in Brown's fiction because they suggested that internal character could be communicated by visible external forms.[7] As Bryan Waterman has explained, Brown's fiction "is fundamentally concerned . . . with interrogating the evidence of the eye." Brown was fascinated with sensory faculties' potential to probe beyond the superficial and into the hidden hearts, minds, and histories of individuals. When misapplied, sensory perceptions could conceal an unknown truth, but when properly honed through "rigor," could also reveal one.[8]

Arguments about Brown's investment in contemporary discourses of visual perception, however, do not fully appreciate the relationship between word and image that Brown cultivated in his early fiction. Like almost all other early American literary books, *Wieland* was published without substantial graphic decoration and without illustration. Neither Brown's publisher, Hoquet Caritat, nor the printers, Thomas and James Swords, found it practical or profitable to illustrate the novel. Despite the fact that his readers did not encounter *Wieland* as an illustrated text, I argue, Brown's conception of it with pictorial accompaniments suggests that visual representation plays a vital role in its structure and development. The first part of this essay introduces Brown's manuscript drawings in an attempt to recover them as fundamental, not incidental, to *Wieland*'s beginnings. I elaborate on the stakes of this reclamation in the remainder of the essay. Through my discussions of the ways these sketches illustrate moments in *Wieland*, I argue for a reading of the novel in which disputes over narrative authority are played out through the experiences of visual perception and representation. The novel offers a fictionalized account of drawing as it relates to narrative practice and evidences the significance both of Brown's visual experience and of the pressing need to integrate more fully a word and image methodology into the study of the early national literary culture.

1. Sketching Utopias

Brown's first draft of *Wieland* is an unfinished outline in an otherwise-ordinary commonplace book. Word lists fill pages 3, 4, and 5, what editors have called the "'Outline' proper" begins on page 6, skips page 9, continues on pages 10 and 11, then reappears on pages 18 and 19, and finally concludes on page 24" (*Wieland*, 421). The few comments that Brown's penchant for skipping pages has generated are usually dismissive. In the first volume in Kent State University's edition of Brown's novels and other works, editors Sydney J. Krause, S. W. Reid, and Alexander Cowie imply that Brown's skipped pages are merely irregular whimsy: "There seems to be no special explanation for the gaps between pages 11 and 18, and 19 and 24" (421). In keeping with their assertion that the page breaks do not matter, Krause, Reid, and Cowie's edition represents the commonplace book in a limited way. It includes facsimiles of the notebook pages on which Brown included textual references to *Wieland*, accompanied by a transcription that has continued to be seen as the gold-standard evidence of *Wieland*'s origins. In its transcribed form, Brown's page breaks and other unfinished sketches disappear into the new text's fabricated unity. Such an attitude toward the material qualities of the commonplace book draft has had profound implications for how we have continued to read the novel. The few editions that attend to the draft at all have ignored its disrupted pagination.[9] Yet the notebook's skipped pages, irregular graphic flourishes, and, most significantly, drawings are as much a part of the initial draft as the novel's more recognizable verbal antecedents. A palimpsest that affirms Brown's early works as experiments with multiple aesthetic forms, the notebook suggests a significant need to read *Wieland* as evidence of Brown's theories of the interrelations between word and image.

Held at the Historical Society of Pennsylvania (HSP) as part of the Brown Family Papers Collection, the small eighty-seven-page notebook shows evidence of Brown's early aesthetic ideas, drafted shortly after the publication of Brown's earliest fiction but before he moved to New York to try his hand at novel writing. In his plans for *Wieland*'s narrative structure, Brown moves from lists of names that test out various spellings (Is it the story of "Wieland" or "Weyland"?), to a loose outline of major plot points and character traits ("A certain gravity & gloominess in them."), and finally to a dramatic structure ("Act 2"). These incomplete notations signal that Brown was still in the earliest stages of composition, testing out various textual forms—lists, outline, narrative prose, and dramatic performance—to build the novel's complex plot. The notebook's drawings are equally scattered and incomplete, ranging from an elegantly rendered two-page topographical map of a watershed area to a crude geometric sketch. Brown's habit of skipping pages and his tendency to leave texts and sketches unfinished left plenty of room for later use. After Brown used it for a few years, the notebook fell into the hands of Brown's father, Elijah Brown, whose dating indicates that he began writing in the book in 1800. Using it both as a commonplace book and as scrap paper, the elder Brown's notations included copied out Quaker sermons and notes for his Philadelphia real estate business. To keep his own notations distinguishable from his son's, he simply drew lines around Brown's notes and sketches. The younger Brown's darker, larger hand remains the more noticeable, as it sprawls over the pages in contrast to his father's lighter, finer writing.

In order to understand the connections between Brown's drawings and his fiction, we need to consider the body of his drawings as a set. While there are only a handful of drawings in the *Wieland* notebook, Brown's sketches accompany several other examples of his early writing. Another notebook held at the HSP that, like the *Wieland* notebook, was later used by Brown's father also contains architectural designs.[10] Several pages show circular designs and overhead views of rooms and buildings. By far the largest collection of Brown's drawings, the Harry Ransom Center at the University of Texas (HRC) collection contains architectural drawings identical in style to those of the HSP holdings.[11] Of the thirty-nine pages of drawings at the HRC, approximately fifteen pages contain one or more designs that are easily identified as neoclassical forms, including buildings plans, curved arches, and other geometric shapes. Three recall the elements of a medieval church more than of neoclassical design, and another three depict full or partial Gothic arches. Of the full collection of Brown's extant drawings, only a handful depict complete buildings.

Like the *Wieland* notebook at the HSP, the HRC's collection of drawings is materially linked to Brown's early fiction. Dated 1793, these fragmentary texts were not Brown's earliest fiction, but they did predate the *Wieland* notes, which were written as early as 1796. While only one file at the HRC is cataloged as containing drawings, another file that holds uncompleted fictional pieces also contains a sketch and the same red and green watercolor stains that appear in the drawings.[12] One of these short fictions, the epistolary "Ellendale fragment," describes the dysfunctional Ellen family and their home Ellendale on the banks of the Schuylkill. The "Ruse, distance, Secrecy" that characterizes their relationships with each other and with their friends gestures to the ideas Brown more fully developed a few years later in *Wieland*. The letters' recipient in the Ellendale piece returns in the other paint-stained text at the HRC, the "Godolphin fragment." Referring to a character named R. H., a likely allusion to Raphael Hythloday, a traveler in Thomas More's *Utopia* (1516), the Godolphin text considers the relationship between poetry and history to advocate for a utopian "community where all are votaries of truth and justice and of consequence where all are happy."[13]

While no specific moment in either the Ellendale fragment or the Godolphin fragment corresponds exactly to the drawings, the utopian themes that drive them also motivate many of the sketches. For instance, one image from the HRC collection appears to resemble the layout for an educational institution in that sections are labeled "Art," "Math," and "Archit." According to Alan Axelrod, "Brown was toying with designs for a school or college, the very architecture of which was intended to reflect his system of pedagogy and his conception of the division of knowledge." "The ambitious utopianism of the drawings and calculations," Axelrod notes, are in keeping with both Brown's teenage interests as a member of the Belles Lettres Society and his much later, and mostly posthumously published, *Historical Sketches* (1803–7).[14] Drawing inspiration from the popular Palladian architecture movement reflected in countless early national constructions, Brown's plans for an educational campus are likely hypothetical; if the measurements are in feet, the buildings could never have been built in his day. Just as Brown's early fictions imagine utopian worlds, Brown's drawings similarly envision an eccentric architecture that would serve those fantastic locales and their inhabitants. Brown's drawings register his deep learning in classical and modern building design, but just as significantly, they insist on his interest in creating fictional worlds that could be represented visually.

The fact that the Ellendale and Godolphin fragments were penned in the same moment, sometimes on the same paper, with the same utopian concerns as Brown's drawings should lead us to consider all of his drawings as central to his early composition processes and his theories about fiction. While the number of drawings that accompany Brown's first draft of *Wieland* are limited, the many illustrations that accompany his other early fiction underscore the relationship between the drawings in the *Wieland* notebook and *Wieland* itself. At the least, Brown's interests in fiction and drawing emerged simultaneously, and at the most, his compositional habits show that Brown thought of them in conjunction and that they derived from the same aesthetic imperative. Recognizing the interrelatedness of Brown's experiments with word and image enables us to move past the drawings as artifacts of a youthful pastime and toward a more materially informed reading of the visual systems at work in *Wieland.*

2. *Architecture in the Margins*

The most visually striking drawing in the notebook in which Brown drafted *Wieland* is the meticulously measured and shaded architectural sketch on pages 46 and 47 (see fig. 1). While almost all of the designs in the *Wieland* notebook are crude and incomplete, Brown's plan for a neoclassical building and archway stands out because of its carefully penned lines and shading. Scaled and labeled, the left half of the design depicts a large semicircular space embellished with semicircles equally spaced around its border while a smaller, full circle is connected by straight lines. The right half of the design appears to be an exterior building facade with capped doorways with gabled cornices. Echoing many contemporary architectural designs for domed buildings, Brown's sketch occupied more than a little of his time.[15] How should we read this image of a complex domed structure, this architectural plan that accompanies Brown's first draft of *Wieland*? What, if any, elements of the narrative does it illustrate?

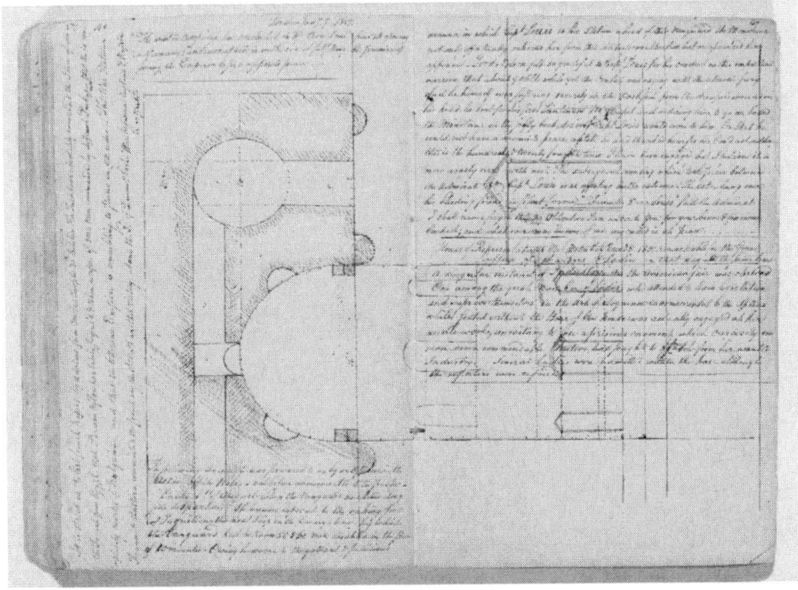

Fig. 1. Architectural Sketch. Charles Brockden Brown and Elijah Brown, Sr. Brown Family Papers, vol. 24. Historical Society of Pennsylvania, Philadelphia.

Critics have pointed out the dramatic ways in which architecture shapes *Wieland*, noting that the family's houses structure many of the novel's central events. As Duncan Faherty has explained, Brown's continual return "to architectural scenes at decisive moments" is a choice that "places possession, intention, and design at the forefront of his narratives." In *Wieland*, in particular, "[t]he fate of the Wielands is inextricably bound together with their various properties," claims Elizabeth Jane Wall Hinds.[16] Familial devastation is a result of an overinterest, but underestimation, of the built environment of the Wieland family estate on the part of those who reside there. While the final version of the novel includes several important buildings, the draft text in the *Wieland* notebook mentions only the temple or summerhouse, whereas Clara's and Theodore's houses are hardly anywhere to be found.

Even in the final version of the novel, the domed temple remains the site of many of the family's most terrible disasters. It is at the temple where the elder Wieland meets his death as the result of unexplained spontaneous combustion and, later, where Carwin is compelled to utter his first act of ventriloquism in the novel, thereby setting in motion events that result in tragedy. Designed and built by the elder Wieland as "the temple of his Deity" (12), the building has a striking presence:

> At the distance of three hundred yards from his house, on the top of a rock whose sides were steep, rugged, and encumbered with dwarf cedars and stony asperities, he built what to a common eye would have seemed a summer-house. The eastern verge of this precipice was sixty feet above the river which flowed at its foot. The view before it consisted of a transparent current, fluctuating and rippling in a rocky channel, and bounded by a rising scene of cornfields and orchards. The edifice was slight and airy. It was not more than a circular area, twelve feet in diameter, whose flooring was the rock, cleared of moss and shrubs, and exactly leveled, edged by twelve Tuscan columns, and covered by an undulating dome. (11)

Situated away from the house, the building is the ideal location for the elder Wieland to meditate on his enthusiastic interpretation of the teachings of the French Huguenot group the Camissards, and, later, for his orphaned offspring to establish a shrine to polite rationalism.

Its topographically elevated location also makes the temple an ideal place for the elder Wieland to survey the grounds of his estate. As a perch to which the Wielands continually retreat, the building would seem to grant them unrestricted views over their land and those who populate it. Brown's inspiration for such an architecture of surveillance might have been, as Peter Kafer has suggested, the buildings erected by millenarianists and radical pietists who found their way to rural Pennsylvania in the 1690s, in particular the "tabernacle" built in 1694 by Johannes Kelpius "and his 'Chapter of Perfection.'" Constructed to accommodate the beliefs of a group who constantly looked for signs of the second coming, the temple of Kelpius and his followers featured "an observatory on the roof, where brethren would sit through the night with a telescope to search for celestial phenomenon, in millennial anticipation of the coming of the 'Bridegroom.'"[17] Regardless of its specific historical inspiration, however, the temple reflects 1790s interest in domed architectures with views of the surrounding landscape. As a fictional representation of the early Republic's many newly constructed domed buildings, the summerhouse reflects a popular interest in the visual possibilities that such architecture could afford. Domes, church spires, and hot air balloons enabled and encouraged Americans to take in the geography of their country from an elevated perspective.[18]

Wieland's temple reverses contemporary models of panoramic viewing, however, so that the building perched on a cliff does not so much provide excellent views of the world below but itself becomes the object to be viewed. Its location "on the top of a rock whose sides were steep" makes it a place ideally situated for advertising the Wielands' secrets and tragedies to distant onlookers. Early on in the novel, the episode of the elder Wieland's death inverts the expected relations between observers and observed. Overcome with worry, Clara's mother sits at her window hoping to see a sign of her absent husband:

> She rose, and seated herself at the window. She strained her sight to get a view of the dome, and of the path that led to it. The first painted itself with sufficient distinctness on her fancy, but was undistinguishable by the eye from the rocky mass on which it was erected. The second could be imperfectly seen; but her husband had already passed, or had taken a different direction. (16)

It is not until disaster strikes and "[a] light proceeding from the edifice, made every part of the scene visible" that Clara's mother and uncle are able to locate her father (16). The light from the temple acts like a gothic beacon: "[A] blazing light was clearly discernible between the columns of the temple" (17). Although Clara frames this incident as a story about her father's actions, what we actually get is information about her mother and uncle. As observers of the domed building, their perspectives take precedence over the elder Wieland's, even despite their minor roles in Clara's narrative. It is because her mother and uncle look up and out toward the domed structure—rather than down from it—that they are able to provide a verbal account of what happened:

> The preclusive gleam, the blow upon his arm, the fatal spark, the explosion heard so far, the fiery cloud that environed him, without detriment to the structure, though composed of combustible materials, the sudden vanishing of this cloud at my uncle's approach—what is the inference to be drawn from these facts? Their truth is not to be doubted. My uncle's testimony is peculiarly worthy of credit, because no man's temper is more sceptical, and his belief is unalterably attached to natural causes. (19)

The "facts" submitted to the reader, Clara writes, are "not to be doubted" because they have been reported by her uncle. His "sceptical" character, as well as the fact of his witnessing the events firsthand—but, significantly, from afar—is what make the perfect recorder and reporter. Readers can trust him, Clara implies, because he was never too close to the event itself. By reversing the qualities of contemporary panoramic viewing inscribed in the temple's elevated position and domed architecture, the death of the Wielands' father posits the ideal narrating position as the result of an ideal viewing position. The best kinds of viewers, and thus narrators, are characters who lack the elder Wieland's magisterial gaze.

Reading the voices of secondary characters as functions of their visual experiences reclaims the significance of those voices, repositioning them as essential to the novel's overall structure. Like their father, the second generation of the Wieland family peers out and down from their lookout, but the alternate viewing and narrative perspective of the other residents of the estate are essential to the novel's development and resolution. Mettingen's inhabitants become important elements to the narrative at the moments when they are out of the Wieland family's line of sight. A central aspect of the novel's approach to storytelling, Brown's removal of characters from Clara's observational standpoint signals her blindness to their significance in her tale. For instance, Clara is incapable of providing a description of her servant Judith, despite her being the only other resident of Clara's house. Clara's inability to integrate Judith into her story confirms her prejudice toward what Ed White has described as the novel's "rural subaltern." In "groping for a vernacular sociology attentive to class formations, geography, material conditioning" and addressing the conditions of sporadic but politically significant local unrest, like the Paxton Boys riots of the 1760s, Brown attempts to portray the experiences of rural Americans such as those living in southwestern Pennsylvania.[19] Clara fails to describe or to recognize the true character of Judith, a young woman who, as Carwin explains, "was taught that the best use of her charms consists in the sale of them," and as a result, Clara is rendered unusually susceptible to the terrifying events that begin to unfold around her (201). Without Judith, Carwin points out during the novel's climax, he would not have been able to play tricks on Clara from her closet. In describing how he created the illusion of murderers plotting in her closet, he explains that there was a third voice, Judith's, who mimicked the "struggles and prayers of the victim" (202). As Carwin notes, Clara's fearful nature causes her to flee rather than to listen more closely to the voices that someone more observant would have been able to discern as belonging to her housemate. Despite her eventual recognition of most of the circumstances leading to the murders, Clara never discusses at any length Judith's moral character or its important role in shaping the mysteries at Mettingen. This oversight on Clara's part, the novel suggests, is symptomatic of her much larger observational and, therefore, narrative failures.

Working-class young women such as Judith populate more of the Mettingen estate than Clara seems to realize, and they are certainly more essential to the novel's plot than she is willing to admit. As a privileged heiress, Clara willfully subordinates information about the people who work for her family. Even when Clara's own life is saved by the actions of a servant girl who resides at her brother's house, she is unable to describe the girl's actions in relation to her own life and family. Like Carwin, the servant learns about the Wielands' secrets from a concealed position in a closet, the ideal architectural space from which to peer into the darkened chambers and equally dark secrets that haunt the Wieland family. But even though she possesses the most accurate account of the murder, the narrative prevents her from telling her story. "A servant-maid who spied the murder of the children from a closet where she was concealed" identifies Wieland as the murderer, but is interrupted when Wieland bursts into the house, "unexpected, unsolicited, and unsought" (162). Although we learn that Wieland has cut short the girl's testimony and "acknowledged his guilt, and rendered himself up to justice," in the secondhand account Clara provides, we never do get Wieland's version of events (162). Wieland's voice is ultimately stifled by the eyewitness account of his social subordinate. Without authentication by the crime's only witness, Wieland's confession might have been seen as the ramblings of a madman, but not necessarily those of a murderer; the servant girl's account damns Wieland by corroborating his confession. As if to make up for her intrusion into what should be the Wielands' story, Clara attempts to minimize the significance of the servant's voice. After recounting her version of the murder, the servant promptly disappears from Clara's narrative.

Critics have argued that Brown's fiction resists privileging the voice of a single narrator whose perspective cannot be trusted and instead promotes multiple narrative perspectives and relations, perspectives that ultimately reveal characters whose histories of events oppose, complicate, and upset those of the leading narrative voice. According to Jared Gardner, Brown's occupation as an editor prompted him to rely on his fiction to "reject any notion of a true voice that would reduce the complex weave of contradictory voices and positions to a monologic discourse." Similarly, Amanda Emerson has stressed the multiplicity of Brown's "fictitious histories," narratives in which "truth will best be conveyed by individual voices, drawn by the writer from among the possibilities of a many-layered past."[20] In *Wieland*, those characters who provide the key pieces of information that unlock the "incredible" mysteries at the novel's heart are also those whose visual perception is keenest (6).[21] Their seemingly subordinate narrative voices intrude on Clara's storytelling and the novel's plot because they reveal these characters to be more visually observant, better able to comprehend the limits of visual sense perception, and better able to communicate past events as stories that matter. The superior viewing—and therefore storytelling—abilities of characters outside the Wieland family circle register in the very distant margins of Clara's narrative because they do not exist in her myopic view of Mettingen.

Even Carwin is posited as a viewer uniquely positioned to take in the estate from a perspective on the ground. Both the reader and Clara are introduced to Carwin as he admires the Wieland family home. Clara's shock at seeing him strolling the grounds results from her notions of what kinds of people she thinks could find visual pleasure in the experience of a "careless and lingering" walk (50). Carwin simply does not fit the bill: "This lawn was only traversed by men whose views were directed to the pleasures of the walk, or the grandeur of the scenery" (50). Carwin's predilection for lurking around her family's estate is motivated, he tells Clara toward the end of the novel, by Mettingen's artful landscapes, which please his practiced viewing tastes. "In all my rambles," Carwin declares, "I never found a spot in which so many picturesque beauties and rural delights were assembled as at Mettingen" (203). The Wieland estate is, as Jeffrey Andrew Weinstock has put it, "initially presented as a sort of idyllic garden of paradise, ripe for the serpent to come calling."[22] And call he does, gaining entrance into the Wieland family circle, first, by sizing up their land and, then, by manipulating the comfort they receive from looking down on all that they own and seem to control. Carwin enacts the exact opposite of the Wielands' mode of viewership when he literally takes up a marginal position by walking "close to the edge of the bank that was in front" of Clara's house (50). Like Judith and the unnamed servant, Carwin comprehends the true nature of the Wieland family by peering at them from unexpected and overlooked locations. As it turns out, the characters best positioned to visually observe, understand, and verbally record the events at Mettingen are those who like Carwin, hover at the novel's spatial and social margins. In following the notebook draft's emphasis on the domed temple as the novel's central architectural structure, we might expand readings of its significance in the novel's final version and, as I have argued, partially explain Brown's habit of sketching domed architecture while composing fiction. Informed by contemporary viewing practices associated with domed architectures, *Wieland* asserts the interdependence between viewership and narration and between drawing and novel writing.

3. Storytelling and Picture Making

Brown's early sketches suggest the transitive qualities of visual and verbal representation in *Wieland*. But they do not in and of themselves theorize drawing as a form of compositional practice. By contrast, the novel interpolates Brown's practice of mixing verbal and visual media by staging not only viewership but also the recording of visual evidence—drawing itself—as a mode of authorship. Clara's narrative failures, in particular, reveal the way drawing informed part of Brown's approach to the definition of narrative authority. Her inability to understand the tricks and limits of her own visual observations is represented as coextensive with her incapacity to accurately record what she sees. Clara's auditory perception falls short, as we might expect, but so does her vision as we learn that her sensory faculties become mobile and unmoored, and she increasingly refuses to signify what is really there. Throughout the novel, Clara not only relates the events at Mettingen but also gives an account of her nearly complete inability to perceive the world around her. She can observe events, remember them, and try to recount them in writing, but her pronounced weaknesses as a narrator stem from her poor sensory perception: she does not understand what she has observed, and so she cannot accurately remember or record past events. Like a "witness's testimony of what she has seen and heard (with all the biases and limitations implied by such an 'interested' role)," Laura H. Korobkin remarks, Clara's narrative records only what she thinks she heard and saw. Even at the novel's end, Clara remains unsure of what has taken place and so, as Ezra Tawil notes, "[she] visit[s] this epistemological instability upon the similarly disoriented reader."[23] Because she tells the story of the tragedies at Mettingen, and significantly, because she herself is unable to comprehend them, Clara encourages frustrated readers to understand her account as one-sided and inaccurate.

Shortly after her first meeting with Carwin, Clara recounts her experience in drawing his portrait and the dissatisfaction she feels in doing so. Her inability to read Carwin's face is secondary to her inability to provide a pen and ink rendering of it:

> This face, seen for a moment, continued for hours to occupy my fancy, to the exclusion of almost every other image. I had purposed to spend the evening with my brother, but I could not resist the inclination of forming a sketch upon paper of this memorable visage. Whether my hand was aided by any peculiar inspiration, or I was deceived by my own fond conceptions, this portrait, though hastily executed, appeared unexceptionable to my own taste.
>
> I placed it at all distances, and in all lights; my eyes were rivetted upon it. Half the night passed away in wakefulness and in

> contemplation of this picture. So flexible, and yet so stubborn, is the human mind. So obedient to impulses the most transient and brief, and yet so unalterably observant of the direction which is given to it! How little did I then foresee the termination of that chain, of which this may be regarded as the first link? (54)

In Clara's telling, Carwin's face is transformed from pure physical characteristics into a fixed picture that pushes "almost every other image" out of her mind. Carwin's face is not simply like an image recalled in one's imagination; it is an image that she has drawn. Clara's description of Carwin's face as imagistic leads to the actions she takes next: "Half the night passed away in the contemplation of this picture." She "placed it at all distances, and in all lights" with her "eyes rivetted upon it," but nevertheless could neither appreciate the image nor understand the identity and character of the person it portrays. In her visual sketch of Carwin, Clara fails to record the information necessary to identify his mysterious character and history, or more crucially, his exact role in the narrative's plot.

Clara focuses intensely on her inability to give proper meaning to the visual representation of Carwin's face, so much so that she becomes obsessed with the image: "I betook myself to the contemplation of this portrait," Clara explains, continuing, "I laid aside my usual occupations, and seating myself at a window, consumed the day in alternately looking out upon the storm, and gazing at the picture" (54). The image itself begins to give off a talismanic aura the longer she stares at it ("its properties were rare and prodigious"), as Carwin's real face becomes less significant than the sketch meant to record it. As if suddenly aware of the implications of her interest in the image, Clara gives voice to imagined accusations:

> Perhaps you will suspect that such were the first inroads of a passion incident to every female heart, and which frequently gains a footing by means even more slight, and more improbable than these. I shall not controvert the reasonableness of the suspicion, but leave you at liberty to draw, from my narrative, what conclusions you please. (54)

Clara does not give assurances against the imaginary charges that claim her devotion to the portrait may seem "the first inroads of a passion"; instead, she prefers to leave the matter to the reader to decide whether her aims in observation are rooted in sexual desire. Her readers are invited to "draw, from my narrative, what conclusions [they] please." Clara creates an explicit link between her capacities for perceiving, understanding, and recording a situation—figured here in the form of her drawing of Carwin's face—and her inability to convey meaning. She is not only unable to understand her own motives in returning to the image she has made but also unwilling ("I leave you at liberty") to provide a verbal account of her own emotional and mental states or her estimation of Carwin's character. Ultimately, Clara's sense of herself as a visual artist parallels her overestimation of herself as an author.

Just as Clara's weaknesses as a narrator unfold through the practice of drawing Carwin's portrait, the tensions between Carwin's and Clara's storytelling abilities likewise emerge from a failure of visual recognition and representation. As the novel's notorious teller of false tales, Carwin tests everyone he encounters, but no character experiences those narrative trials quite like Clara. Their competing accounts of events are what set and keep the plot in motion. Clara's problems with perception begin when Carwin arrives, to be sure, but they really get going once he starts hiding in her house. It is in this setting that Clara's perceptual misrecognition and Carwin's dissimulating voices are at their most dramatic. Like many rural houses built in the eighteenth century in the Delaware Valley, Clara's home is a "wooden edifice, consisting of two stories," each with two rooms "separated by an entry, or middle passage, with which they communicated by opposite doors" (56). And then there is her closet. So significant is this architectural feature, that Brown devotes a full paragraph to describing it:

> The opposite wing is of smaller dimensions, the rooms not being above eight feet square. The lower of these was used as a depository of household implements, the upper was a closet in which I deposited my books and papers. They had but one inlet, which was from the room adjoining. There was no window in the lower one, and in the upper, a small aperture which communicated light and air, but would scarcely admit the body. (56)

It is worth lingering over that "small aperture." Nearly identical to the room beneath it, Clara's closet is differentiated by the small but significant window. Homes built by German immigrants in Pennsylvania sometimes included a similar architectural feature, "Seelenfensteren" ("spirits-windows"), which were built into the most private room of houses for the purpose of allowing a recently deceased inhabitant's soul to escape the structure.[24] By contrast, the very real and very alive Carwin uses the opening to force his disembodied vocal presence into the room. The window was, he tells Clara at the novel's end, "scarcely large enough to admit the head, but it answered my purpose too well" (202).

As a resident of America's urban centers, however, Brown was likely less familiar with architectural folkways than he was with the booming industry in popular optical devices sold, circulated, and exhibited in Philadelphia and New York.[25] Brown imagines an architectural structure in Clara's house that draws on the advertisements and descriptions of camera obscura instruments and, in doing so, further positions Clara's authorial weaknesses as a function of her inability to comprehend visual representations.[26] Camera obscura machines were frequently used as drawing aids by artists who traced images projected from the devices. Despite their popularity, however, camera obscura instruments were an imperfect tool because they generally produced a distorted version of an original figure so that artists had to consciously adjust for the devices' failings. Brown himself was aware of the altering effects of these machines, reprinting a notice in 1805 that happily announced the invention of "several improvements in the camera obscura," including a new "contrivance" that "placed objects which appear reversed in their natural position."[27]

Just as she cannot adequately represent Carwin in the visual medium of portraiture, Clara is equally unable to negotiate the figurative camera obscura that is her bedroom. She simply cannot discern that her repeated and confusing experiences are illusions projected from an unseen operator through the aperture that is her closet window. Heading to her closet during one of her wakeful nights, Clara suddenly freezes, recalling "what had lately passed in this closet" and noting that she is "alone, and defenceless" (84). What Clara worries will happen if she does open the door is completely unimaginable to her, but her fears of the unknown are paradoxically figured as imagistic. She explains: "My fears had pictured to themselves no precise object. It would be difficult to depict, in words, the ingredients and hues of that phantom which haunted me" (84). The "terrific image" that she imagines is indescribable through language. The closest Clara can come to giving a description of the imagined "phantom" lurking in her closet is a picture without a subject. Lacking a specific image in her mind, verbal narrative skills fail the novel's narrator at the critical moment.

Even when she finally does witness Carwin at work, Clara remains characteristically befuddled. Approaching the house after an evening walk, she notices that there is a "light from the window of my own chamber" (145). Carwin has entered her house, Clara reasons, and made himself comfortable enough to put on a light and wait in her bedroom. Outraged by this idea, Clara proceeds to the house, enters, and fearlessly begins to ascend the stairs, only to find that the same mysterious voice she has heard before calls out the "piercing exclamation of *hold! hold!*" (147). Pivoting to identify the source, Clara is positioned to observe the hidden mechanics of Carwin's sensory tricks:

> I had not closed the door of the apartment I had just left. The staircase, at the foot of which I stood, was eight or ten feet from the door, and attached to the wall through which the door led. My view, therefore, was sidelong, and took in no part of the room.
>
> Through this aperture was an head thrust and drawn back with so much swiftness, that the immediate conviction was, that thus much of a form, ordinarily invisible, had been unshrowded. (147)

The "aperture" and limited sight lines signal the visual and auditory qualities of her experience as yet another figurative camera obscura. Clara catches a crucial glimpse of the operator who controls the illusions she fears, but she does not know what to make of what she has seen. "What conclusion could I form?" she asks (148). Actually seeing Carwin "in the very act of utterance" during one of his deceptions ultimately does not amount to much for Clara; she is still as perplexed as ever and cannot apprehend the chamber of illusions that Carwin has created in her home (214). By the novel's end, it has become apparent that Clara Wieland is not in control of her stories or her visual sensory abilities. Produced by a sensory illusion, the nighttime terrors emanating from Clara's bedroom closet take shape in a figurative camera obscura space that links image production with narrative development.

Reading *Wieland* as a novel composed in conjunction with a series of illustrations of specific buildings, I have argued, reestablishes the temple as the novel's central architectural space. As a site of various modes of visual surveillance, the domed construction helps reveal the storytelling abilities of characters that view and speak from the distanced margins. Often positioned literally out of sight in Clara's narrative, these characters comprehend the world around them far more clearly than Clara does, and they relate what they see to greater effect. Considering the fact of Brown's habit of sketching fictions and drawings simultaneously, we can appreciate the parallels between his narrative strategies and Clara's. Not just a function of her perceptual weaknesses, Clara's inabilities as a narrator are figured in her equally wanting talents as a visual artist. Brown, by contrast, honed his literary skills even while he was busy making drawings.

NOTES

For their help with earlier versions of this essay, I thank Philip Barnard, Jim Green, Yvette Piggush, Matthew Sivils, and the anonymous readers at *LEAR*. Research for this essay was supported by an American Society for Eighteenth-Century Studies and Andrew W. Mellon Fellowship at the Harry Ransom Center at the University of Texas at Austin and a Society for the History of the Early Republic Fellowship at the Historical Society of Pennsylvania and the Library Company of Philadelphia

1. Dunlap, *Life of Brown*, 2:89–90. Brown, *Wieland*, ed. Krause, Reid, and Cowie, 3. Subsequent references to this edition will appear parenthetically in the text.

2. See Barnard, Kamrath, and Shapiro, *Revising Brown*; Gardner, "The Literary Museum," Slawinski, *Validating Bachelorhood*; Warner, *Letters of the Republic*; and Waterman, "Mervyn's Medical Repository."

3. My discussion of the relations between print and manuscript is informed by D. F. McKenzie's concept of the "speech—manuscript—print" relationship, in which interactions between media change as new media emerge, but new media forms do not supplant older modes. Speech and manuscript communication modes existed and continued to inform one another and the new media of print, even as they were affected by the ways print changed readers', writers', and booksellers' understanding spoken and handwritten communication. McKenzie, "Speech-Manuscript-Print."

4. Gustafson, "Emerging Media of Early America," 341.

5. Family plays a key role in a number of readings of *Wieland.* As Shirley Samuels has argued, for instance, Brown writes "national concerns" as "domestic dilemmas, since in order to preserve the nation it was conceived as necessary to preserve the family as a carefully constituted supporting unit." Samuels, "*Wieland,*" 50.

6. See, especially, Davidson, *Revolution and the Word*; Fliegelman, *Declaring Independence*; Galluzzo, "Brown's *Wieland* and the Aesthetics of Terror"; Judson, "A Sound of Voices"; Kazanjian, "Brown's Biloquial Nation"; Looby, *Voicing America*; Ruttenburg, *Democratic Personality*; and Wolfe, "Ventriloquising Nation."

7. Lukasik, *Discerning Characters*, 105–20.

8. Waterman, "Mervyn's Medical Repository," 230–31.

9. Brown, *Wieland*, ed. Waterman, 307–12.

10. Brown Family Papers, vol. 25.

11. Charles Brockden Brown Papers, 1.4.

12. Charles Brockden Brown Papers, 1.2, 1.4.

13. Brown, "Ellendale fragment"; Brown, "Godolphin fragment."

14. Axelrod, *Charles Brockden Brown*, 101.

15. Written at approximately the same time as the drawings, Brown's poem "Devotion" (1794) includes an image of a dome as an example of sublime architecture.

16. Faherty, *Remodeling the Nation*, 50; Hinds, *Private Property*, 12.

17. Kafer, *Brown's Revolution*, 117.

18. For a discussion of the popularity of such viewing practices, see Bellion, *Citizen Spectator*; Bellion, "'Extend the Sphere'"; and Oettermann, *The Panorama.*

19. White, "Carwin the Peasant Rebel," 44. White characterizes Carwin as a "peasant rebel," a character who stands in for the unruly residents of rural localities who questioned, and sometimes violently opposed, government and the process of federal unification.

20. Gardner, "The Literary Museum," 745; Emerson, "The Early American Novel," 128.

21. To some extent, the numerous voices of outsider characters embody what Edward Cahill has described as the positive aspects of the imagination: "Brown finds the technologies of aesthetic experience to be highly complex and ambiguous, but he also assumes the imagination's eminent ability to comprehend such complexity and ambiguity, and to elaborate its central relation to national polity and social transformation." Cahill, "Adventurous and Lawless Fancy," 35.

22. Weinstock, *Charles Brockden Brown*, 37.

23. Korobkin, "Murder by Madman," 724; Tawil, "'New Forms of Sublimity,'" 120.

24. Weaver, "The Pennsylvania German House," 259–60.

25. Among the most popular visual devices in Brown's lifetime, camera obscura machines and solar microscopes depended on darkened rooms with small apertures for daylight. While such optical devices had been around for centuries, account books and other records from leading makers and importers of visual devices show a huge spike in production and sales in the early republic. Using lenses, and sometimes mirrors, fitted into small apertures in exterior walls, exhibits in the early Republic showed how camera obscura machines could project magnified, inverted images of the outside

world for visitors in darkened rooms. Other, smaller, devices designed for tabletop use became standard parlor fare, as elite young women increasingly used them to improve their drawing skills. See Bellion, *Citizen Spectator*; Crary, *Techniques of the Observer*; Hammond, *The Camera Obscura*; and Steadman, *Vermeer's Camera.*

26. Andrew Newman finds the descriptions of dark spaces and light in Brown's *Edgar Huntly* similarly reminiscent of the camera obscura, but reads Brown's allusion to the device as a program for literary criticism. Newman notes that the historical fictional qualities of Brown's novels suggest an "obscure space like the camera" and thus "part of the historicist critic's task is to locate and uncover its apertures, the points where the language seems to open up onto a phenomenal world of events, people, and other texts." Newman, "'Light might possibly be requisite,'" 325–26.

27. Brown, "Recent European Intelligence," 474.

BIBLIOGRAPHY

Axelrod, Alan. *Charles Brockden Brown: An American Tale.* Austin: University of Texas Press, 1983.

Barnard, Philip, Mark L. Kamrath, and Stephen Shapiro, eds. *Revising Charles Brockden Brown: Culture, Politics, and Sexuality in the Early Republic.* Knoxville: University of Tennessee Press, 2004.

Bellion, Wendy. *Citizen Spectator: Art, Illusion, and Visual Perception in Early National America.* Chapel Hill: Published for the Omohundro Institute for Early American History and Culture, Williamsburg, VA, by the University of North Carolina Press, 2011.

——. "'Extend the Sphere': Charles Willson Peale's Panorama of Annapolis." *Art Bulletin* 86.3 (2004): 529–49.

Brown, Charles Brockden. "Architectural Drawings and Notes." Transcribed by Sarah Blythe. Personal e-mail. June 2011.

——. Charles Brockden Brown Papers, Collections 1.2 and 1.4. Harry Ransom Center at the University of Texas at Austin.

——. "Devotion (To [Debby Ferris])." 4 October 1794. Charles Brockden Brown Papers. George J. Mitchell Department of Special Collections and Archives, Bowdoin College Library, Brunswick, ME.

——. "Ellendale fragment." In *Collected Writings of Charles Brockden Brown*, vol. 1: Letters and Early Epistolary Fragments, edited by Philip Barnard, Elizabeth Hewitt, and Mark L. Kamrath. Lewisburg, PA: Bucknell University Press, 2013.

——. "Godolphin fragment." In *Collected Writings of Charles Brockden Brown*, vol. 1: Letters and Early Epistolary Fragments, edited by Philip Barnard, Elizabeth Hewitt, and Mark L. Kamrath. Lewisburg, PA: Bucknell University Press, 2013.

——. "Recent European Intelligence, Literary and Philosophical." *Literary Magazine* 4 (1805): 471–75.

——. *Wieland and Memoirs of Carwin the Biloquist.* Edited by Jay Fliegelman. New York: Penguin, 1991.

——. *Wieland and Memoirs of Carwin the Biloquist.* Edited by Bryan Waterman. New York: Norton, 2011.

——. *Wieland: or, the Transformation, an American Tale; Memoirs of Carwin, the Biloquist.* Bicentennial Edition. Edited by Sydney J. Krause, S. W. Reid, and Alexander Cowie. Kent: Kent State University Press, 1977.

Brown, Charles Brockden, and Elijah Brown Sr. Brown Family Papers. Vols. 24 and 25. Historical Society of Pennsylvania, Philadelphia.

Cahill, Edward. "An Adventurous and Lawless Fancy: Charles Brockden Brown's Aesthetic State." *Early American Literature* 36.1 (2001): 31–40.

Crary, Jonathan. *Techniques of the Observer: Vision and Modernity in the Nineteenth Century*. Cambridge, MA: MIT Press, 1990.

Davidson, Cathy N. *Revolution and the Word: The Rise of the Novel in America*. Rev. ed. New York: Oxford University Press, 2004.

Dunlap, William. *The Life of Charles Brockden Brown, Together with Selections from the Rarest of His Printed Works, from His Original Letters, and from His Manuscripts before Unpublished.* 2 vols. Philadelphia: James P. Parke, 1815.

Emerson, Amanda. "The Early American Novel: Charles Brockden Brown's Fictitious Historiography." *Novel: A Forum on Fiction* 40.1/2 (2006): 125–50.

Faherty, Duncan. *Remodeling the Nation: The Architecture of American Identity, 1776–1856.* Durham: University of New Hampshire Press, 2007.

Fliegelman, Jay. *Declaring Independence: Jefferson, Natural Language, and the Culture of Performance*. Stanford, CA: Stanford University Press, 1993.

——. Introduction. In Brown, *Wieland*, ed. Fliegelman, vii–xlii.

Galluzzo, Anthony. "Charles Brockden Brown's *Wieland* and the Aesthetics of Terror: Revolution, Reaction, and the Radical Enlightenment in Early American Letters." *Eighteenth-Century Studies* 42.2 (2009): 255–71.

Gardner, Jared. "The Literary Museum and the Unsettling of the Early American Novel." *ELH* 67.3 (2000): 743–71.

Goddu, Teresa. *Gothic America: Narrative, History, and Nation*. New York: Columbia University Press, 1997.

Gustafson, Sandra M. "The Emerging Media of Early America." In *Cultural Narratives: Textuality and Performance in American Culture before 1900*, edited by Sandra M. Gustafson and Caroline R. Sloat, 341–65. Notre Dame, IN: University of Notre Dame Press, 2010.

Hammond, John H. *The Camera Obscura: A Chronicle*. New York: Taylor and Francis, 1981.

Hinds, Elizabeth Jane Wall. *Private Property: Charles Brockden Brown's Gendered Economics of Virtue.* Newark: University of Delaware Press, 1997.

Judson, Barbara. "A Sound of Voices: The Ventrioloquial Uncanny in *Wieland* and *Prometheus Unbound.*" *Eighteenth-Century Studies* 44.1 (2010): 21–37.

Kafer, Peter. *Charles Brockden Brown's Revolution and the Birth of American Gothic.* Philadelphia: University of Pennsylvania Press, 2004.

Kazanjian, David. "Charles Brockden Brown's Biloquial Nation: National Culture and White Settler Colonialism in *Memoirs of Carwin the Biloquist.*" *American Literature* 73.3 (2001): 459–96.

Korobkin, Laura H. "Murder by Madman: Criminal Responsibility, Law, and Judgment in *Wieland.*" *American Literature* 72.4 (2000): 721–50.

Looby, Christopher. *Voicing America: Language, Literary Form, and the Origins of the United States.* Chicago: University of Chicago Press, 1996.

Lukasik, Christopher. *Discerning Characters: The Culture of Appearance in Early America.* Philadelphia: University of Pennsylvania Press, 2010.

McKenzie, D. F. "Speech-Manuscript-Print." *Library Chronicle of the University of Texas* 20.1/2 (1990): 86–109.

Newman, Andrew. "'Light might possibly be requisite': *Edgar Huntly*, Regional History, and Historicist Criticism." *Early American Studies* 8.2 (2010): 322–57.

Oettermann, Stephen. *The Panorama: History of a Mass Medium.* Translated by Deborah Lucas Schneider. New York: Zone Books, 1997.

Ruttenburg, Nancy. *Democratic Personality: Popular Voice and the Trial of American Authorship.* Stanford, CA: Stanford University Press, 1998.

Samuels, Shirley. "*Wieland*: Alien and Infidel." *Early American Literature* 25.1 (1990): 46–66.

Schmidt, Leigh Eric. *Hearing Things: Religion, Illusion, and the American Enlightenment.* Cambridge, MA: Harvard University Press, 2000.

Slawinski, Scott. *Validating Bachelorhood: Audience, Patriarchy, and Charles Brockden Brown's Editorship of the Monthly Magazine and American Review.* New York: Routledge, 2005.

Steadman, Philip. *Vermeer's Camera: Uncovering the Truth behind the Masterpieces.* New York: Oxford University Press, 2001.

Tawil, Ezra. "'New Forms of Sublimity': *Edgar Huntly* and the European Origins of American Exceptionalism." *Novel: A Forum on Fiction* 40.1/2 (2006): 104–24.

Warner, Michael. *Letters of the Republic: Publication and the Public Sphere in Eighteenth-Century America.* Cambridge, MA: Harvard University Press, 1990.

Waterman, Bryan. "Arthur Mervyn's Medical Repository and the Early Republic's Knowledge Industries." *American Literary History* 15.2 (2003): 213–47.

Weaver, William Woys. "The Pennsylvania German House: European Antecedents and New World Forms." *Winterthur Portfolio* 21.4 (1986): 243-64.

Weinstock, Jeffrey Andrew. *Charles Brockden Brown.* Cardiff: University of Wales Press, 2011.

White, Ed. "Carwin the Peasant Rebel." In *Revising Charles Brockden Brown: Culture, Politics, and Sexuality in the Early Republic*, edited by Philip Barnard, Mark L. Kamrath, and Stephen Shapiro, 41–59. Knoxville: University of Tennessee Press, 2004.

Wolfe, Eric A. "Ventriloquising Nation: Voice, Identity, and Radical Democracy in Charles Brockden Brown's *Wieland.*" *American Literature* 78.3 (2006): 431–57.

James Fenimore Cooper, American English, and the Signification of Aristocracy *in a Republic*

Allan M. Axelrad
California State University, Fullerton

THE American Revolution severed long-standing ties with an entitled and privileged Old World aristocracy. The upheaval that resulted saw significant political, social, economic, and cultural changes in the New World. Even the common language was affected. Democratic revolutions were bound to affect the use of language, Alexis de Tocqueville observed. With a new social order, traditional authorities would lose their standing, the "rules" of "style" would lose their force, words would be employed "indiscriminately," and "confusion" would develop "in language as in society."[1] James Fenimore Cooper shared some of Tocqueville's concerns about "confusion" over social decorum; however, the American author was generally more optimistic than the French social philosopher about the future of American English. Yet he recognized that there were real issues that would certainly arise.

In "the aftermath of the American Revolution," Jill Lepore observed, "Americans faced the same problem many postcolonial nations face today: speaking the language of the now-despised mother country."[2] Some words were especially affected because they had been poisoned by their unique association with the old regime. The words *aristocracy*, *aristocrat*, and *aristocratic* are a case in point, since their meanings were so deeply rooted in the sociopolitical fabric of the hated former colonial tyrannizer. The ensuing dispute over what they

Literature in the Early American Republic: Annual Studies on Cooper and His Contemporaries
Volume 6, 2014. Copyright © 2014 by AMS Press, Inc. All rights reserved.

now meant touched an ideological nerve in the new republic and had a considerable impact on Cooper and his legacy.

When the new United States separated from England after the Revolution, the great projects of establishing a postcolonial society, creating an American culture, and instituting a republican government were all linked in some degree to the unprecedented task of determining the form and content of American English. Begun by Founding Fathers, and heavily influenced by the work of Noah Webster, the debate over American English continued into the nineteenth century, enlisting a variety of literary voices, including Cooper's.[3] While their views could be situational, in some measure it might be said that traditionalists sought to purify the English language by eliminating Americanisms; unionists sought to standardize the language for the entire new nation; and others, like Cooper, spoke for a republican language that accommodated popular usage.[4]

In 1828 in *Notions of the Americans*, Cooper spoke of the futility of "purists" who sought to avoid "innovations" in language. His view was pragmatic. "I think when words once get fairly into use," he wrote, "their triumph affords a sufficient evidence of merit to entitle them to patronage."[5] In all, Cooper provided a generally positive review of American English in *Notions of the Americans*. He noted that there were regional, class, ethnic, racial, and gender differences; but instead of advancing an argument for standardizing American English, he showed pride in the fact that different constituencies in the new nation understood each other clearly. Cooper was fully aware that language was socially constructed. In postcolonial America, neologism was virtually inevitable in the form of new words, new phrases, and new usages for existing words. In Cooper's view, creating an American English was part and parcel of the larger postcolonial project of creating a new culture for a new nation. While often recognized as a literary pioneer for his contribution to the development of the western, the sea story, and the novel of social criticism, Cooper was also a literary pioneer in the development of American English.

In his 1845 novel *Satanstoe*, in a footnote on the recently coined American English word *sleigh*, Cooper proclaimed: "Twenty millions of people not only can make a word, but they can make a language."[6] Cooper was a very interested and quite thoughtful witness to the creation of this language. In rejecting the position taken by language "purists," he enthusiastically employed Americanisms in his novels, frequently providing footnotes to aid potentially puzzled readers of English across the Atlantic.[7] Such Americanisms included "*beaver dam*," "*betterments*," "*blazed*," "*brave*," "*chicker-berry*," "*clearings*," "*down countries*," "*flood-wood*," "*half-breed*," "*long-knives*," "*patent*," "*pathfinder*," "*portage*," "*posse*," "*rattler*," "*relish*," "*squatter*," "*sugar camp*," "*trapper*," "*warwhoop*," and "*wood-path*."[8]

Cooper was particularly attentive to American-Indian usage. Among the Native Americanisms in the early Leather-Stocking novels, Cooper introduced the color-coded racial expressions that were created by Native Americans for themselves and for European Americans. The use of the color designation *red*—as in *red men* or *red people*—had spread among American Indians over the course of the eighteenth century, as they sought to distinguish between themselves and the people who came from Europe who considered themselves *white*.[9] In *The Pioneers*, Chingachgook refers to Indians as "red-men." However, Chingachgook also uses two brand new Native-American racial expressions: "red-skin" for Indians and "white-skin" for European Americans.[10] The terms *red-skin* and *white-skin* had just appeared together in print for the first time in 1821 when *The Literary Gazette* published a speech by Black Thunder, a Fox Indian.[11] *The Pioneers* was completed in 1822 and published in 1823. The next Leather-Stocking tale, *The Last of the Mohicans*, appeared in 1826. Throughout this novel, Indians continue to refer to themselves as *red-men* and *red-skins*. Instead of *white-skins*, the Indian leaders—the *good* Indian, Chingachgook; the *bad* Indian, Magua; and the neutral Indian, Tamenund—now call European Americans *pale-faces*. This novel marked the first appearance in print of *pale-face*, another new American Indian term for European Americans.[12] The racial nomenclature *red-skins* and *pale-faces* originated in Native American culture and reached a popular audience in Cooper's early Leather-Stocking novels, becoming new Americanisms for a rapidly evolving American English language. Long before *red-skins* and *pale-faces* became standard racial signifiers in Hollywood westerns, *red-skins* would switch from a term connoting pride in American Indian identity to a pejorative term employed by biased or insensitive European Americans. While he was aware that there were risks, Cooper nonetheless insisted that language must be open ended, that it must respond to historical change and the rich cultural diversity of the American people.

Cooper's disinterest in the argument for a standardized American language went hand in hand with his genuine appreciation of American diversity. In his first Leather-Stocking novel, *The Pioneers*, Cooper entertained his readers with a wide variety of American dialects and figures of speech reflecting differences in race, ethnicity, class, and region. Showing Cooper's attentiveness to actual Indian speech, Chingachgook speaks a sometimes poetic and sometimes guttural American-Indian English. Natty Bumppo speaks backwoodsman vernacular, which includes occasional Native Americanisms. Agamemnon speaks black English. Major Frederick Hartmann speaks with a German-American accent. Mrs. Hollister has a decided Irish brogue. Monsieur Le Quoi speaks with a French-American accent. Remarkable Pettibone speaks lower-class New England regional dialect. Benjamin Pump speaks English sailor Cockney. Judge Temple occasionally says thee and thou, divulging his Quaker roots. Dirck Van der School speaks with a New York Dutch accent. The next generation New York gentry, Elizabeth Temple and Oliver Effingham, are well educated and well spoken, much like their upper-class counterparts in England.[13] However, Dr. Elnathan Todd, who was educated with the help of "'Webster's Spelling Book,'"[14] speaks with a pompous and rather foolish New England voice.

Noah Webster believed that a rationally constituted national language was essential for a successful national government, and he sought to systematize American English by standardizing the written and spoken word. Cooper was right to suppose that Webster sought to impose New England regional English upon the rest of the country. He disliked the reliance on euphemism and the pretentiousness of New England speech, and he resisted Webster's notion that written and spoken English should be consistent. Cooper continued to satirize Websterian English in *The Monikins* (1835), wherein the leadership in the land of Leaplow uses words to deceive and manipulate the people, and in the Littlepage trilogy (1845–46), by following the shenanigans of multiple generations of ambitious Newcomes who seek fame and fortune in upstate New York.[15] The first Newcome, Jason in *Satanstoe*, is a migrant from New England. He is ill educated and vulgar, but also pretentious and ambitious. Like Webster, Jason was born in Connecticut, attended Yale, and is a pedagogue and language reformer who wants to standardize and harmonize pronunciation and spelling.[16] In the subsequent Littlepage novels, *The Chainbearer* (1845) and *The Redskins* (1846), the Newcomes becomes increasing demagogic and dangerous, as they artfully manipulate language for economic gain and political power.[17]

The Founding Fathers had understood that republics were especially vulnerable to demagogues who skillfully manipulated language to control and direct the electorate for the sake of their own personal ambition. In a question that appears to be rather puzzling, John Adams asked: "What are demagogues and popular orators but aristocrats?" Aristocrats presumably belonged in aristocracies, not republics; in the Old World, not the New World, at least after the Revolution. The new republic did not recognize aristocratic titles and special privileges of class. Here, there were no dukes and duchesses, lords and ladies, barons and baronesses, marquises and marchionesses. Yet Adams's fear of indigenous aristocrats and a nascent aristocracy was already widespread in the early years of the new nation.[18]

In 1835, according to Susan Fenimore Cooper, her father delivered a "Lecture on Language" at the Court House in Cooperstown. All that remains is a fragment of the manuscript in Cooper's handwriting, with the title, location, and date of the talk identified in the handwriting of his daughter.[19] As her father's literary executor, she took it upon herself to cut his manuscripts into pieces to satisfy requests by autograph seekers.[20] While fragments of these manuscripts continue to turn up, it is doubtful in cases such as his "Lecture on Language" that the complete manuscript can ever be reconstituted. Nevertheless, we can see in the surviving fragment the gist of the issues involving American English that would preoccupy him throughout his literary career. Cooper took it for granted that the English language would evolve differently in the New World. "Separated as we are by distance, opinions, habits, usages, wants, resources and institutions from the mother country," he explained, "discrepancies in the uses of words as well as the forms of speech" would naturally occur. Neologisms were inevitable. And Cooper saw that neologisms could be a source of strength for a fiction writer intent on establishing an American literature. The new nation would quite naturally create new words, and the meaning of some words would undergo mutation. The conflation of "demagogues" and "aristocrats" by Adams is an example of a postcolonial mutation. Cooper himself frequently conflated *demagogues* and *aristocrats*. But he also saw that, in a republic, "changes in signification" were not always "to be desired,"[21] most especially when language mischaracterized the social order and created ambiguity and confusion about the interconnection of economic and political power. In this regard, "changes in signification" of the word *aristocrat* proved to be a double-edge sword.

1.

Great manorial estates once dominated much of eastern New York, most notably the Hudson Valley. The estates were farmed by tenants who owed rent to their landlords. Hoping to realize the economic promise of the American Revolution for themselves, tenants actively sought to replace leasehold with freehold, and intermittently resorted to force. At the height of the anti-rent strife in the 1840s, tenants disguised as Indians violently resisted rent collection. Their costumes evoked the Boston Tea Party, republican values, and the Founding Fathers' heroic defiance of aristocracy. These masquerading Indians—along with many of their contemporaries and subsequent historians—saw their rebellion against landlords and leases as a repudiation of the last stronghold of aristocratic entitlement in the northern states.

In his 1846 novel, *The Redskins; or Indian and Ingin*,[22] Cooper stretched the signification of the newly popular Americanism *red-skin* to include anti-renters disguised as Injins. In the actual Anti-Rent Wars, the rebelling tenants practiced *charivari*, a local tradition of ritualistic, costumed, mob action, in which young men dressed up in fear-inspiring disguises. But their masquerade also built on a long-standing tradition of white men playing Indian to express an authentic American identity and validate their deep historical claim to the land.[23] The real *red-skins* in Cooper's novel are unswayed by the dress-up *red-skins* and instead support the landlords. Even though the ancient *red-skin* sage Susquesus sides with the landlords against their rebellious tenants, he continually questions the legitimacy of the landlords' original claim to Indian land. He knows his people are its rightful owners.[24]

While complicated by the competing claims of landlords, masquerading *red-skins*, and real *red-skins*, Cooper's novel is intended as a lesson on property rights and republican values. It is also about what it means to be thought aristocratic in America. This is recognized in the *Dictionary of American Regional English* in providing the following passage from *The Redskins* as its first example of the American usage of the word *aristocratic*:

> Ravensnest . . . [was] termed an "aristocratic residence." This word "aristocratic," I find since my return home, has got to be a term of expansive signification, its meaning depending on the particular habits and opinions of the person who happens to use it.[25]

The passage contains observations by the first-person narrator of the novel, Hugh Littlepage, landlord of Ravensnest. It begins with a fragment of a sentence that establishes that "Ravensnest" was thought "aristocratic." In England, this would have suggested lower-class envy of upper-class elegance. On the American side of the Atlantic, meanings varied and were situational; in this case, it suggests criticism of unrepublican ostentation.[26] The concluding sentence of the passage calls attention to the "expansive signification" of the "word 'aristocratic'" in America. It also appears to contain a complaint: if "its meaning" depends "on the particular habits and opinions of the person who happens to use it," there is license for abuse.

In truth, Cooper complained repeatedly about the "expansive signification" of the words *aristocratic*, *aristocrat*, and *aristocracy*, and he repeatedly aired his opinions about their proper *signification*. Most of Cooper's contemporaries were deaf to what he had to say. Most scholars have been deaf as well. Yet almost everybody—Cooper, other New Yorkers, later scholars—thought that the Anti-Rent Wars had to do with aristocracy. Most placed the aristocrats on the landlords' side. But Cooper thought that the aristocrats were on the side of the tenants. Despite vast differences, all parties agreed that to be aristocratic was to be elitist and undemocratic, and even, some felt, un-American.

This is not surprising since the American Revolution had been fought against an aristocratic regime. Before the Revolution (though often from a transatlantic distance), aristocracy had to do with class prerogatives—ranging from the establishment of taste to economic and political power—that became problematic after the Revolution. But postrevolutionary changes in status, the arbitration of taste, and political and economic power also took place within a context of a burgeoning commercialism that rapidly transformed the new republic into a dynamic capitalist civilization. New forms of power and prestige brought new challenges to republicanism and also renewed charges of aristocracy, as Cooper and his contemporaries continued to use the term *aristocratic* to denounce unrepublican behavior. The confusion over *signification* resulted from the variety of contexts for the word *aristocrat*, ranging from the old European caste system to nineteenth-century capitalism. Cooper was caught up in this confusion for personal and ideological reasons, and our understanding of his legacy has remained confused as well.

In the following pages, I will attempt to clear up this confusion, looking first at what others, past and present, have had to say about Cooper and aristocracy and then at what Cooper himself had to say. His writings contain a surprising amount of commentary on the *signification* of the terms *aristocratic*, *aristocrat*, and *aristocracy*. At times, the commentary takes the form of lighthearted banter on manners and mores in the young republic; at other times, the tone is more serious, with topics ranging from politics to economics, from Congress to capitalism. Cooper seemed to be obsessed with aristocracy. It behooves us to understand why he cared so much.

2.

When the Cooper family returned to America in 1833 after living in Europe for seven years, in Lewis Leary's considered opinion, "they must have seemed aloof and aristocratic, their attitude insinuating criticism of American ways. Everything about them was strange, their clothes, the furniture they imported, their foreign servants, and the manners of the children—'Even the cat was French.'"[27] Though sounding like caricature, this is a common construction of what James

Fenimore Cooper and his family seemed like on their return: they had "aristocratic" airs. This image was strengthened by their 1836 move to Otsego Hall, the family home in Cooperstown, which had been renovated and remodeled and was now a Gothic mansion. It was reinforced in 1837 by Cooper's quarrel with townsfolk over access to family property known as Three Mile Point. And the image of the aristocrat was further fixed in the popular mind in 1838 by his novel *Home As Found*, which disparaged the manners and ideas of the local populace of Templeton, a thinly disguised fiction for Cooperstown.

In 1833, in preparing his attack upon the charter of the Bank of the United States, the Democratic President Andrew Jackson had warned of "an aristocracy" that "insidiously employed" its wealth and influence to subvert the political system. The Jacksonians believed that the Bank represented a corrupt, tyrannical, moneyed aristocracy.[28] Adopting their opponents' strategy, the Whigs, in turn, sought to discredit the Democrats by making them appear to be the aristocratic party. Cooper might have been a literary hero, but he also was thought to be a Democrat; in the highly charged political atmosphere of the day, even the author of *The Last of the Mohicans* was considered fair game for Whig sharpshooters. Accusations against the seemingly aristocratic author were played out in the press. Cooper's "aristocratical airs" are "monstrous," *The New-Yorker* reported in 1839, adding that they just "would be ludicrous" if not so "peevish and malignant."[29] Newspaper insults multiplied and Cooper filed libel suits against the Whig press in Cooperstown, Albany, and New York City. In the spirit of this acrimony, the epithet *aristocrat* was hurled back and forth.

Cooper's adversarial relationship with the press and public was partly the outcome of partisan politics. But Cooper's criticism of America after his return from Europe, for the remainder of the 1830s and into the early 1840s, fed into their political strategy.[30] Americans were proud of their egalitarian society and easily offended by Cooper's patrician pronouncements. Americans are to be "reproached," he stated in *The American Democrat* in 1838, for "want of a proper deference for social station"; moreover, he thought it was "unreasonable to expect high breeding in any but those who are trained to it" from early childhood onward.[31] "The class" at the top of the social hierarchy, he lectured his readers—and fully believed—"is the natural repository of the manners, tastes, tone, and, to a certain extent, of the principles of a country" (84). As a member of that class, he undertook his obligation to elevate less-well-bred Americans. The enrichment Cooper offered was not received with gratitude. His unappreciative contemporaries instead thought him aristocratic.

By the mid-1840s, the clamor over Cooper's aristocratic behavior and pronouncements had subsided, and the press all but ignored writings of his containing inflammatory subject matter, such as the attack on anti-rentism in *The Redskins*.[32] Cooper's contemporaries had lost their interest in aristocratic-Cooper-baiting. But his reputation was now well set. Thus, for example, the historian Dixon Ryan Fox called Cooper "a whole-hearted and vociferous aristocrat," one of "the last among well-known Americans to take an unequivocal stand for aristocratic principles." And the literary critic Leslie A. Fiedler thought him "the most class-conscious of all American writers," yet "class-conscious the way only a provincial New York aristocrat could be." From the first full-length biography of Cooper in 1882 by Thomas R. Lounsbury right up into our own time, literary scholars and historians have continued to label Cooper an aristocrat or associate him with aristocracy; in recent years, their number includes two Pulitzer Prize winners in history, Alan Taylor for *William Cooper's Town* (1995) and Daniel Walker Howe for *What Hath God Wrought* (2007).[33] In the judgment of a wide variety of scholars, Cooper was an aristocrat in his personal tastes and/or an advocate of some combination of social or economic or political aristocracy. They have located the source of Cooper's aristocratic inclinations and appetites in his birthright or marriage or lifestyle, and they have identified aristocratic opinions and preferences in his early writings as well as his later work.[34] A few scholars have found Cooper at least somewhat conflicted between aristocratic and republican values. "Every aspect of his life—his home, his gardens, his dress, and his deportment—would exemplify aristocratic taste," wrote William P. Kelly, who nonetheless found him to be politically "republican." Somewhat similarly, Richard L. Bushman reported that, although Cooper was "devoted to republican principles," he "campaigned for an American aristocracy as energetically as anyone."[35] Several other scholars have found him conflicted in a different way: even though he was an aristocrat himself and/or an advocate of an American aristocracy, he nonetheless did not like (other) aristocrats and/or foreign aristocracy.[36] And a few scholars, swayed by Cooper's own vehement disclaimers, have insisted that he was not an aristocrat or an advocate of aristocracy and that his dislike of both was unequivocal.[37] On the subject of Cooper and aristocracy, such divergence in opinion seems puzzling at first. However, in their usage of American English, *all are correct.* Thus the problem of "expansive signification" that plagued Cooper in his own day would appear to have cast a shadow of confusion over his legacy as well.

Cooper had an abiding interest in the proper use of American English,[38] but he was extraordinarily insistent on getting the meaning of these words right. He used the terms *aristocratic*, *aristocrat*, and *aristocracy* regularly in his writings from the late 1820s onward. Sometimes he satirized their misuse, sometimes he lectured his readers on their correct use, and he used these terms in ways that undoubtedly puzzled some of his contemporary readers and some modern scholars as well. Whatever else the terms might mean for others, we will see that Cooper was quite clear about what they meant to him.

3.

Meanings and manners were a bit confused in America, Cooper realized. "In this part of the world," he thus complained, "it is thought aristocratic not to frequent taverns, and lounge at corners, squirting tobacco juice."[39] Similarly, a character in *The Redskins* reports that it was considered "excessively aristocratic" for one "to pretend not to blow one's nose with his fingers" (164). "Wa-a-l," another confesses, "I hear a great deal about aristocrats, and I read a great deal about aristocrats, in this country, and I know that most folks look upon them as hateful, but I'm by no means sartain I know what an aristocrat is" (146). Thus, a character in *The Ways of the Hour* (1850) laments, "not one in a thousand knows the meaning of the word" *aristocrat.*[40]

In his 1843 novella, *The Autobiography of a Pocket Handkerchief*, Cooper poked fun at the widespread misuse of the word *aristocratic.* The tale is what has come to be know as an *it-narrative* because it is narrated by an inanimate object, in this case a very feminine handkerchief. She is also "an exceedingly aristocratick pocket handkerchief." As the narrator, she is aided by "mesmeretick powers"—that is, "'handkerchiefly speaking'"—that enable her to see and hear and provide insightful commentary on what is happening around her, even when she is stuffed in a drawer.[41] The pocket handkerchief cuts to the core of the problem: being thought "aristocratic" in the United States, she says, "ranks as an eighth deadly sin, though no one seems to know precisely what it means." To be so "stigmatized" is to be "tainted" with a "crime" that no "governor would dare to pardon" (18). Though "nothing is considered so disreputable in America as to be 'aristocratic,' a word of very extensive signification, as it embraces the tastes, the opinions, the habits, the virtues, and sometimes the religion of the offending party," the handkerchief observes, "on the other hand, nothing is so certain to attract attention as nobility" (88). Americans seemed to be both repelled by and drawn to aristocracy. The "*nouveaux riches*" (19) most commonly fell under the spell of aristocracy and sought to acquire what they thought were aristocratic status symbols. In Cooper's *Pocket Handkerchief*, Eudosia Halfacre, who wishes to "pass for aristocratic," pays one hundred dollars to buy "the highest priced handkerchief, by twenty dollars, that ever crossed the Atlantic" (54, 52). By contrast, Anne and Maria—"the daughters of a gentleman of very large estate," who "belonged to the true *elite* of the country"—turn down the opportunity to buy this fabulously expensive handkerchief: "They do n't believe that a nightcap is intended for a bed quilt" (49, 50).

Cooper maintained that the old New York *elite* were rural gentry. But their superior taste, manners, and education did not necessarily mean that they were aristocrats. In his 1821 novel, *The Spy*, he did acknowledge that there were some aristocrats in old New York society; however, he believed that their "aristocratical" character was due to their Englishness, which explained why they were Loyalists during the American Revolution.[42] In 1821, his position on aristocrats was nonjudgmental. His attitude toward aristocrats would permanently change based on firsthand observations that he made during a visit to England from late February to late May 1828. Drawing on what he learned, Cooper now expressed outright distaste for aristocrats and aristocracy, publishing his newly formed ideas about English aristocracy in brief in *Notions of the Americans* in June 1828 and more expansively in his English travel book, *Gleanings in Europe: England*, in 1837.[43] In the travel book, he noted that England was "an aristocracy of wealth" (139). But wealth alone was not enough. The "aristocracy," he explained, "is identified by blood, intermarriages, possessions," and, most especially, by "authority in the government" (151). In the formulation that he first articulated in 1828 and would maintain thereafter, *wealth combined with political power* was the key to aristocracy. What Cooper saw in England was a figurehead monarch, whereas the aristocracy—which was made up of a collection of self-interested, interrelated families—ruled the land from Parliament. Some of the aristocrats bore titles, others were commoners; this politically dominant group of Englishmen, in his view, included nobles, merchants, manufacturers, and even rural gentry.

When it came to America, however, Cooper insisted on distinguishing between a business and a landed elite, as well as between aristocrats and gentlemen. In Europe, aristocrats were often highly educated and culturally refined; in America, gentlemen were refined and educated while aristocrats were often boorish businessmen. For many of Cooper's contemporaries, as well as later scholars, this distinction between an aristocrat and a gentleman was not at all clear.[44] But it did seem clear to Cooper. He was quick, as we have seen, to take issue with what, in *The American Democrat*, he called "perversions of significations" of "American language" (110). One such perversion was the conflation of gentry and aristocracy. "To call a man who has the habits and opinions of a gentleman, aristocrat," he declared in *The American Democrat*, "is an abuse of terms" (88). Gentry were not aristocrats, Cooper believed; they lacked political power. "The highest birth, the largest fortune, the most exclusive association, would not make an aristocrat," a character in *The Redskins* explains, "without the addition of a narrow political power" (472). "Aristocracy means exclusive political privileges in the hands of a few," a character in *The Ways of the Hour* confirms, "and it means nothing else" (117). Cooper was not alone. The danger posed by unchecked political power was widely understood and greatly feared in postrevolutionary America. Cooper was cautiously hopeful, however, that, under the *correct* form of government, the opportunities for aristocrats to obtain political power might be minimized.

In an April 1831 letter, Cooper named the basic forms of government. "Now there are but three forms of government known," he told Charles Wilkes: "Monarchy, Oligarchy and Republican. You may modify these forms more or less," he explained, "but they are, in the nature of things, all the *generic* forms of government that can exist, since either One must rule—or a minority must rule, or the Majority."[45] In *The Politics*, Aristotle also named three "correct" forms of government: "aristocracy," "kingship," and "polity." Each "correct" form had a degenerative form: "oligarchy from aristocracy," "tyranny from kingship," and "democracy from polity."[46] For Aristotle, oligarchy was the degenerative form of aristocracy. For Cooper, however, oligarchy and aristocracy were actually the same; the term he most often employed was *aristocracy*, but in his usage, *aristocracy* and *oligarchy* were equivalent terms for government by minority rule. Moreover, where Aristotle claimed three "correct" and three degenerative forms, Cooper claimed only two *correct* forms, monarchy and republic, and one *degenerative* form, aristocracy. "It is to be regretted the world does not discriminate more justly in its use of political terms," Cooper stated in 1831 in his preface to *The Bravo*: "Governments are usually called either monarchies or republics."[47] Most importantly, they share the same degenerative form: aristocracy. "Republicks" are either "democratical" or "aristocratical," he explained in *The American Democrat* (11), and he considered aristocracy the degenerative form of monarchy as well.[48]

Cooper believed that, after the Glorious Revolution of 1688, England began to change "its form of government, from that of a monarchy to that of an exceedingly oppressive aristocracy." He thought that attempts by the aristocracy to oppress the colonies produced the American Revolution. He also believed that the French Revolution resulted from aristocrats conspiring to overthrow the monarchy. All over Europe, Cooper maintained, aristocrats were conspiring to overthrow monarchies; soon aristocracy would become the only form of government.[49]

Cooper worried about the United States. "Aristocracies are oftener republicks than any thing else," he wrote in *The American Democrat*, while observing that "they have been among the most oppressive governments the world has ever known" (19–20). In his view, this was because aristocrats were particularly adept at manipulating the democratic masses. "Demagogues and editors" were a prime example of such "aristocrats," he pointed out in *The Redskins* (472); in political affairs, these aristocrats were motivated by economic self-interest, not the real interests of the people. Cooper believed that the legislature was the center of their political power, so he was anxious about legislative infringement on executive rights. To counter the threat of aristocracy, he advocated executive power in the hands of a strong president such as Andrew Jackson. The office and the man, he hoped, would have the strength to withstand the intrigues of aristocratic demagogues.

Cooper was particularly concerned about the interconnectedness of business and Congress, for he was certain that the chief threat of aristocracy in America came from the commercial sector. "It is a mistake to suppose commerce favorable to liberty," he explained in *The American Democrat*, because "the polity" preferred by "every community of merchants" was "a monied aristocracy" (160). Both as "a class" and "as politicians," he wrote his English publisher in 1835, American merchants "are aristocrats."[50] In a richly revealing 1836 letter to the sculptor Horatio Greenough, he exclaimed: "Alas! my good Greenough, this is no region for poets, so sell them your wares, and shut your ears. The foreigners have got to be so strong, among us, that they no longer creep but walk erect. They throng the presses, control one or two of the larger cities, and materially influence public opinion all over the Union." Cooper was no nativist. "By foreigners, I do not mean the lower class of Irish voters," he explained, "but the merchants and others a degree below them, who are almost to a man hostile in feeling to the country, and to all her interests, except as they may happen to be their interests."[51] The real "foreigners" to American democracy, in his opinion, were not Irish-Catholic immigrants but native-born Protestant merchants, businessmen, and bankers; fast accumulating influence and power, they sought to turn America into an aristocracy.

Like numerous letters in the mid-1830s to family, friends, and *The Evening Post*, in *A Letter to His Countrymen* (1834), Cooper addressed the growing danger of aristocracy and the subversion of the Constitution. In response to Cooper, a newly elected Whig Congressman from Massachusetts, Caleb Cushing, authored a pamphlet titled *A Reply to the Letter of J. Fenimore Cooper by One of His Countrymen*. Speaking to Cooper's central political issue, Cushing wrote: "What I specially deny and impugn is the strange heresy [your letter] puts forth,—a misconception so palpable as not even to possess the faint lustre of mere paradox,—that, in the United States, the great object of public suspicion and watchfulness should be the legislative, rather than the executive, department of government." As an anti-Jacksonian Whig partisan and legislator, Cushing worried about "executive usurpation" and "tyranny" in President Andrew Jackson's "*monarchical*" behavior.[52] And he was right, of course, that Congress was "the great object" of this Jacksonian democrat's fears and "suspicion."

Cooper believed that Congress was the biggest threat to the Constitution and American liberty. Congress represented the business community and financial interests and was naturally inclined toward aristocracy. The president was elected by the people and represented the country as a whole, not just the aristocratic minority. Unfortunately, everywhere Cooper looked in the western world, legislators seemed to be trespassing on executive rights and promoting moneyed aristocracies.[53]

It is for this reason that the idyllic island community that comes into existence for a time in Cooper's 1847 South Pacific novel, *The Crater*, has no legislature and the chief executive is elected for life. Even so, the government of this remote island is unable to withstand the forces of change. A two-house legislature, frequent elections, and other "fundamental" changes are introduced by lawyers, editors, and merchants. These new "élites" are "demagogues"; like "aristocrats" in "the state of New York," they rely on cant, their "new constitution" reflecting Cooper's low opinion of the New York State Constitution of 1846. The original governor, who "did not blow his nose with his fingers," is accused of "aristocracy" and deposed; and we, as readers, bear witness to the rise and fall of a good society.[54]

The society in Cooper's 1831 novel *The Bravo* is fallen from the start. The narrative transports the reader into a labyrinth of moral incoherence, thereby providing a nightmarish vision of an evil aristocracy. The story takes place in eighteenth-century Venice, and it is plain that the ancient republic long ago lost its youth and vigor and is now far advanced in the inevitable cycle that civilizations follow, with the Venetians themselves fearing "the final consummation of their artificial condition" (251). Even though "the bank flourishes with goodly dividends" (255), indicative of a wealthy commercial aristocracy, signs of decay are rampant. Cooper seizes every opportunity to inform his readers that the Venetian "days of glory and greatness exist no longer" (148). Venice is on "a downward course," he writes, and its "incipient lethargy," "fallen fortunes," and "fading circumstances" suggest that, like other "states which have crumbled beneath the weight of their own abuses," the end is near (6, 93, 128).

Cooper observes in *The Bravo* that "all human things"—people and political states alike—follow a natural cycle of generation, growth to maturity, and decay (250). *The Crater*, modeled on Thomas Cole's series of five paintings, *The Course of Empire*, describes one complete cycle, from the birth to the death of the island civilization.[55] In *The Bravo*, as elsewhere, he uses organic analogies and metaphors to illustrate the cyclic nature of historical change. First, there is "the feebleness of infancy"; once passed, "the child attains the age" of a reasonable life expectancy. Even the "empire of China" was once "as youthful as our own republic," he notes—with a pointed lesson for his own land—though now if suffers "from decrepitude which is a natural companion of its years" (250, 251). Like China, Venice is "aged" and "tottering with its years" (14, 168). Outwardly, the city is glittery and dazzling, blinding the populace to its true condition. Despite "increasing feebleness," Cooper explains, "communities, like individuals, draw near their dissolution, inattentive to the symptoms of decay, until they are overtaken with that fate, which finally overwhelms empires and their power in the common lot of man" (93).

The epigraph to the opening chapter, from Lord Byron's *Childe Harold's Pilgrimage* (1812) characterizes Venice in its "dying glory" by its "palace" and its "prison." Symbolically linked by "the Bridge of Signs," the palace and the prison represent royalty and servitude (5). However, in Venice, royalty is an illusion and a sham. In *The Bravo*, the Doge is chief of state in name only; he is merely "a puppet" and "a tool of the aristocracy" (342, 343). Much like the King of England, according to Cooper, the Doge's power was long ago usurped by a "luxurious and affluent aristocracy" (90). Real power in Venice resides in the Senate—a small, self-serving, hereditary aristocracy that controls government, business, and finance. Pairing natural enemies of republics,

Cooper likens the "director of a monied institution" in his relation "to his corporation" to an "aristocrat"/"senator" in his "relation to the state" (76, 77). With their power and their disdain for republican values, taken separately, in Cooper's view, financial institutions, corporations, aristocrats, and senators are all potentially dangerous threats to the integrity of a sound republic. But, in *The Bravo*, they are one and the same, and they control the Venetian State.

Much like a twentieth-century totalitarian regime, the Venetian State has eliminated all historically sanctified, institutional buffers between the people and an all-powerful government. The family has been compromised. The church is powerless. The Venetian aristocracy in *The Bravo* has deprived the people of their rights. It invades their privacy with secret police and informants; by one character's "tally every second man in Venice is well paid for reporting what the others say and do" (84). The state wields power through fear and by skillfully manipulating the people through systematic lying and deceit. There is no protection of the law. Trials and executions are secret, except when the aristocracy chooses otherwise. Jacopo, the Bravo, is secretly tried and convicted, but sentenced to a public execution. Even when his head is placed upon the block, a last minute reprieve is expected, since a priest, Father Anselmo, has provided authorities with incontrovertible proof of his innocence. For that reason, when the palace gave a signal, the Bravo's sweetheart, Gelsomina, "uttered a cry of delight, and turned to throw herself upon the bosom of the reprieved." Instead of a reprieve, "the head of Jacopo rolled upon the stones as if to meet her" (357). At that moment, with the reader expecting a happy ending, Cooper completes his civic lesson on the character of an absolute aristocracy.

Cooper's choice of this city-state for this lesson in political science is reflected in his observation in *The American Democrat* that "aristocracy" is more likely to develop in a "metropolitan" environment (53, 54), and it also reflects his fear of urbanization in America. Though set in eighteenth-century Venice, Cooper claimed that "the Bravo" was "*in spirit, the most American book I ever wrote*."[56] Concerned that his novel was misunderstood, Cooper clarified the "moral" of the tale in *A Letter to His Countrymen* (14). He noted that throughout history, republics had been transformed into aristocracies. It had happened to the Republic of Venice. It could happen in America as well. "I had an abundant occasion to observe that the great political contest of the age was not" between "monarchy and democracy" as most think, he wrote. He explained that monarchy, "except" when "fraudulently maintained as a cover" by "aristocrats," was "virtually extinct in Christendom" (11). As a result, as Cooper saw it, the real political contest of the nineteenth century was between aristocracy and democracy. What had happened overseas to Venice in *The Bravo* gave warning to Americans of the threat of aristocracy at home, a threat issuing from the dangerous combination of business interests and the legislature.[57] The dark genius of the Venetian aristocracy, much like demagogic aristocrats in the United States, was their skill in manipulating the masses for their own purposes, rather than representing the real interests of the people.

Venice had been a model of the good republic for American colonists, at least into the early years of the eighteenth century. But by the era of the American Revolution, Venice had become a symbol in republican thought of what could happen to a free people who were not vigilant about their rights. Parallels were seen between the development of an oppressive government in Venice and the development of an oppressive government in England. For intellectual architects of the new republic such as John Adams, Alexander Hamilton, Thomas Jefferson, and James Madison, Venice provided an example of a former republic that had degenerated into a despotic state ruled by a tyrannous aristocracy. To avoid such a fate, the new republic would have to be especially vigilant. Like Cooper, the Revolutionary generation believed that history is cyclical, and they readily understood the transitory nature of institutions, states, and empires.[58] At the heart of the republican ideology of the Founding Fathers was an intense awareness of both the preciousness and the fragility of the liberty for which they fought. Like the Founding Fathers, Cooper drew on the lesson of Venice in *The Bravo* to express his fear of a business and financial aristocracy, the effacement of the Constitution, and the ensuing loss of liberty.

The Bravo presents his worst-case scenario. Yet Cooper granted that a mixed government—monarchy and aristocracy or democracy and aristocracy—might be tolerable if the aristocracy was mild. States such as Virginia might "be termed representative democracies" from the perspective of "their white population," he pointed out in *A Letter to His Countrymen*; nonetheless, he concluded, "they are in truth, even now, mild aristocracies, when considered in reference to their whole population" (61). The problem, of course, was slavery. Cooper recognized an affinity between aristocracy and slavery. "So long as slavery exists in the country," he observed in *The American Democrat*, "some portion of this aristocratic infusion will probably remain" (20–21). In his view, an "aristocracy" built upon slavery was "more" compatible with "republicanism than democracy." He believed that full citizenship was restricted in a republic; in a democracy, it was open to all men. For that reason, Cooper thought that slavery belonged to America's republican past, not its democratic future. "It is opposed to the spirit of the age," he thus concluded.[59]

In the main, however, his fears of aristocracy were generated by business activity in the North, particularly when such activity benefited from legislative patronage and entailed the creation or expansion of corporations. From the 1780s onward, Americans had heatedly debated the growing presence of corporations in their land. For many, corporations were anti-republican, because they corrupted the political system, and aristocratic, because they received special privilege.[60] In his own day, the proliferation of corporations reinforced and graphically illustrated Cooper's fear of aristocrats subverting America's political system. Legislatures granted corporate privileges by special charter; thus acts of incorporation required the active complicity of businessmen and legislators. Like "all corporate bodies," according to Susan Fenimore Cooper, her father thought that "aristocracy" tended to be "coldly selfish, tyrannical, and treacherous."[61] Specifically linking "aristocracy" and "corporations," *The Bravo* looked into Europe's past to caution against a future America ruled by a "tyrannic" and "soulless corporation" (128, 129, 130, 131).[62] With great concern and a sense of urgency, Cooper repeatedly warned his countrymen of the threat of a business aristocracy. Had he belonged to a later generation, he would have called this peril *capitalism*.[63]

At first glance, Cooper's *The Autobiography of a Pocket Handkerchief* appears to make lighthearted fun of aristocrats and aristocratic pretensions. On closer inspection, the work seems more somber, for it is a tale about capitalist exploitation.[64] Eudosia Halfacre, the nouveau riche American, who paid one hundred dollars for the handkerchief, calls upon trickle-down economics to rationalize such extravagance. "The luxuries of the rich," she thinks, "give employment to the poor, and cause money to circulate." She innocently assumes that workers receive a fair return on their labor. "Now, this handkerchief of mine," she says, "no doubt has given employment to some poor French girl for four or five months, and, of course, food and raiment." She confidently but naively asserts that the seamstress must have "earned" as profit "fifty of the hundred dollars" that she "paid" (60). The pocket handkerchief knows better. "Alas, poor Adrienne!" says the handkerchief, thinking of the unfortunate young woman who had labored for months on the embroidery: "Thou didst not receive for me as many francs, as this fair calculator gave thee dollars" (61). As evidence, Cooper inserted a table itemizing expenses and profits associated with the production and sale of the pocket handkerchief. The figures in the table solidly support the handkerchief's understated determination that Adrienne would have been "richer" and "much happier" had she never begun the project and "spared" herself "so many, many hours of painful and anxious toil!" (61)

Adrienne had been born into a good family that fell onto hard times after the Revolution due to the subversion of the French monarchy by aristocrats. The old order gave way to industrial capitalism, and the family chateau was turned into a factory. Nearly destitute and the sole supporter of her aged grandmother, Adrienne worked by day for a milliner who paid her poorly, keeping her "in ignorance of her own value" (29). By night, she embroidered the pocket handkerchief. In both cases, the products were sold at a considerable profit, but in neither case did she receive a fair return on her labor. In assessing the cost of aristocratic "frivolities," the pocket handkerchief explains that "their luxuries, have two sets of victims to plunder, the consumer, and the real producer, or the operative" (28).

Though "misery" and "oppression" (28, 29) are the worker's usual lot, this tale ends otherwise. Fortunately, good breeding, not money, is the key to true upper-class membership. Adrienne crosses the Atlantic to be a governess, falls in love with a New York gentleman of large estate (who turns out to be a distant cousin), reunites with the pocket handkerchief, and presumably lives happily ever after. The story concludes with Adrienne recovering her birthright. However, the fairy-tale ending does not mask the ascendant economic forces that drive the narrative: inadequate wages, dehumanized labor, charging a market price rather than a fair price, reckless speculation, and a generally unfeeling and irresponsible system that objectifies people and desensitizes businessmen to the human consequences of their activities. Moreover, we recognize that Adrienne was quite lucky to have escaped the "*slavish*" labor (28; emphasis added) that had seemed to be her fate. Thinking back to her "days of want and sorrow" when she was a "trodden on and abused hireling," Adrienne says, "I toiled for bread like an Eastern *slave*" (101; emphasis added). Linking capitalism and slavery, her lament contains a damning indictment of the system that had exploited her labor and reduced her to such desperate circumstances.

4.

Fear of slavery was a marked concern in antebellum republican thought. This fear had multiple sources. Most obvious was slavery in the South, for it provided a constant reminder to all Americans what loss of freedom meant. However, Cooper was well aware of the condition in the North known as wage slavery. Wage slavery occurred in factories, or, potentially, wherever there was hired labor. Banks, corporations, monopolies were other forms of economic enterprise that were often thought to be harbingers of slavery at this time.[65] Southern plantations, northern industry, banks, corporations, and monopolies were all included under the rubric *aristocracy* in Cooper's lexicon, and all were linked to slavery.

Fear of slavery had been a fundamental concern in the republican ideology of the leaders of the American Revolution.[66] Cooper was a conservative republican,[67] ideologically closer to that generation than his own. The nineteenth-century author clung to an idealized vision of an eighteenth-century New York that was led by rural gentry motivated by noblesse oblige. If this world were turned upside down, the old order would be replaced by an urban, business aristocracy. As imaginative constructs, for Cooper, these worlds were polar opposites. The pastoral world of the gentry could be characterized by a warm paternalism, republican virtue, human dignity, and liberty. The urban world of the aristocracy could be characterized by corporate impersonality, business (or capitalist) greed, human degradation, and slavery.

It is no wonder, in *The American Democrat*, that Cooper railed against the "vulgar use" of "the term aristocracy" that "perverted its signification" to include "gentry of democracies" (54) like himself. Venting his frustration over the widespread misnomer equating "a refined gentleman" with an "aristocrat," a character in *The Ways of the Hour* exclaims: "Aristocracy, forsooth! If there be aristocracy in America, the blackguard is the aristocrat" (316). He was right, for in postcolonial America "the blackguard" was "the aristocrat." *Aristocrat* was a term of opprobrium used to vilify political or economic enemies. While most everybody disapproved of aristocrats, opinions differed widely on their identity. Like most of his fellow countrymen, Cooper detested *aristocrats*, agreed that *aristocratic* behavior was unrepublican, and was vehemently opposed to *aristocracy*. Cooper's *aristocrats* were businessmen. We might call them capitalists. In *The Redskins* landlord Littlepage, disguised as a German for protection against anti-renters, further explains: "[D]em as vat you calls dimigogues be der American arisdograts. Dey gets all der money of der pooblic, und haf all der power" (154). Using oratory and the press to manipulate public opinion, they sought economic privilege for themselves. If their legislative power was unchecked, the republic would degenerate into an *aristocracy*.

Fear of aristocracy caused Cooper to worry about increasing commercialism and, particularly, about the spread of monopolistic corporations. From his early writings onward, he warned about "congress" granting "monopoly," which would cause exploitation and ultimately "tyranny."[68] The problem was capitalism, most especially, corporate capitalism. "Aristocracies," he stated in *The American Democrat*, exhibited "the irresponsible nature of corporations." They were devoid of "personal feelings" or "human impulses" (59). And they had an insatiable appetite for economic and political power. Under aristocracy, the people could be callously exploited, deprived of basic rights, and even reduced to slavery. In his proto-totalitarian novel, *The Bravo*, Cooper looked into the past to imagine a future society in which the aristocracy had deprived an entire people of their freedom. That was the consummate *signification* of aristocracy for Cooper.

5.

If the Anti-Rent Wars and Cooper's novel *The Redskins* were both about aristocracy, they were also both about capitalism. As many commentators have noted, New York's great manorial estates obstructed economic development in agriculture, commercial enterprise, and industry. Arguing for the public's interest in the development of the country, corporations had called upon the power of eminent domain to build turnpikes, canals, and railroads, thus providing a serviceable model for tenants seeking their right to unrestricted enterprise. In this manner, small entrepreneurs and corporations found common cause under the banner of capitalism against great estates and old wealth. The tenants' desire to become independent entrepreneurs was supported by foresighted leaders of New York's political parties. Landlordism spoke to the past. Anti-rentism spoke to the economic future of the state. Of course, the landlords had also practiced capitalism, in seeking profit from private property based on inherited privileges. The landlords' defeat in the Anti-Rent Wars signaled the succession of a newer and more dynamic form of capitalism, the rearrangement of the social structure, and reconstitution of economic and political power in the State of New York.[69]

Cooper was fearful of these changes. He responded with a powerful case about the threat to republican values and the republic itself posed by the emerging capitalist system. With the vantage of hindsight, we can easily appreciate his insight into the potentially dangerous nexus of corporate capitalism and Congress, though we are not as sanguine as he was about the capacity of the Executive to transcend economic influence. We can also see that Cooper responded to the emerging economic and political order with a comfortable and reassuring myth of old New York based on a romanticized rural gentry tradition. In situating himself in a tradition supposedly untarnished by capitalism, he had to ignore his own family background—his father's rise to wealth as a real-estate entrepreneur and the commercial basis of his wife's DeLancey family fortune—as well as his own sharp business dealings as a professional author in a literary marketplace.[70] In truth, all parties in the anti-rent debate supported *capitalism*; in its *expansive signification* in American English, a wide variety of Americans, including parties on both sides of the anti-rent debate, could be linked to *aristocracy* as well.

NOTES

I would like to thank Lance Schachterle for his thoughtful suggestions in his review of this essay for *LEAR*. I would also like to thank Jeffrey Walker for examining the handwritten manuscript of Cooper's "Lecture on Language" and for correcting my transcription errors.

1. Tocqueville, *Democracy in America*, 551.

2. Lepore, *A Is for American*, 18.

3. See Baron, *Grammar and Good Taste*; Cmiel, *Democratic Eloquence*; Gustafson, *Representative Words*; J. Howe, *Language and Political Meaning*; Kramer, *Imagining Language in America*; Lepore, *A Is for American*; Looby, *Voicing America*; and Simpson, *Politics of American English*.

4. Gustafson, *Representative Words*, 39.

5. Cooper, *Notions of the Americans*, 369.

6. Cooper, *Satanstoe*, 206.

7. Schachterle, "Cooper on the Languages of the Americans."

8. Simpson, *Politics of American English*, 170–77.

9. See Shoemaker, "How Indians Got to be Red"; Shoemaker, *A Strange Likeness*, 130–40.

10. Cooper, *The Pioneers*, 403, 402, 403, 421. The only other character who uses the racial designation "red-skin" is Chingachgook's longtime companion, Leather-Stocking. For examples, see Cooper, *The Pioneers*, 26, 452, 455. For the sake of consistency, I will adhere to the spelling *red-skin*, except in direct quotations and titles.

11. Goddard, "'I Am a Red Skin,'" 15.

12. *The Last of the Mohicans* is the first historical example of *pale-face* given in *Dictionary of American English*, 3:1672. In *The Oxford English Dictionary*, 9:93, *The Last of the Mohicans* is the second historical example of *pale-face*. The first historical example is 1822; however, the source is George A. McCall, *Letters from the Frontiers*, which was not published until 1868. In this volume, a letter written in Pensacola, Florida, to "Dear H----," probably McCall's sister, Harriet, records "an Indian chief of noble proportions" as using the term "*Paleface*" to address an army captain. There is no reason to believe that anyone saw the letter besides the recipient, "H." It also appears that the letter was written in January 1823, rather than in 1822. Nonetheless, McCall's letter suggests that *pale-face* originated in Native American culture by establishing that it was used by an Indian several years before Cooper's novel appeared. See McCall, *Letters from the Frontiers*, xiii, 72, 66. For examples of Chingachgook's, Magua's, and Tamenund's uses of the term *pale-face* for European Americans, see Cooper, *The Last of the Mohicans*, 313, 349, 350. As in *The Pioneers*, Leather-Stocking also uses the Indians' color-coded racial terms.

13. On Cooper's careful research into and accurate replication of Native American figurative expression, see John T. Frederick, "Cooper' Eloquent Indians." On Cooper's

perception of the similarity in spoken English of upper-class Americans and their English counterparts, see Schachterle, "Cooper on the Languages of the Americans," 60, 63–64.

14. Cooper, *The Pioneers*, 72.

15. Lepore, *A Is for American*, 3–41; Simpson, *Politics of American English*, 52–90, 186–92; Gustafson, *Representative Words*, 335–38.

16. Cooper, *Satanstoe*, 41–44.

17. Gustafson, *Representative Words*, 337–38.

18. Quoted in Gustafson, *Representative Words*, 147; also see, Fraser, *Wall Street*, 142–46.

19. Cooper, "Lecture on Language."

20. Axelrad, "'The Lumley Autograph.'"

21. Cooper, "Lecture on Language."

22. The original full title of the American first edition was *The Redskins; or Indian and Ingin: Being the Conclusion of the Littlepage Manuscripts*. See Spiller and Blackburn, *Descriptive Bibliography*, 145.

23. Huston, *Land and Freedom*, 116–24; Huston, "The Parties and 'The People,'" 250–52; Deloria, *Playing Indian*, 5–9, 38–41, 69.

24. Schachterle, "Themes of Land and Leadership," 96, 119, 120, 123.

25. *Dictionary of American Regional English*, 1:85. The example is quoted exactly as it appears in the dictionary; nothing is added or deleted. The identical quote from Cooper's *The Redskins* also was used as the first example of the American meaning of *aristocratic* in the *Dictionary of American English*, 1:73. For the source of the quote, see Cooper, *The Redskins*, 164. Subsequent quotations from *The Redskins* are noted parenthetically in the text.

26. The American meaning of *aristocratic* is "Stylish; culturally superior" according to the *Dictionary of American Regional English*, 1:85. The closest English counterpart to the American meaning of the word *aristocratic* is "Befitting an aristocrat; grand, stylish" according to *The Oxford English Dictionary*, 1:630. Where the American examples show a range of possible meanings and suggest disapproval for deviating from republican simplicity, the English examples represent a lower-class view of upper-class lifestyle.

27. Leary, *Soundings*, 277.

28. Quoted in Meacham, *American Lion*, 267. Also see Brooke, *Columbia Rising*, 445; Ashworth, *"Agrarians" and "Aristocrats,"* 127–31.

29. *The New-Yorker*, 323. The Whig attack on Cooper was based on the perception that he was a Democrat. While generally sympathetic to the principles of the Democratic Party, Cooper was not a party Democrat. Instead, he considered himself a democrat with a small *d*. See McWilliams, *Political Justice*, 191–94. While not a democrat with a capital *D*, in fearing rule by the wealthy, Cooper was anti-Whig and pro-Jackson; see Franklin, "Fathering the Son," 157. For the classic study of Cooper branded an aristocrat by the Whig press, see Waples, *Whig Myth*.

30. This is especially the case in *A Letter to His Countrymen* (1834); *The Monikins* (1835); all five European travel books (1836–38); *The American Democrat* (1838); and the Effingham novels, *Homeward Bound* and *Home As Found* (1838). The Effingham

controversy continued into 1842, with Cooper responding to ongoing ridicule in the press with a series of letters in *Brother Jonathan* plus a "Lost Chapter" of *Home As Found.*

31. Cooper, *The American Democrat*, 145, 143. Subsequent quotations from *The American Democrat* are noted parenthetically in the text.

32. An exception, the *Albany Freeholder*, the official anti-rent organ, issued a vigorous denunciation of *The Redskins*. See Christman, *Tin Horns and Calico*, 256–57.

33. Fox, "Cooper, Aristocrat," 20; Fiedler, *Love and Death*, 184; Lounsbury, *James Fenimore Cooper*, 82; Taylor, *William Cooper's Town*, 291; D. W. Howe, *What Hath God Wrought*, 233.

34. For examples from the 1920s into the twenty-first century, see Parrington, *Main Currents* (1927), 215, 223; Spiller, *Fenimore Cooper* (1931), ix, 212, 301, 311; Canby, *Classic Americans* (1939), 117; Brooks, *World of Irving* (1944), 263; Cowie, *Rise of the American Novel* (1948), 118, 156, 157; Smith, *Virgin Land* (1950), 212; Chase, *American Novel* (1957), 54; Williams, *Contours of American History* (1961), 181; Baym, "Women of Cooper's Leatherstocking Tales" (1971), 700; Sundquist, *Home As Found* (1979), 3, 19; Slotkin, *Fatal Environment* (1985), 105; Kazin, *A Writer's America* (1988), 99; Long, *James Fenimore Cooper* (1990), 194; Cawelti, "Cooper and the Frontier Myth and Anti-Myth" (1993), 158; Johnson, *History of the American People* (1997), 405; and Hecht, "Rents in the Landscape" (2005), 39–42.

35. Kelly, *Plotting America's Past*, 40; Bushman, *Refinement of America*, 417.

36. See Kaul, *American Vision*, 95, 100; Marder, *Exiles At Home*, 26, 28, 59.

37. See House, *Cooper's Americans*, 9; Levine, *Conspiracy and Romance*, 61; and Ringe, *James Fenimore Cooper*, 121–22. For a particularly helpful discussion of the importance of the terms *aristocrat* and *aristocracy* for Cooper, see McWilliams, *Political Justice*, 46–48, 148–54, 173–82, 228–29, 298–305.

38. For discussion of Cooper's fascination with American English, see Gustafson, *Representative Words*, 334–39; Kramer, *Imagining Language in America*, 18, 23, 28, 29; Schachterle, "Cooper on the Languages of the Americans"; and Simpson, *Politics of American English*, 149–229.

39. Quoted by Taylor, *William Cooper's Town*, 426.

40. Cooper, *Ways of the Hour*, 316. Subsequent quotations from *The Ways of the Hour* are noted parenthetically in the text.

41. Cooper, *Pocket Handkerchief*, 88, 79. Subsequent quotations from *Pocket Handkerchief* are noted parenthetically in the text. For a helpful discussion of *it-narratives* and the femininity of the pocket handkerchief, see the historical introduction by Matt Sivils and James P. Elliott to Cooper's *Pocket Handkerchief*, xiv–xv, xxiv–xxv.

42. Cooper, *The Spy*, 36.

43. Although Cooper also visited England in 1806, 1807, 1826, and 1833, it was during his 1828 visit that he formulated his views of English aristocracy that he immediately articulated in *Notions of the Americans* and later articulated in his 1837 English travel book. See Ringe and Staggs's historical introduction in Cooper's *Gleanings: England*, xvii; Cooper, *Notions of the Americans*, 530–32; Cooper, *Gleanings: England*, 136–41, 151–54, 203–5. Subsequent quotations from *Gleanings: England* are noted parenthetically in the text.

44. On the difficulty of distinguishing between aristocrats and gentlemen in popular discourse in postrevolutionary and antebellum America, see Cmiel, *Democratic Eloquence*, 39–57.

45. Cooper to Charles Wilkes, 27 April 1831, in *Letters and Journals*, 2:73, hereafter cited as *L&J*.

46. Aristotle, *The Politics*, 119–20.

47. Cooper, *The Bravo*, 1. Subsequent quotations from *The Bravo* are noted parenthetically in the text.

48. In his view, England was a monarchy that had degenerated into an aristocracy. America was a democratic republic, not an aristocratic republic. Yet he sometimes made a simple distinction between "Aristocracy" in England and "Democracy" in America. For example, see *Notions of the Americans*, 282. Moreover, he was not perfectly consistent. He sometimes distinguished democracy from republic on the basis of its broader franchise and thought of democracy as a type of republic, though he also used the terms interchangeably. The republican/democratic form of government, in his opinion, was at least as good and possibly better than monarchy. Their wider base of support gave republics/democracies an advantage over monarchies; their disadvantage was the ease with which moneyed aristocrats might manipulate the masses through demagoguery and thus create an aristocracy. He thought that monarchies were better fortified against this danger.

49. Cooper, *Letter to His Countrymen*, 88. Subsequent quotations from *A Letter to His Countrymen* are noted parenthetically in the text. Though he no doubt meant the Glorious Revolution of 1688, in *A Letter to His Countrymen*, he mistakenly referred to the change in government in England as the "revolution of 1668" (65). Elsewhere he correctly dates the change from monarchy to aristocracy as 1688; see Cooper to Mrs. Peter Augustus Jay, 16 June 1831, in *L&J*, 2:107. See Cooper, *Homeward Bound* (1838), 421; Cooper, *Gleanings: Switzerland* (1836), 108; Cooper to Benjamin Silliman, 10 June 1831, in *L&J*, 2:94–98.

50. Cooper to Richard Bentley, 6 April 1835, in *L&J*, 3:143.

51. Cooper to Horatio Greenough, 14 June 1836, in *L&J*, 3:220.

52. Cushing, *Reply to Cooper*, 5–6, 62, 61.

53. On "the great danger we have to apprehend" in "legislative usurpation" in the United States, see Cooper to Micah Sterling, 27 October 1834, in *L&J*, 3:59. Also see Cooper to William Cullen Bryant and William Leggett, for *The Evening Post*, 8 January 1835, in *L&J*, 3:84. On legislative usurpation of executive authority in the United States and Europe, see Cooper to William Cullen Bryant and William Leggett, for *The Evening Post*, 28 March 1835, in *L&J*, 3:132.

54. Cooper, *The Crater*, 440, 441, 442, 438, 450. See Philbrick's footnote on the New York State Constitution of 1846, in Cooper, *The Crater*, 441.

55. See Axelrad, *History and Utopia*, 1–47.

56. Cooper to Rufus Wilmot Griswold, 27 May–June 1844, in *L&J*, 4:461.

57. See Diggins, *Lost Soul of American Politics*, 180–91; Levine, *Conspiracy and Romance*, 71–103; McWilliams, *Political Justice*, 154–66; Ringe Introduction to *The Bravo*; Ringe, *James Fenimore* Cooper, 40–49; Schachterle, "The 'soulless corporation.'"

58. Eglin, *Venice Transfigured*, 180–82; Bailyn, *Ideological Origins*, 64; Persons, "Cyclical Theory of History."

59. Cooper, "New York," 30.

60. Brooke, *Columbia Rising*, 445–46; Maier, "Revolutionary Origins of the American Corporation," 52, 62, 66, 72; Welter, *Mind of America*, 77–80, 89, 168–69.

61. Susan Fenimore Cooper, *Pages and Pictures*, 249.

62. On the Venetian corporation in *The Bravo*, see Levine, *Conspiracy and Romance*, 75–96; Schachterle, "The 'soulless corporation.'"

63. The term *capitalism* was not part of Cooper's vocabulary. However, he used the term "capitalists" as early as 1821. See Cooper's book review, "(Commercial Restrictions)," 26, 29. Dictionary examples of the first appearance of the term *capitalism* in English are dated after Cooper's death: in 1854 in the *O.E.D.*, 1:334; in 1886 in the *Dictionary of American English*, 1:418.

64. See Grossman, *James Fenimore Cooper*, 170–75; Meyers, *Jacksonian Persuasion*, 82–84.

65. Roediger, *Wages of Whiteness*, 66–67.

66. In the words of Bernard Bailyn, "'Slavery' was a central concept in eighteenth-century political discourse. As the absolute political evil, it appears in every statement of political principle, in every discussion of constitutionalism or legal rights, in every exhortation to resistance." Bailyn, *Ideological Origins*, 232.

67. For discussion of Cooper's conservative republican ideology, see Axelrad, *History and Utopia*, 49–54; Diggins, *Lost Soul of American Politics*, 180–91; Levine, *Conspiracy and Romance*, 58–103; McWilliams, *Political Justice*, 143–54, 185–216; and Meyers, *Jacksonian Persuasion*, 57–100.

68. Cooper, "(Commercial Restrictions)," 37, 38, 40. On Cooper's linkage of economic monopoly, political power, and exploitation, also see Cooper, *Gleanings: England*, 146, 149; Cooper, *The American Democrat*, 60.

69. Bonomi, *A Factious People*, 5–10, 69–75, 179–200; Bruegel, "Unrest"; Christman, *Tin Horns and Calico*, 39, 318; Ellis, *Landlords and Farmers*, 274–75, 287; Fox, *Decline of Aristocracy*, 438; Hall, *Magic Mirror*, 100; Horwitz, *Transformation of American Law*, 31, 63–66, 259–61; Huston, *Land and Freedom*, 5–8, 71, 74, 135–45, 189–92, 200–217; McCurdy, *Anti-Rent Era*, xiv–xv, 49–51, 110–116, 131–35, 331–32; Kim, *Landlord and Tenant*, 234–80.

70. On the economic enterprise of Cooper's father, William Cooper, and the creation of the family's estate, see Taylor, *William Cooper's Town*. On the role of old New York merchant families such as the DeLanceys, see Bonomi, *A Factious People*, 60–68. On Cooper as a professional author in a literary marketplace, see Charvat, "Cooper As Professional Author"; Franklin, *James Fenimore Cooper*, 252–69, 351–57, 491–521; Franklin, "'One More Scene'"; Harthorn, "Cooper, Carey, Lea and Blanchard"; Harthorn "The Pathfinder," and Schachterle, "Cooper's Work in Print."

BIBLIOGRAPHY

Aristotle. *The Politics*. Translated by Carnes Lord. Chicago: University of Chicago Press, 1984.

Ashworth, John. *"Agrarians" and "Aristocrats": Party Political Ideology in the United States, 1837–1846*. London: Royal Historical Society, 1983.

Axelrad, Allan. *History and Utopia: A Study of the World View of James Fenimore Cooper*. Norwood, PA: Norwood Editions, 1978.

______. "'The Lumley Autograph' and the Great Literary Lion: Authenticity and Commodification in Nineteenth-Century Autograph Collecting." In *Susan Fenimore Cooper: New Essays on Rural Hours and Other Works*, edited by Rochelle Johnson and Daniel Patterson, 22–38. Athens: University of Georgia Press, 2001.

Bailyn, Bernard. *The Ideological Origins of the American Revolution*. Cambridge, MA: Harvard University Press, 1967.

Baron, Dennis E. *Grammar and Good Taste: Reforming the American Language*. New Haven, CT: Yale University Press, 1982.

Baym, Nina. "The Women of Cooper's Leatherstocking Tales." *American Quarterly* 23.4 (1971): 696–709.

Bonomi, Patricia. *A Factious People: Politics and Society in Colonial New York*. New York: Columbia University Press, 1971.

Brooke, John L. *Columbia Rising: Civil Life on the Upper Hudson from the Revolution to the Age of Jackson*. Chapel Hill: University of North Carolina Press, 2010.

Brooks, Van Wyck. *The World of Washington Irving*. New York: Dutton, 1944.

Bruegel, Martin. "Unrest: Manorial Society and the Market in the Hudson Valley, 1780–1850." *Journal of American History* 82.1 (1996): 1393–1424.

Bushman, Richard L. *The Refinement of America: Persons, Houses, Cities*. New York: Random House, 1992.

Canby, Henry Seidel. *Classic Americans: A Study of Eminent American Writers from Irving to Whitman*. 1939; New York: Russell and Russell, 1959.

Cawelti, John G. "Cooper and the Frontier Myth and Anti-Myth." In *James Fenimore Cooper: New Historical and Literary Contexts*, edited by W. M. Verhoeven, 151–60. Atlanta: Rodopi, 1993.

Charvat, William. "Cooper As Professional Author." In *James Fenimore Cooper: A Re-Appraisal*, edited by Mary E. Cunningham, 128–43. Cooperstown: New York State Historical Association, 1954.

Chase, Richard. *The American Novel and Its Tradition*. Garden City: Doubleday, 1957.

Christman, Henry. *Tin Horns and Calico: A Decisive Episode in the Emergence of Democracy* New York: Holt, 1945.

Cmiel, Kenneth. *Democratic Eloquence: The Fight over Popular Speech in Nineteenth-Century America*. Berkeley: University of California Press, 1990.

Cooper, James Fenimore. *The Amerian Democrat*, Introduction by H. L. Mencken and J. Perry Leavell, Jr. New York: Minerva Press, 1969.

______. *The Autobiography of a Pocket Handkerchief*. Edited with a historical introduction by Matthew Wynn Sivils and James P. Elliot. New York: AMS Press, 2012.

______. *The Bravo. A Venetian Story*. Edited by Lance Schachterle and James A. Sappenfield; historical introduction by Kay Seymour House; explanatory notes by Anna Scannavini. New York: AMS Press, 2011.

______. "(Commercial Restrictions). An Examination of the New Tariff by *One of the People.*" In *Early Critical Essays (1820–1822)*, edited by James F. Beard Jr. Delmar, NY: Scholars' Facsimiles and Reprints, 1955.

______. *The Crater or Vulcan's Peak.* Edited by Thomas Philbrick. Cambridge: Harvard University Press, 1962.

______. *Gleanings in Europe: England.* Historical introduction and explanatory notes by Donald A. Ringe and Kenneth W. Staggs; text established by James P. Elliott, Kenneth W. Staggs, and Robert D. Madison. New York: State University of New York Press, 1982.

______. *Gleanings in Europe: Switzerland.* Historical introduction and explanatory notes by Robert E. Spiller and James F. Beard; text established by Kenneth W. Staggs and James P. Elliott. Albany: State University of New York Press, 1980.

______. *Homeward Bound.* New York: Putnams, 1906.

______. *The Last of the Mohicans; A Narrative of 1757.* Historical introduction by James Franklin Beard; text established with explanatory notes by James A. Sappenfield and E. N. Feltskog. Albany: State University of New York Press, 1983.

______. "Lecture on Language delivered at the Court House." Manuscript fragment, Cooperstown, 1835. Identified and dated in the handwriting of Cooper's daughter, Susan Fenimore Cooper.

______. *The Letters and Journals of James Fenimore Cooper.* Edited by James Franklin Beard. 6 vols. Cambridge, MA: The Belknap Press of Harvard University Press, 1960–68.

______. *A Letter to His Countrymen.* New York: Wiley, 1834.

______. "New York." *Spirit of the Fair*, 7 April 1864.

______. *Notions of the Americans: Picked Up by a Travelling Bachelor.* Text established with historical introduction and textual notes by Gary Williams. Albany: State University of New York Press, 1991.

______. *The Pioneers, or the Sources of the Susquehanna; A Descriptive Tale.* Historical introduction and explanatory notes by James Franklin Beard; text established by Lance Schachterle and Kenneth M. Andersen Jr. Albany: State University of New York Press, 1980.

______. *The Redskins.* New York: Putnams, 1906.

______. *Satanstoe, or The Littlepage Manuscripts: A Tale of the Colony.* Historical introduction by Kay Seymour House; text established with explanatory notes by Kay Seymour House and Constance Ayers Denne. Albany: State University of New York Press, 1990.

______. *The Spy: A Tale of the Neutral Ground.* Historical introduction by James P. Elliott; explanatory notes by James H. Pickering; text established by James P. Elliott, Lance Schachterle, and Jeffrey Walker. Albany: State University of New York Press, 2002.

______. *The Ways of the Hour.* New York: Putnams, 1906.

Cooper, Susan Fenimore. *Pages and Pictures, From the Writings of James Fenimore Cooper.* New York: Townsend, 1861.

Cowie, Alexander. *The Rise of the American Novel.* New York: American Book Company, 1948.

Cushing, Caleb. *A Reply to the Letter of J. Fenimore Cooper by One of His Countrymen.* Boston: Buckingham, 1834.

Deloria, Philip J. *Playing Indian.* New Haven, CT: Yale University Press, 1998.

A Dictionary of American English on Historical Principles. Edited by Sir William A. Craigie and James R. Hulbert. 4 vols. Chicago: University of Chicago Press, 1938–44.

Dictionary of American Regional English. Edited by Frederic C. Cassidy. 2 vols. Cambridge, MA: Harvard University Press, 1985.

Diggins, John P. *The Lost Soul of American Politics: Virtue, Self-Interest, and the Foundations of Liberalism.* Chicago: University of Chicago Press, 1984.

Eglin, John. *Venice Transfigured: The Myth of Venice in British Culture, 1660–1797.* New York: Palgrave, 2001.

Ellis, David Maldwyn. *Landlords and Farmers in the Hudson-Mohawk Region, 1790–1850.* 1946; New York: Octagon Books, 1967.

Fiedler, Leslie A. *Love and Death in the American Novel.* 1960; rev. ed. New York: Stein and Day, 1966.

Fox, Dixon Ryan. *The Decline of Aristocracy in the Politics of New York, 1801–1840.* 1919; New York: Harper and Row, 1965.

______. "James Fenimore Cooper, Aristocrat." *New York History* 22.1 (1941): 18–35.

Franklin, Wayne. "Fathering the Son: The Cultural Origins of James Fenimore Cooper," *Resources for American Literary Study* 27.2 (2001): 149–78.

______. *James Fenimore Cooper: The Early Years.* New Haven, CT: Yale University Press, 2007.

______. "'One More Scene': The Marketing Context of Cooper's 'Sixth' Leather-Stocking Tale." In *Leather-Stocking Redux; Or, Old Tales, New Essays,* edited by Jeffrey Walker, 225–52. New York: AMS Press, 2011.

Fraser, Steve. *Wall Street: America's Dream Palace.* New Haven, CT: Yale University Press, 2008.

Frederick, John T. "Cooper's Eloquent Indians." *PMLA* 71.5 (1956): 1004–17.

Goddard, Ives. "'I Am a Red Skin': The Adoption of a Native American Expression (1769–1826)." *European Review of Native American Studies* 19.2 (2005): 1–20.

Grossman, James. *James Fenimore Cooper: A Biographic and Critical Study.* 1949; Stanford, CA: Stanford University Press, 1967.

Gustafson, Thomas. *Representative Words: Politics, Literature, and the American Language, 1776–1865.* New York: Cambridge University Press, 1992.

Hall, Kermit L. *The Magic Mirror: Law in American History.* New York: Oxford University Press, 1989.

Harthorn, Steven P. "James Fenimore Cooper, Carey, Lea and Blanchard, and the Fable of the Indulgent Publisher." *James Fenimore Cooper, His Country and His Art* 16 (2007): 29–43.

______. "The Pathfinder *and Cooper's Return to Popular Literature.*" In *Leather-Stocking Redux; Or, Old Tales, New Essays,* edited by Jeffrey Walker, 193–224. New York: AMS Press, 2011.

Hecht, Roger. "Rents in the Landscape: The Anti-Rent War in Melville's *Pierre.*" *ATQ* 19.1 (2005): 37–50.

Horwitz, Morton J. *The Transformation of American Law, 1780–1860*. Cambridge, MA: Harvard University Press, 1977.

House, Kay Seymour. *Cooper's Americans*. Columbus: Ohio State University Press, 1965.

Howe, Daniel Walker. *What Hath God Wrought: The Transformation of America, 1815–1848*. New York: Oxford University Press, 2007.

Howe, John. *Language and Political Meaning in Revolutionary America*. Amherst: University of Massachusetts Press, 2004.

Huston, Reeve. *Land and Freedom: Rural Society, Popular Protest, and Party Politics in Antebellum New York*. New York: Oxford University Press, 2000.

______. "The Parties and 'The People': The New York Anti-Rent Wars and the Contours of Jacksonian Politics." *Journal of the Early Republic* 20.2 (2000): 241–71.

Johnson, Paul. *A History of the American People*. 1997; New York: Harper Collins, 1998.

Kaul, A. N. *The American Vision: Actual and Ideal Society in Nineteenth-Century Fiction*. New Haven, CT: Yale University Press, 1963.

Kazin, Alfred. *A Writer's America*. New York: Knopf, 1988.

Kelly, William P. *Plotting America's Past: Fenimore Cooper and the Leatherstocking Tales*. Carbondale: Southern Illinois University Press, 1983.

Kim, Sung Bok. *Landlord and Tenant in Colonial New York: Manorial Society, 1664–1775*. Chapel Hill: University of North Carolina Press, 1978.

Kramer, Michael P. *Imagining Language in America: From the Revolution to the Civil War*. Princeton, NJ: Princeton University Press, 1992.

Leary, Lewis. *Soundings: Some Early American Writers*. Athens: University of Georgia Press, 1975.

Lepore, Jill. *A Is for American: Letters and Other Characters in the Newly United States*. New York: Knopf, 2002.

Levine, Robert S. *Conspiracy and Romance: Studies in Brockton Brown, Cooper, Hawthorne, and Melville*. Cambridge, UK: Cambridge University Press, 1989.

Long, Robert Emmet. *James Fenimore Cooper*. New York: Continuum, 1990.

Looby, Christopher, *Voicing America: Language, Literary Form, and the Origins of the United States*. Chicago: University of Chicago Press, 1996.

Lounsbury, Thomas R. *James Fenimore Cooper*. Boston: Houghton, Mifflin, 1882.

Maier, Pauline. "The Revolutionary Origins of the American Corporation." *William and Mary Quarterly* 50.1 (1993): 51–84.

Marder, Daniel. *Exiles at Home: A Story of Literature in Nineteenth Century America*. Lanham, MD: University Press of America, 1984.

McCall, Major General George A. *Letters from the Frontiers*. Introduction by John K. Mahon. Gainesville: University Presses of Florida, 1974.

McCurdy, Charles W. *The Anti-Rent Era in New York Law and Politics, 1839–1865*. Chapel Hill: University of North Carolina Press, 2001.

McWilliams, John P., Jr. *Political Justice in a Republic: James Fenimore Cooper's America*. Berkeley: University of California Press, 1972.

Meacham, Jon. *American Lion: Andrew Jackson in the White House*. New York: Random House, 2008.

Meyers, Marvin. *The Jacksonian Persuasion: Politics and Belief*. 1957; Stanford, CA: Stanford University Press, 1960.

The New-Yorker 4 (2 Feb. 1839).

Oxford English Dictionary. 2nd ed. Prepared by J. A. Simpson and E. S. C. Weiner. 20 vols. Oxford, UK: Oxford University Press, 1989.

Parrington, Vernon Louis. *Main Currents in American Thought: The Romantic Revolution in America, 1800–1860*. 1927; New York: Harcourt, Brace, 1954.

Persons, Stow. "The Cyclical Theory of History in Eighteenth Century America." *American Quarterly* 6.2 (1954): 147–63.

Ringe, Donald A. Introduction to *The Bravo*. 5–16. 1831; New Haven: College and University Press, 1963.

______. *James Fenimore Cooper: Updated Edition*. Boston: Twayne, 1988.

Roediger, David R. *The Wages of Whiteness: Race and the Making of the American Working Class*. New York: Verso, 1991.

Schachterle, Lance. "Cooper's Work in Print." In *Reading Cooper, Teaching Cooper*, edited by Jeffrey Walker, 158–81. New York: AMS Press, 2007.

______. "James Fenimore Cooper on the Languages of the Americans: A Note on the Author's Footnotes." *Nineteenth-Century Literature* 66.1 (2011): 37–68.

______. "The 'soulless corporation' in Venice, England, France, and America: Cooper's *The Bravo (1831)*." *James Fenimore Cooper Society Miscellaneous Papers* 28 (2011): 7–14.

______. "The Themes of Land and Leadership in 'The Littlepage Manuscripts.'" *Literature in the Early American Republic: Annual Studies on Cooper and His Contemporaries* 1 (2009): 89–131.

Shoemaker, Nancy. "How Indians Got To Be Red." *American Historical Review* 102.3 (1997): 625–44.

______. *A Strange Likeness: Becoming Red and White in Eighteenth-Century North America*. New York: Oxford University Press, 2004.

Simpson, David. *The Politics of American English, 1776–1850*. New York: Oxford University Press, 1986.

Slotkin, Richard. *The Fatal Environment: The Myth of the Frontier in the Age of Industrialization, 1800–1890*. New York: Atheneum, 1985.

Smith, Henry Nash. *Virgin Land: The American West as Symbol and Myth*. 1950; Cambridge, MA: Harvard University Press, 1970.

Spiller, Robert E. *Fenimore Cooper: Critic of His Times*. New York: Minton, Balch, 1931.

Spiller, Robert E., and Philip C. Blackburn. *A Descriptive Bibliography of the Writings of James Fenimore Cooper*. New York: Bowker, 1934.

Sundquist, Eric I. *Home As Found: Authority and Genealogy in Nineteenth-Century American Literature*. Baltimore, MD: Johns Hopkins University Press, 1979.

Taylor, Alan. *William Cooper's Town: Power and Persuasion on the Frontier of the Early American Republic*. New York: Knopf, 1995.

Tocqueville, Alexis de. *Democracy in America*. Translated by Arthur Goldhammer. 1835, 1840. New York: Library of America, 2004.

Waples, Dorothy. *The Whig Myth of James Fenimore Cooper*. New Haven, CT: Yale University Press, 1938.

Welter, Rush. *The Mind of America*. New York: Columbia University Press, 1975.

Williams, William Appleman. *The Contours of American History*. 1961; New York: Viewpoints, 1973.

Patriotism and Caste in The Chainbearer: *Cooper's Fifth Revolutionary War Novel*

LANCE SCHACHTERLE
Worcester Polytechnic Institute

> "You t'ink, sah, dis part of 'e country been talk too much lately 'bout Patty Rism and 'e country, sah?"
>
> "I am afraid Patty has been overdone here, as well as in most other counties." (1:30)

> "It's on equity, I want to put this very matter, Major—I know the law is ag'in me—that is, some people say it is; but, some think not, now we've had a revolution—but, let the law go as it may, there's such a thing as what I call right, between man and man." (1:179)

> While it is scarcely possible that either man, or woman, should not see how grave a barrier to wedded happiness is interposed by the opinions and habits of social castes, it is seldom that any one, in his or her own proper sphere, feels that the want of money is an insurmountable obstacle to a union—more especially when one of the parties is provided with the means of maintaining the household gods. The seniors may, and do often have scruples on this score, but the young people rarely. (2:118)[1]

TO promote James Fenimore Cooper's fifth novel, *Lionel Lincoln*, published in February 1825, Charles Wiley began as early as December 1823 to advertise that he would "shortly put to press the first of a series of Tales called 'Legends of the Thirteen Republics.' Tale first—Lionel, or Boston Beleaguered."[2] Wiley's notice implied that

Literature in the Early American Republic: Annual Studies on Cooper and His Contemporaries
Volume 6, 2014. Copyright © 2014 by AMS Press, Inc. All rights reserved.

Cooper intended a novel for each of the thirteen colonies, starting with Massachusetts. Weak sales for *Lionel Lincoln*—in large part because of a twisted plot where the hero, Waverley-like, sides with imperial authority at the end and the chief rebel spokesman is revealed to be a madman—probably was a factor in Cooper's never fulfilling this thirteen-part plan. His next novel, *The Last of the Mohicans* (1826), proved a popular and critical success to this day and confirmed the "Indian romance" as a sure authorial moneymaker.[3]

With *The Spy* (1821), Cooper had invented the American Revolutionary War novel by placing the heroic deeds of the Virginian cavalry against British troopers in the context of romantic entanglements involving sisters split between allegiance to the rebel cause and to the king. Cooper, however, qualified the straightforward rebel heroics both by probing the troubled patriotism of the shrewd but misunderstood Harvey Birch and by foregrounding the depredations of the Skinners, guerillas supposedly supporting the Revolution but exploiting both sides with their thuggery. Cooper built on his first success with war themes by inventing American sea fiction in *The Pilot* (1824), a romance involving the fictional portrayal of John Paul Jones taking the war to the British coastline only to be frustrated by the young American naval officers caring more about pursuing their girlfriends than about prosecuting the war. And in 1843, he returned explicitly to the Revolutionary War with *Wyandotté*, though there his concern had shifted more to the conflict between New York landowners and greedy Yankees seeking their real estate than with fighting British colonial masters.[4] But other than in *Wyandotté*, Cooper never set another novel in the time period of the Revolution after 1825.[5]

In at least two sea novels after 1825, *The Red Rover* (1827) and *The Water-Witch* (1830), Cooper depicted colonial sea captains whose rebellion against British authority may prefigure the Revolution. Captain Heidegger in *The Red Rover* redeems his life of piracy against British commerce by dying in service to the rebel cause in the war while the "Skimmer of the Seas" in *The Water-Witch* repeatedly outwits and outsails the British naval vessels trying to arrest him for smuggling. And, of course, Cooper chronicled in detail the war as fought at sea in *The History of the Navy of the United States of America* (1839) and celebrated the rare American successes in the war at the hands of

John Paul Jones in his *Lives of Distinguished American Naval Officers* (printed separately in *Graham's Magazine*, 1842–45; published in book form by Carey and Hart, Philadelphia, 1846).

1. The Chainbearer *as a Revolutionary War Novel*

In his article on the proposed but never written "Sixth" Leather-Stocking Tale, Wayne Franklin remarks that Cooper excluded Natty Bumppo from *Wyandotté* because the author "had in a sense written out his interest in the Revolution. One notes that he omitted it from the Littlepage series."[6] My argument here is that *The Chainbearer* (1845) does present Cooper's take on the Revolution, both in descriptions early in the novel of Mordaunt Littlepage, the hero, participating in numerous Revolutionary War battles and, more importantly, in reconstituting what "revolution" meant to Cooper in the 1840s.

"The Littlepage Manuscripts," of which *The Chainbearer* is the second of three volumes, constitutes Cooper's most carefully constructed multivolume achievement in fiction. Writing to Richard Bentley on 22 January 1845, Cooper at length argued that the proposed trilogy would contain exciting incidents and political reflections likely to please a British audience. Cooper required all his powers of persuasion to engage Bentley in yet another large publishing project; cheaply produced literature was coming to dominate publishing following the economic troubles of the late 1830s, and many new authors such as Charles Dickens were competing with established figures. Furthermore, in 1838, Bentley had protested strongly against the Home novels morphing into two volumes, since "[m]y experience has always proved that sequels do not sell to the same extent as the earlier portion."[7]

Thus Cooper tried his best to present "the Littlepage Manuscripts" as independent yet related novels:

> "The Family of Littlepage" will form three complete Tales, each perfectly distinct from the other as regards leading characters, love story &c, but, in this wise connected. I divide the subjects into the "Colony," "Revolution" and "Republic," carrying the same family, the same localities, and the same things generally through the three

> different books, but exhibiting the changes produced by time &c. In the Colony [*Satanstoe*], for instance, the Littlepage of that day, first visits an estate of wild land, during the operations of the year 1758, the year that succeeded the scenes of the Mohicans, and it is there that the most stirring events of the book oc[c]ur. In the "Revolution" [*The Chainbearer*] this land is first settled, and the principles are developed, on which this settlement takes place, showing a book, in some respects resembling the Pioneers, though varied by localities and incidents—In the "Republic" [*The Redskins*] we shall have the present aspect of things, with an exhibition of the Anti-Rent commotion that now exists among us, and which certainly threatens the destruction of our system—You know I write what I think, in these matters, and I shall not spare "The Republic" in all in which it is faulty and weak, as faulty and weak it has been to a grievous extent in these matters.
> ... These books will be perfectly distinct as Tales, and each will make an ordinary sized novel, though I hope the interest of one will be reflected on the others. (*L&J*, 5:7)

This letter to Bentley clearly states that the governing theme of *The Chainbearer* is revolution: "In the 'Revolution' this land is first settled, and the principles are developed, on which this settlement takes place, showing a book, in some respects resembling the *Pioneers*, though varied by localities and incidents." Because the action of the novel occurs in 1784, Cooper's associating the novel with the "Revolution" cannot refer to the time of the actual Revolutionary War, concluded with the peace treaty of 1783. However, the novel's hero, the then-college-age Mordaunt Littlepage—son of Corny Littlepage and Anneke Mordaunt, who marry at the end of *Satanstoe* (1845)—fights in several important battles early in the war and observes the fall of Yorktown.

While Cooper does not narrate in *Chainbearer* any historical battles in detail—as he did the opening skirmishes of Concord, Lexington, and Bunker Hill in *Lionel Lincoln*—in the first chapter, Mordant mentions participating under his father's command in two important American victories in New Jersey, at Trenton and at Princeton. (In *Chainbearer*, the Corny Littlepage of *Satanstoe* is now a colonel and at the end of the war is brevetted to a general, the title by which he is always referenced as a reminder of the Littlepage service on the patriot side.) Mordaunt emphasizes how it took him six years to graduate from Nassau Hall (Princeton) because of extended absences from college to participate in several battles; Cooper patriotically names at least eight Revolutionary War encounters that were at least draws for the Americans without mentioning Mordaunt's presence at a single instance of their many defeats.

Later, in chapter 18, Mordaunt seeks to impress the squatter Aaron Thousandacres by adverting to fighting in the crucial American victory at Saratoga—where Thousandacres with his numerous sons had also fought on the rebel side (2:37–38). Further, in the opening chapter, Mordaunt also refers to the quarrel between Generals Horatio Gates and Philip Schuyler, backed respectively by New England and New York militants. In the second chapter, he recalls the withdrawal of the last British forces in America, from New York on 25 November 1783, and to Washington's dramatic suppression of the potential officers' rebellion at Newburgh, New York, earlier in the same year. Finally, when the Chainbearer succumbs to his gunshot wound in chapter 29, he reverently names other heroes who died in the war itself: "Yes, lat, t'ere wast a time when I shoult haf peen glat to haf peen shot on t'e fielt, and to haf diet wit' Montgomery, ant Laurens, ant Wooster ant Warren, and sich-like gallant heroes" (2.197).[8] Thus memories of the American actions and sacrifices in the war suffuse the novel.

2. Revolution and Caste: The Anti-Rent Controversy

Consistent with the practices of the day, Cooper narrated the war from the point of view exclusively of the officers; the rank and file who fought and died are never mentioned.[9] And Mordaunt never forgets his caste and its social obligations: he is a landowner in his own right, and as only son of Corny Littlepage and Anneke Mordaunt, presumptive heir to Lilacsbush, Ravensnest, and Mooseridge—the latter two properties he has been sent into the northern wilderness of New York to oversee surveying and sales or lease. As a gentleman and military officer (always addressed as "Major"), several times he tells the reader he restrains himself from physically resisting the Thousandacres squatters who hold him captive because such resistance is beneath his dignity. Despite his whole family siding with the patriot cause, he accedes to a suitor for his younger sister's hands, Tom Bayard, who is a mild Loyalist because Bayard accepts Mordaunt's defense of the Revolution (1:51–52) with gentlemanly courtesy.[10]

Patriotic fervor is a given among the moderately wealthy Littlepages, but not necessarily among the lower classes. In an amusing incident in chapter 2, Mordaunt recounts his distress while on a military mission in finding his pocket filled mainly with near-worthless Continental currency. He and his faithful slave Jaap consider doubtfully whether the locals will accept this hyperinflated currency for an evening's lodgings, with an appeal to their patriotism:

> **Jaap:** "You t'ink, sah, dis part of 'e country been talk to[o] much lately 'bout Patty Rism and 'e country, sah?"
> **Mordaunt:** "I am afraid Patty has been overdone here, as well as in most other counties." (1.30)

Thus the quick-thinking Jaap conjures up a solution by entertaining the locals at the inn (1:30–31) and collecting enough coins to pay their bill. Mordaunt resolves, however, never to use this Twain-like scam again and repairs to a substantial house where the genteel owner unhesitatingly advances him five silver dollars on the basis of their shared caste identity.

As *The Chainbearer* develops, the full scope of Cooper's primary concern here with "Revolution" is disclosed: the novel is not mainly a glance back to the issues and events of 1775–83, but instead a manifestation of the author's fears that anti-rentism will soon cause a new and dire revolution in the newly united States. Cooper's 22 January letter announcing the trilogy to Bentley described the aim of the third novel—and by implication all three interrelated tales—as "an exhibition of the Anti-Rent commotion that now exists among us, and which certainly threatens the destruction of our system." Thus Cooper shows in *The Chainbearer* how the seeds of the anti-rent revolution were planted by the flood of New England emigrants who sought the comparatively more fertile soil of upper New York state and were free to move there after the war's end. Mordaunt first learns of squatters on his Ravensnest estate in chapter 7 from the cagey landlady Mrs. Tinkum, a recent squatter whose dialect betrays her New England origin. Mrs. Tinkum justifies her "title" through bartering for the "betterments" (improvements) of the previous squatter who ran the very modest local tavern and censures the Chainbearer for refusing to survey "their" land when he learns they hold no legitimate title (1:94).

Chapter 9 firmly establishes the revolutionary threat to New York landholders from New Englanders by introducing the Connecticut emigrant Jason Newcome. Now installed as the agent (a corrupt one, we eventually discover) of the Littlepages on the family lands Mordaunt has come to survey, Newcome, by exploiting the people's misplaced faith in the "Majority," manipulates the vote for the denomination of the "meetin' us" the locals are about to raise, to favor the "Old Connecticut Standing Order," or Congregationalists. Demagoguery, always Cooper's most fearful threat to constitutional democracy, is alive and well on these new lands.

And while Newcome's role in the Revolution has largely been profiting by selling supplies to both sides, he firmly believes that revolution may render moot his contract with the Littlepages:

> "It's on equity, I want to put this very matter, Major—I know the law is ag'in me—that is, some people say it is; *but, some think not, now we've had a revolution*—but, let the law go as it may, there's such a thing as what I call right, between man and man." (1.179; emphasis added)

Newcome embodies Cooper's deepest fears in the 1840s: that the Revolution may justify ending those contractual arrangements for property he sees as enshrined in the Constitution of 1789. In volume 2 of the novel, he encounters the gravest threat, as expounded on page 2 of his preface, that "the capital error is becoming prevalent, which holds the pernicious doctrine that this is a government of men, instead of one of principles."

In volume 2, chapter 16, the lawless squatters of the Thousandacres family come to dominate the book physically. (Their family name is Timberman, but they are known as Thousandacres for their success in appropriating as much of other people's lands as they can use.) The Thousandacres are the archetypical "back country" people J. Hector St. John de Crèvecoeur, Henry Brackenridge, Charles Brockden Brown, Timothy Dwight, and others depicted as morally degenerate. So did

Cooper; in chapter 16, when first introducing Aaron,[11] he never missed an opportunity to describe Thousandacres and his squatter clan as wild animals.[12] Broadly, Cooper characterized these Vermont Yankees in the war as "manifest[ing] a spirit favourable to the colonies" but "declar[ing] themselves neutral" (2:7) after the war as they sought to secure their illegal land claims by seeking favorable terms with both the new American government and the old British one in Canada. While Aaron is proud of fighting against Burgoyne, he is even more proud of diverting to his own use—rather than returning to the Continental army—precious supplies the British have seized.[13]

The patriarchal Thousandacres repeatedly argues in chapter 23 with Cooper's surrogate, the surveyor Andries Coejemans (the "Chainbearer"), that squatter possession is based on the Genesis grant of the land to mankind, to do with what he likes. Thousandacres's argument is that "Possession is every thing, and I call it possession, to crave a spot, and to make some sort of calkerlations, or works near it" (2:96). When Chainbearer gets the better in the argument by insisting on the prior legal rights of the Littlepages, Thousandacres sends him back to confinement. The Chainbearer expostulates in excited Dutch dialect: "Oh! You're a true son of Liperty!. . . a true son of Liperty, according' to your own conceit! You want efery t'ing in your own way, and efery t'ing in your own pocket. T'e Lort's law is a law for T'ousantacres, put not a law to care for Cornelius Littlepage" (2:98). Later, in chapter 25, when the Dutchman reminds Thousandacres that the Littlepages have "fou't gallantly for "liperty," the squatter makes clear that he thinks the Revolution allows taking and using whatever land he can find:

> If he's [Mordaunt] a fri'nd of liberty, he should be a fri'nd of liberty's people; should give liberty and take liberty. Now, I call it liberty to let every man have as much land as he has need on, and no more, keepin' the rest for them that's in the same sitiation. If he and his father be true fri'nds of liberty, let 'em prove it like men, by giving up all claims to any more land than they want. That's what I call liberty! Let every man have as much land as he's need on; that's my religion, and it's liberty, too. (2:138–39)

Lest, like John Milton's Satan, Thousandacres's rebellious rhetoric here be too appealing, Cooper immediately adds a long footnote in his guise as editor, rejecting such views as inimical both to the Tenth Commandment and to "the spirit of the institutions of the country." Thousandacres ultimately can silence Chainbearer's persuasive defense of property rights only by shooting him, thus reenacting the incident Cooper records in his "Preface" of the killing of a sheriff sent to arrest real squatters like the fictional Thousandacres.[14]

To Mordaunt and to his author, such views threaten a violent revolution of the have-nots against the haves:

> It is this gradual undermining of just opinions [on "the supremacy of law"], that forms the imminent danger of our social system . . . false notions on that of personal rights, and the substitution of numbers for principles, bidding fair to produce much the most important revolution that has ever yet taken place on the American continent. (2.177)

Thus Cooper ensures in the plot that Thousandacres will die an unrepentant latter-day Puritan, stubborn but consumed by guilt for murdering the Chainbearer, and that his family will be dispersed and their "betterments" seized by the Littlepages. This justice is administered in summer 1784, well before anti-rent agitation spread throughout the old Patroon estates in New York, but clearly Cooper intends the defeat of the squatters to prefigure what he hoped would be a similar justice visited on the anti-rent agitators of his own day.

3. Revolution and Caste: Can Mordaunt Littlepage Marry a Working-Class Girl?

When in the last chapter the squatters have been ejected and all the Littlepages are gathered at Ravensnest to celebrate their victory, Mordaunt's father, General Littlepage (the resourceful and flexible Corny Littlepage of *Satanstoe* now morphed into a genteel patriarch), opens his campaign to get Mordant to marry the genteel Priscilla Bayard and establish social order on the new frontier:

> Nothing contributes so much to the civilization of a country as to dot it with a gentry, and you will both give and receive advantages by adopting such a course. It is impossible for those who have never been witnesses of the result, to appreciate the effect produced by one gentleman's family in a neighbourhood, in the way of manners, tastes, general intelligence, and civilization at large. (2:213)

Mordaunt's younger sister Anneke, engaged to Tom Bayard, made clear in chapters 3 and 4 that she and all her family hoped Mordaunt would fall in love with Tom's sister, Pris (Priscilla). While attracted to Pris physically, Mordant is puzzled by Pris's careful distancing of herself from him, which he cannot decide is winningly artless or deceptively artful. Later, in chapter 7, Cooper enacts a scene right out of the romance playbook by having Mordaunt enthralled by a hidden singing female voice in the wilderness. In the next chapter, he meets the source of this enchanting melody, Ursula or Dus Malbone, the Chainbearer's niece—the very young woman, with whom old Andries has been urging Mordaunt to fall in love throughout their service in the Revolution.

And so he does. But herein Cooper has set himself a challenging problem: while he has given Dus an education in the same boarding school that Pris Bayard attended, Dus enters the novel dependent on her uncle Andries and has sunk to the menial job of being a chainbearer herself. (The novel's title is usually taken to refer to Andries Coejemans but it equally defines Ursula Malbone, as Cooper stresses at 2:179 and 2:193.) How then to make Ursula fit Mordaunt's caste-bound formula for an appropriate wife, as defined in chapter 14:

> The wife of an educated man should be an educated woman; one fit to be his associate, qualified to mingle her tastes with his own, to exchange ideas, and otherwise to be his companion, in an intellectual sense. These are the higher requisites; a gentleman accepting the minor qualifications as so many extra advantages, if kept within their proper limits; but as positive disadvantages if they interfere with, or in any manner mar the manners, temper, or mental improvement of the woman whom he has chosen as his wife, and not as his domestic. (1:185)

Had novel editors existed in the mid 1840s, surely the second sentence would have been challenged; the context here seems to mean that a genteel wife should know how to supervise domestic arrangements without getting her own hands unduly soiled. Thus the next paragraph assures us that Dus ably manages housekeeping at Ravensnest, such that "the negroes [slaves, to be sure] removed all necessity for her descending to absolute toil" (1:185).

To promote Dus Malbone above Pris Bayard in the affection of Mordaunt—and the reader—Cooper must balance her energy and courage (as in chapter 10, when she saves the roof raising by dashing in to support a fallen brace at a crucial moment) with her genteel domestic qualifications (as in chapter 11, when she serves tea using the only surviving Malbone treasure, their silver plate). Cooper largely does succeed in balancing these two sides of Dus, at least to Mordaunt's satisfaction, as emblemized at 1:155, where Dus's laugh is at first "a wild melody" to which in the manuscript Cooper added "but subdued." Mordaunt seems to like "wild but subdued." Mordaunt thus overcomes his shock at Dus's carrying chain because he convinces himself that Dus's early genteel education trumps her later menial occupation: early education not present occupation assigns caste.

Further—in a social revolution Cooper seems to be at least adumbrating—caste equality does not require financial equality:

> While it is scarcely possible that either man, or woman, should not see how grave a barrier to wedded happiness is interposed by the opinions and habits of social castes, it is seldom that any one, in his or her own proper sphere, feels that the want of money is an insurmountable obstacle to a union—more especially when one of the parties is provided with the means of maintaining the household gods. The seniors may, and do often have scruples on this score, but the young people rarely. (2:118)[15]

Mordaunt knows his caste demands that his family agree to his marrying Dus, and she has promised her dying uncle not to wed unless the Littlepages approve. Cooper deftly handles this resolution by introducing Dus to "the seniors" by her beautiful singing, followed immediately by their witnessing her brother Frank and Pris arm in arm, thus removing her as candidate for their son. Further, Pris, Dus's friend from her early boarding-school days, warmly endorses her character and genteel origins, so the former chainbearer becomes mistress of all the lands to be surveyed as the source of the family's future wealth. Thus in *The Chainbearer*, gentility and land titles defeat squatting and kidnapping, though Cooper stretches conventional ideas of gentility to allow Mordaunt to marry well below his social station and without financial gain.[16]

4. Conclusion: Which Revolution?

When Cooper established the tripartite themes for the proposed Littlepage trilogy in his letter to Bentley of 22 January 1844—"Colony," "Revolution," and "Republic"— his primary concern with "Revolution," I believe, was not the military and political conflicts of 1775–81 but the events of the 1840s that Cooper regarded as the most momentous and threatening to the Republic, the "Anti-Rent" controversy. To us today, the resolution of this conflict, with the large landowners of New York relinquishing those aspects of their contracts that many of their tenant found "feudal," seem reasonable and equitable, a step in the direction of healthy economic diversity. But to Cooper, "Anti-Rent" was far the gravest threat to the Constitution, as it placed the rule of men over the rule of law by usurping the (to him) sacred rights of property. His letters make clear that he believed revolution would follow, which if the country were to survive, would have to be suppressed by bayonets.[17]

However, reminders of the status-upending Revolution of 1775–81 suffuse *The Chainbearer*, from the opening chapters with Mordaunt's establishing his bone fides as a patriot by naming the battles in which he fought to the constant reminder of the war so recently ended in the addressing of the Littlepages and their genteel friends by their military ranks. Cooper seems to be asking: Did the patriots sacrifice to create a republic under a constitution only to lose the rule of law to lawless greed? Will Thousandacres's claims that the Revolution nullified earlier land titles and make squatter possession—especially by those who fought on the patriot side—justified in law (an opinion shared by Jason Newcome) be shown to be true? *The Chainbeare*r rejects those claims and restores property, and order, at least to Cooper's satisfaction. By making the titular character and his niece chainbearers—essential functions in eighteenth-century surveying—Cooper thematically reinforces his sense that civilization requires clear boundaries to suppress the greed of those not bound by education and caste.[18]

NOTES

1. This essay draws on work on a scholarly edition for the Cooper Edition of *The Chainbearer*, edited by myself and James P. Elliott. We have not yet determined the final lineation and pagination for that text, so citations to the novel will be from the two volumes of the first edition, printed by Burgess, Stringer and Co, New York, 1845. Subsequent page references to this edition will be cited parenthetically in the text by volume and page.

2. Cooper, *Lionel Lincoln*, xxi.

3. In my article "Cooper and the American Revolutionary War Novel, 1784–1825," I argue that *The Spy* (1821) was the first novel to foreground the revolutionary military struggle, but that, by the time of writing *Lionel Lincoln* (1825), Cooper was having serious reservations about the motivations of the American "patriots."

4. Wayne Franklin brilliantly contrasts *Wyandotté* (1843), published two decades after *The Pioneers* (1823), as demonstrating Cooper's much darker vision of the Revolution, with greed, self-deception, and paradox displacing the author's earlier optimism about the prospects for founding a stable new community fulfilling the promises of the Revolution. See his *New World of Cooper*, 150–82.

5. An interesting question about Cooper's occasional returns to writing about the Revolutionary War is why he left a gap in Natty Bumppo's life corresponding to his service in the Revolution. Steven P. Harthorn discovered at the American Antiquarian Society a half-sheet of Cooper's notes for a new novel ("Hints for the New Book") that he identified as *Wyandotté*. One line here reads "Leatherstocking listening and at a loss to decide" ("What Happened?" 58). Harthorn attributed the author's apparent decision not to include Natty Bumppo in his fourth Revolutionary War novel to his associating Bumppo with the Tory Effinghams in *The Pioneers*. Wayne Franklin, in "'One More Scene,'" reviews the same evidence Harthorn used for Cooper's considering a sixth Leather-Stocking Tale set in the Revolution but points to small hints in the earlier Tales that Natty could have participated in the war on the patriot side. Franklin concludes that Cooper did not proceed with this prospect because his publishers in the late 1840s, Stringer and Townsend, rejected it.

6. Franklin, "'One More Scene,'" 252n46.

7. For Bentley's letter, see Cooper, *Letters and Journals of James Fenimore Cooper*, 3:307n2. Further references to this edition are cited parenthetically in the text as *L&J*.

8. General Richard Montgomery (1738–75) died while leading the unsuccessful attack on Quebec; John Laurens (1754–82) was killed in one of the last actions of the war at Combahee Ferry, SC; General David Wooster (1711–77) was mortally wounded at Danbury, CT; and Dr. Joseph Warren (1741–75), a leader of the Boston

patriots, died at the outbreak of fighting. Warren appeared in *Lionel Lincoln* (1825) as a forceful advocate for the Revolution whose death at Bunker Hill was deeply lamented. The deaths of Montgomery and Warren were the subjects of widely admired historical paintings by John Trumbull (1756–1843).

9. A singular anomaly is Herman Mann's *The Female Review: or, Memoirs of an American Young Lady* (1797). But Mann's book, a fictional account based on the real woman-warrior Deborah Sampson, is the exception which proves the rule by depicting the titillating story of a woman disguised as a common Revolutionary War soldier, not a male in the ranks. Mann conveys some sense of Sampson's everyday life in camp, but the main interest is with her sexual identity. Another early Revolutionary War novel, John Neal's *Seventy-six* (1823), narrates several actual battles—the defeat at Brandywine on 9 September 1777 in considerable and gory detail—but focuses only on four genteel officers, none below the rank of captain.

10. While chapter 2 is interesting for disclosing Cooper's nuanced analysis of the causes that motivated both Whig rebels and Tory loyalists, the narrative tone never challenges the decision of the Littlepages to side with the rebels. In contrast, Cooper's father, raised a Quaker but early leaving that faith, never participated in the war; instead, he founded his landholding wealth by acquiring the Otsego patent, with questionable strategies, from their loyalist owners. For the full story of how the author's father established and lost his vast land speculations, see Alan Taylor, *William Cooper's Town*. And, of course, Cooper knew well the Loyalist side from the family of his wife, Susan De Lancey, many of whose relatives fought for the king; in the third paragraph of the first chapter, the De Lanceys are listed first in naming prominent families who lost lands to confiscation after the successful conclusion of the war.

11. In the manuscript, Cooper initially named Thousandacres as "Ishmael"—the first name of a similar but ultimately effective patriarchal lawgiver in *The Prairie* (1827)—but soon recognized the significance of the earlier name and shifted to "Aaron."

12. See, for example, Cooper's description of the Thousandacres' matriarch Prudence and her "brood," at their introduction in the text:

"Miss Thousandacres," as the squatter sometimes magnificently called his consort, or the dam of his young brood, was far from receiving us with either smiles, or welcomes. . . . In all the intercourse I subsequently had with her family, the manner of this woman was anxious, distrustful, watchful, and bore a strong resemblance to that of the dam that is overseeing the welfare of its cubs. . . . My example [of eating without polite discourse] was imitated by all around our own particular board, it being the refined and intellectual, only, who habitually converse at their meals. The animal had too great a preponderance among the squatters, to leave them an exception to the rule. (2:18)

As for Prudence, she walked away, and I soon heard her calling all her younger children, by name, to collect them near her person, as the hen gathers its chickens beneath the wing. (2:29)

13. While imprisoned for several days in the Thousandacres' "store-us," Mordaunt tries to win their sympathy by conversing about his role in the Revolution, where they too fought against the British. He begins by recounting his presence at the two crucial

British surrenders of the war, Burgoyne's and Cornwallis'. The suspicious Aaron then queries him (2:38), "Which rijiment was on the right, Hazen's or Brookes's, in storming the Jarmans [at Bemis' Heights]—Tell me that, and I will soon let you know whether I believe you, or not?" Mordaunt replies that in the smoke of battle, he could not tell, but Cooper the historian probably knew that the correct answer was the troops under Lt. Colonel John Brooks (1752–1825), who broke the Hessian lines at the battle of Bemis' Heights. By inserting such details from the conflict, Cooper assures that we do not forget the larger context of the battles of 1775–81; by having Aaron regale the audience with his oft-told tale of being pressed into service by the British to transport seized American war stocks but eluding the British to bring them home as his own trophies, Cooper reminds us that Thousandacreas puts personal advantage above "Patty Rism."

14. In his introduction to the period in which Cooper authored "the Littlepage Manuscripts," James Franklin Beard records that a band of locals resisting legal sanctions on tenants "shot and killed Deputy Sheriff Osman Steele as he collected the farmer's cattle for a forced sale" (*L&J*, 5:3). This murder, on 7 August 1845 when Cooper was at work on *Chainbearer*, must have confirmed the novelist's dire forebodings of a revolution aimed at replacing a government of law with a government of a majority that encouraged mob rule.

15. Frank Malbone's happy fate at the end of the novel is both to marry his beloved, Pris Bayard, and then to benefit from a succession of never-before-heard-of distant relatives who providentially die off and leave him a wealthy man. The implication is that the "one of the parties" who has the money should be the man.

Interestingly, the most complex authorial second thought in the manuscript is Cooper's introduction of Frank Malbone. Cooper introduced Dus by name in chapter 2 as the daughter of the Chainbearer's sister and a handsome wastrel, Bob Malbone. Cooper rewrote a paragraph in manuscript to bring Frank into the novel as a half brother to Dus, born of his father's first wife. Cooper apparently realized someone like Frank was required to serve the role of Pris Bayard's secret love and thus the reason for her coolness to Mordaunt.

16. In my view, gentility collapses in the face of the new economy Cooper recognized and feared in the 1840s. In *The Redskins* (1845), set in the 1840s, the final Littlepage generation—consisting of Mordaunt's second son and his nephew, the son of Mordant's first son, who died young—live off the profits of the capital in land and shares amassed by the foresight of their ancestors. But they have become ineffectual esthetes, unable to manage their holdings in the face of the anti-rent movement, and their unearned legacies are preserved only through the audacious comedy of the ancient Susquesus and his redskin friends saving their bacon. For discussion, see my "Themes of Land and Leadership in 'The Littlepage Manuscripts.'"

17. Two letters of Cooper to total strangers who sided with him on the anti-rent controversy document that his gravest fear for the demise of constitutional government in the 1840s was the success of the anti-rent movement. Responding on 1 January 1847 to an unsolicited letter from the Hosmer sisters who had written on 26 November 1846 to praise his work, Cooper opined, "As to anti-rentism, in my judgment it is to be the test of the institutions. If men find that by making political

combinations they can wipe out their indebtedness, adieu to every thing like liberty or government. The[re] will be but one alternative, and that will be the bayonet" (*L&J*, 5:184). He drew out the bayonet again the next year when predicting revolution on 4 November 1848 in response to an inquiry from Thomas Warren Field regarding Field's loss of lands near the fictional Ravensnest and Mooseridge:

How far this downward tendency [assault on landowners' rights] will go, I do not pretend to say; but I think it quite clear that, unless arrested, it must lead to revolution[s] and bloodshed. This State of things has long been predicted, and he who can look back for half a century [as Cooper did in the trilogy], must see that a fearful progress has been made towards anarchy and its successor tyranny, in that period. Another such half century will, in my judgment, bring the whole country under the bayonet. (*L&J*, 5:388)

18. Modern literature is far less likely to ennoble those who mark out boundaries to ensure the profit of oligarchs: see Franz Kafka's *The Castle* (1926) and Thomas Pynchon's *Mason & Dixon* (1997). But then recall that the author of *Walden* was proud of his precision as a land surveyor.

BIBLIOGRAPHY

Cooper, James Fenimore. *The Chainbearer*. New York: Burgess, Stringer and Company, 1845.

———. *The Letters and Journals of James Fenimore Cooper*. Edited by James Franklin Beard. 6 vols. Cambridge, MA: Belknap Press of Harvard University Press, 1960–68.

———. *Lionel Lincoln; or, The Leaguer of Boston*. Edited with historical introduction and explanatory notes by Donald A. Ringe and Lucy B. Ringe. Albany: State University of New York Press, 1984.

———. *The Redskins; Or Indian and Injin*. New York: "The Darley Edition." Townsend, 1860. Preliminary work in the Cooper Edition is under way on this, the final novel of "The Littlepage Manuscripts."

Franklin, Wayne. *James Fenimore Cooper: The Early Years*. New Haven, CT: Yale University Press, 2007.

———. *The New World of James Fenimore Cooper*. Chicago: University of Chicago Press, 1982.

———. "'One More Scene': The Marketing Context of Cooper's 'Sixth' Leather-Stocking Tale." In *Leather-Stocking Redux; Or, Old Tales, New Essays*, edited by Jeffrey Walker, 225–52. New York: AMS Press, 2011.

Harthorn, Steven P. "What Happened to Cooper's Sixth Leatherstocking Tale?" In *James Fenimore Cooper: His Country and His Art. Papers from the 2005 Cooper Seminar*, edited by Hugh MacDougall and Steven P. Harthorn, 55–61. Oneonta, NY: State University of New York College at Oneonta, 2006.

Mann, Herman. *The Female Review: or, Memoirs of an American Young Lady; whose life and character are peculiarly distinguished—being a continental soldier, for nearly three years, in the late American war. During which time, she performed the duties of every department, into which she was called, with punctual exactness, fidelity and honor, and preserved her chastity inviolate, by the most artful concealment of her sex. With an appendix, containing characteristic traits, by different hands; her taste for economy, principles of domestic education, &c. By a citizen of Massachusetts.* Dedham, MA: Nathaniel and Benjamin Heaton, for the Author, 1797.

Neal, John. *Seventy-six.* Baltimore: Joseph Robinson, 1823.

Schachterle, Lance. "Cooper and the Revolutionary War Novel, 1784–1825." *Literature in the Early American Republic: Studies of Cooper and His Contemporaries* 4 (2012): 227–80.

———. "The Themes of Land and Leadership in 'The Littlepage Manuscripts." *Literature in the Early American Republic: Studies of Cooper and His Contemporaries* 1 (2009): 89–131

Taylor, Alan. *William Cooper's Town: Power and Persuasion in the Frontier of the Early American Republic.* New York: Knopf, 1995.

Foreign Friendship: James Fenimore Cooper and America's International Origins

Sarah Sillin
University of Maryland

JAMES Fenimore Cooper's novels—famous for their pairings of Indians and European Americans—also represent numerous affiliations among Americans and English, French, Dutch, and African characters, among others. In his Revolutionary War stories, sea tales, and travel narratives, Cooper returns again and again to characters who form strong attachments across national lines. Critics such as Leslie Fiedler and Ivy Schweitzer have argued persuasively for the importance of friendship to both Cooper's fiction and the shifting social and political landscape of the early national period.[1] However, the significance of Cooper's emphasis on international friendships, in particular, remains unexplored. While these relationships clearly have sources in the colonial American setting that his historical romances often depict, friendships between Americans and foreigners took on particular significance during the early national period when Cooper first emerged as a novelist. Following the War of 1812 and the Transcontinental Treaty of 1819, Americans sought to establish new policies articulating the nation's relation to Europe, such as the Monroe Doctrine of 1823, which warned against European interference in North and South America. Cooper proves an important figure for examining the America of the 1820s because his work reflects a profound engagement with the interrelationship of domestic and foreign politics. In novels such as *The Pilot; A Tale of the Sea* (1823) and

Literature in the Early American Republic: Annual Studies on Cooper and His Contemporaries
Volume 6, 2014. Copyright © 2014 by AMS Press, Inc. All rights reserved.

The Prairie: A Tale (1827), Cooper responds to anxieties about foreign influence by asserting that the nation is capable of navigating affiliations with an array of peoples, even profiting from such relationships, while preserving its recently established independence.

In Cooper's work, friendship provides readers with a metonym for international affiliations. The affinities that emerge in his novels consistently define Americans through their encounters with the foreign. Notably, friendship was a popular trope of literature in the early national period, often used to consider what connects the members of a society or nation. For example, Hannah Foster's *The Coquette* (1797) is told largely through the exchange of letters among friends. The protagonist's correspondence links her to a social sphere as she shares her opinions and receives advice from loved ones. Her friendships prove so intimate that she fears any other attachment will interrupt them, declaring, "Marriage is the tomb of friendship."[2] Likewise, Catharine Maria Sedgwick imagines powerful friendships, representing these relationships as a motive for heroic self-sacrifice in *Hope Leslie, or Early Times in Massachusetts* (1827). She envisions friends so strongly sympathetic that they relinquish their lovers and risk death for one another. Numerous other writers, such as Lydia Maria Child, Susan Warner, and Frederick Douglass, explore how friendships help incorporate individuals into the nation and motivate them to act in their shared interests.[3] Cooper's portraits of international friendships contribute to this broader body of literature by suggesting that similarly powerful affinities can unite foreign peoples into an international community and by exploring how such attachments could further the nation.

By engaging the trope of friendship, Cooper and his contemporaries drew on its well-established political significance. Enlightenment philosophers had theorized that, in emergent republics, the bonds between fellow citizens would function as friendships and thereby foster a sense of connection to the country in the absence of feudal bonds. Adam Smith defined friendship as "a natural sympathy, from an involuntary feeling that the persons to whom we attach ourselves are the natural and proper objects of esteem and approbation." He argued that sympathy depends upon moral judgment: we must approve of others' feelings as the appropriate response to a given experience in order to feel they are worthy of friendship. In a similar vein, David Hume argued that elective affiliations are the result of "a certain sympathy which always arises betwixt similar characters."[4] As recent historical and literary studies suggest, early Americans also understood friendship as based in sympathy stemming from a strong sense of resemblance. Men and women of the same class, education, and faith developed affinities for one another that were thought to inspire republican virtue by uniting meritorious citizens and encouraging them to act in the broader national interest.[5] As a double who could not be conflated with the self, the friend served two primary functions essential to the nation: he affirmed one's own value and fostered one's sympathetic connection to the larger world.[6] Cooper's fictional friendships operate along parallel lines—his characters' sympathy for one another demonstrates their moral approval of each other—while asserting that such shared traits could also foster a sense of similarity and equality across national divisions. His portraits of European Americans' relationships with the British and Native Americans presume that these friends share the same disposition and virtues.

In addition to illuminating interconnections between the domestic and the foreign, Cooper's depictions of friendship further our understanding of the role that sympathy played in defining the nation. While a long line of theorists have explored how feeling connects citizens to one another and thereby creates a cohesive nation, Cooper represents international sympathy as central to America's development.[7] In other words, he imagines that his American characters' ability to feel for and enter into the experiences of foreign peoples help them to perceive their common global interests. My point here is not that Cooper's emphasis on sympathy for foreigners is inherently progressive. Indeed, critical debates about Cooper's representations of relationships between European American and Native American characters (whom, regrettably, he often depicts as "foreign") remain contentious: these relations are interpreted either as a failure to acknowledge how Americans violently dispossessed Natives of their lands or as a means to decry this very loss.[9] Nonetheless, such friendships between disparate peoples—including American and British characters such as *The Pilot*'s Manual and Bourroughcliffe, as well as Native American and European American characters such as

The Prairie's Hard-Heart and Natty—suggest an alternative to the historical violence of cross-cultural encounter. Given that Cooper is often identified as a father of American literature and literary nationalism, it is important to understand that his narratives express complex desires for both national power and egalitarian affiliation. Even as these texts can prove troubling justifications of violence, they also acknowledge the value of foreign cultures.

Cooper's faith in Americans' capacity to benefit from and contribute to international alliances informs his letters and pamphlets, as well as his travel narratives on Europe and America.[9] For example, in a pamphlet on the French finance controversy in 1831, Cooper explicitly advocates for republican government in France while hazarding the attacks of those who believe that republicanism should not be exported to Europe or that America should influence the spread of reform only by example.[10] Notably, he frames his participation in these debates as an attempt to support the position of his friend General Lafayette. Elsewhere he describes the influence of their transatlantic friendship, writing that it motivated Cooper's involvement in French and Polish revolutions and provided him with insight into foreign cultures that he used to critique the United States.[11] This is not to say that his novels fictionalize his own relationships, but rather that Cooper consistently evinces a belief that nationalism goes hand in hand with foreign affiliations and should never be merely isolationist. His representation of friendships across borders are worth exploring in order to understand how literary tropes could be used to reimagine Americans' global role.

1.

The Pilot and *The Prairie* prove useful examples for examining what Cooper believed connected the nation to other peoples and what it could gain from foreign affiliation. Though these novels are rarely considered in relation to each other, they share an engagement with global sympathy. *The Pilot* recounts fictional battles of the Revolutionary War and imagines how this conflict forged new relations between Britain and America. No longer the children of the British, but rather their potential friends and equals, Cooper's Americans assert their political independence while retaining a basis for affiliation with Europeans. *The Prairie* takes place in newly acquired US territories where a network of friendships emerges as national expansion brings new groups into contact. Cooper imagines how such interactions can cultivate respect for cultural differences, which the novel suggests is important to both national expansion and foreign relations. This perspective allows some groups, namely, the former Spanish colonists, to be subsumed into the nation, whereas other peoples, such as the Pawnee Loup, preserve their difference even as they form affiliations with Americans. Finally, as a point of contrast, I turn to *The Deerslayer or, The First War-Path* (1841), which offers a grimmer, more violent portrait of cross-cultural encounter during the French and Indian War while nonetheless conveying the value of sympathy through the famous friendship between Natty Bumppo and Chingachgook. The pattern of international friendship that emerges from the earlier texts suggests that a history of cross-cultural encounter provides Americans with the basis to participate in the global sphere: to continue expanding, building trade routes, and forming military and economic alliances. Thus, if we conceive of nations as dependent upon "a rich legacy of memories" and "a heroic past," as Ernest Renan argues, Cooper contributes to the development of the US nation through his representations of Americans successfully navigating global conflicts and alliances.[12]

The Pilot's depiction of international relations insists that individuals' sympathies can transcend national borders, even as the novel notes the potential for such relationships to cause ruptures in the nation. The plot centers on Barnstable and Griffith, two Americans fighting for independence as they court the cousins Katherine and Cecilia. The courtship has been interrupted by the Revolutionary War, which prompted the young women's guardian, the Tory Colonel Howard, to remove them from America and to forbid these revolutionaries' pursuit of his wards. Barnstable and Griffith follow their love interests to England, where the men are allied with John Paul Jones (disguised as "Mr. Gray"), who spearheads a mission to capture various British lords. Jones, like Barnstable and Griffith, encounters an old love interest in England, Alice Dunscombe. However, his participation in the Revolution ultimately keeps the two from reconciling. Though the military mission fails, Barnstable, Griffith, and Jones break down

Howard's defense of his estate and win sea battles against the British. Howard dies near the end of the novel, blessing his wards' marriages and conceding that the American Revolution may be just. While this narrative is primarily concerned with reconciling divisions between Americans, namely, between loyalists and patriots, it simultaneously reconsiders the relationship between Britain and America, concluding with a sentimental vision of an American-British friendship that evokes a sense of national equality.[13]

Cooper shows that establishing affiliations outside of the nation can be quite costly, as Jones's simultaneous ties to the American Revolution and a British past, including his love interest, come into conflict. Indeed, Alice insists that one's national loyalties and personal affections are intimately connected. As she laments Jones's support for the American Revolution, she conflates his betrayal of his nation with his relinquishment of love for her and God, proclaiming, "Are not the relations of domestic life of God's establishing, and have not the nations grown from families, as branches spread from the stem, till the tree overshadows the land! 'Tis an ancient and sacred tie that binds man to his nation, neither can it be severed without infamy."[14] Alice expresses an important conception of nationalism—based on the belief that the nation develops from the family—that conveys the centrality of personal relationships to larger political and religious structures. This becomes a problem when Jones proves more willing to support the American cause for independence than to fight for the nation of his birth; he sees her sense of loyalty as too narrow. Her insistence that nation and family are one therefore precludes the possibility for Jones to ally himself with America while retaining a sense of familial connection to Britain by rekindling his relationship with her. Alice's arguments do not win Jones back to Britain's side. Still, they resonate with recurring themes in Cooper's fiction, which often links the nation to the family by representing happy marriages as the foundation for a flourishing national future. For instance, Barnstable's marriage to Katherine and Griffith's marriage to Cecilia evoke a sense of optimism for America at *The Pilot*'s conclusion, as these women support their husbands, who construct the new republic.

Though Cooper's novels often suggest that familial ties, including those of marriage, should be of a piece with one's national loyalties,

The Pilot evokes the possibility for ties of friendship to extend beyond the nation. Over the course of the novel, an international friendship develops between two of the novel's minor characters: the British Major Borroughcliffe and the American Captain Manual. Their relationship offers insight into Cooper's understanding of what constitutes the bases and benefits of such an affiliation. Through this friendship, Cooper revises the parent-child metaphors so often used to describe the hierarchical relationship between Britain and America in the eighteenth century, and which Cooper earlier invokes by setting the youthful rebels in opposition to the elderly loyalist Howard. The British-American friendship instead imagines the two nations linked by amiable equality, though Borroughcliffe and Manual first meet while fighting on opposing sides of the war. Their encounters—in which the Americans' mission is defeated, even as they best the British at sea—suggest that military prowess renders the Americans and British equals. Moreover, these scenes create a shared history between the two men; in the words of Borroughcliffe, "[W]e have drank together, and we have fought; surely there is nothing now to prevent our being sworn friends!" (372). Notably, Cooper transforms the Revolution into the basis for new affiliations. The effect is twofold: first, suggesting that the foundations for future relations are laid not just in a history of British imperialism, but also in the meeting of equals on the battlefield, and, second, establishing that this violent past need not produce suspicion and anxiety, as its conflicts have been resolved.

The novel's concluding chapters, which function like an epilogue, extend the transatlantic friendship well beyond the Revolution. When Manual and Borroughcliffe assume adjacent posts at forts along the Saint Lawrence a decade later, Cooper writes that, to facilitate the friendship, "a log cabin was erected on one of the islands in the river, as a sort of neutral territory, where their feastings and revels might be held without any scandal to the discipline of their respective garrisons" (421). The creation of neutral territory frees their friendship from the formal strictures of their official, national roles. Nevertheless, it also reinforces the sense that these men's similar stations, what Cooper refers to as their "mutual situations" (421), afford them an equality that, along with their shared military experience, provides a basis for their relationship. Manual and Borroughcliffe can create a neutral space of affiliation because each holds authority within a national military force from which he can separate himself *temporarily*.

This relationship suggests a new equality between the two nations' military might, but does not eliminate the possibility for conflict between the British and the Americans. Cooper writes, "In this manner year and year rolled by, the most perfect harmony existing between the two posts, notwithstanding the angry passions that disturbed their respective countries" (422). While the "angry passions" go unexplained, the men's amity expands outward via synecdoche, so that their feelings for each other come to characterize their garrisons. This moment is striking given that scholars often note Cooper's critical distance from England, especially during the 1820s and 1830s.[15] The scene suggests that such friendship, though not the predominate feeling between the English and Americans at the turn of the century, might nonetheless prove influential. Borroughcliffe and Manual's relationship implies that the American characters and their nation have overcome the Revolution's uncertainties by establishing enforceable national borders and creating the possibility for neutral territory beyond them. Both sweet and comic, their friendship comes to resemble a marriage without threatening their national loyalties.

Their affection lasts until Manual's death, which is followed shortly thereafter by Borroughcliffe's. The nearly synchronized deaths again suggest the men's equivalence, and the two bachelors are buried side by side, evoking a continuation of their friendship in the afterlife. This friendship provides a corrective model to the events of 1812 that threatened such affiliation through contestations over national borders, including that between the United States and Canada. The two men are able to protect this national division while participating in exchanges through simple forms, such as using their national trade routes to share their favorite malts and wines. Cooper's faith in the potential for such affiliation is notable given the anxiety many of his contemporaries expressed about the relation between America and Europe.

The Pilot does reflect concerns about the influence of foreign empires; in particular, Cooper employs the friendship forged between the American patriot Griffith and John Paul Jones to delimit the sway of the British Empire and express an ardent US nationalism. Griffith and Jones's affinity proves critical to America's future; as an ally, Jones works toward the larger cause of the Revolution, resolves the conflict between Griffith and Barnstable, and helps promote marriages that represent the nation's future. Surprisingly, though, the British rebel offers a model of what Americans should *not* become. Even as he is an important figure of international friendship, Jones is the subject of criticism for his very support of the Americans. Griffith's final remarks about Jones attribute his courageous participation in the war, as well as his desire to have the secret of his name preserved, largely to his "desire of distinction," a "foible" (426) of character likely shaped by his imperfect education. Through Griffith's characterization of Jones, Cooper balances his depiction of foreign contributions to the Revolutionary War with a sense of US exceptionalism. A more celebratory depiction of the British hero would risk the possibility of his usurping all credit for Americans' independence. Instead, Griffith's criticism implies that America possesses a special ability to foster selfless patriotism. This view distinguishes the nation from Britain and explains why Cooper's American characters are able to reconcile the potential conflicts between their personal and national allegiance, unlike Jones, who remains permanently estranged from Alice and Britain. Thus, while British influence proves essential to the plot, John Paul Jones does not dominate the narrative of America's national origins; the novel's concluding marriages redirect readers' attention to the nation's future and its new leaders.

Friendship's function in *The Pilot*—expressing equality between America and Britain at the moment of national independence—elucidates why the trope was of particular interest during the early national period. As Caleb Crain argues, the language of friendship allowed Americans to express identities as equals within a republic, equals capable of forming sympathetic attachments that would clarify their new political and social relations to each other.[16] Attending to transatlantic sympathies reveals that the figure of the friend also offered important reassurance that Americans could assess foreign peoples, could determine who would become America's political allies and who would share their national and global concerns. Moreover, this language conveys confidence that America could form such affiliations without being subsumed into a foreign empire.

Cooper's *The Prairie*, published four years later in 1827 and set just after the Louisiana Purchase, shifts the focus to friendships that form within the context of national expansion. Here, friendship appears all the more central to America's future because Cooper thoroughly integrates foreign affinities with domestic marriages, thus representing intranational relations as dependent upon international affiliations. The novel opens with a general description of settlers' rapid entrance into newly acquired American territories, which is then exemplified by the Bush family's journey onto the prairie. In this frontier context, individuals' loyalties quickly become suspect, and the novel follows the conflict between three parties: the Bush family of settlers, the Sioux, and an international band that forms around Cooper's famous protagonist, Natty Bumppo. Natty's band includes two young men, Duncan Uncas Middleton and Paul Hover, following the settlers in order to recover their love interests: Inez Middleton and Ellen Wade. Inez—a Spanish aristocrat—is the captive of Abiram White (brother of the Bush matriarch), who plans to sell her. She eventually flees her captors with their niece Ellen. The two women join their friends, and this group is aided in their escape by Hard-Heart, a Pawnee Loup chief. Conflict intensifies as Ishmael and Esther Bush believe that Natty has killed their eldest son, in reality murdered by Abiram. Colluding with the settler family, the Sioux chief Mahtoree takes the band of friends captive; he threatens to kill some of the men and hopes to marry Inez and Ellen. Instead, Hard-Heart kills Mahtoree, evoking the importance of cross-cultural affiliations to protecting US interests. The Bush family recognizes Ellen's and Inez's rights to liberty, and all the European Americans except Natty return to the settlements. Natty alone chooses to remain on the prairie with the Pawnee tribe until his death. The reabsorption of characters into the settlements attests to the idea that the cross-cultural affiliations and conflicts occurring on the frontier in turn influence domestic relations.

Cooper foregrounds the Louisiana Purchase as the historic incident giving rise to the novel's plot and thematic concerns. This allows him to represent how expansion produced close relations between the young republic and foreign peoples, including former Spanish colonists and native tribes. *The Prairie* also calls attention to the centrality of marriage as a means of creating national coherence during this moment of expansion and exchange: "[S]ome little time was necessary to blend the discrepant elements of society. In attaining so desirable an end, woman was made to perform her accustomed and grateful office. The barriers of Prejudice and religion were broken through by the irresistible power of the Master Passion, and family unions, ere long, began to cement the political tie."[17] Here Cooper renders explicit the role that the marriage between the Protestant Middleton and Catholic Inez plays in representing a route to national unity. Notably, the band of sympathetic characters facilitates such marriage through their network of friendships, integrating Americans' foreign relations with their domestic future. Moreover, this alliance helps protect Inez against the unsought advances of Mahtoree, who is as enamored of her as both Middleton and Hard-Heart. Cooper thus insists that the nation's future is expansive enough to incorporate the Spanish/Creole woman through marriage, as well as Native allies such as Hard-Heart through friendship, but delimits such relations by refusing the possibility of a European American's marriage to a Native American.[18]

Though prior studies of male friendship on the frontier in Cooper's fiction often argue that he situates such homosocial relations in opposition to romantic, heterosexual relations, Cooper's early novels depict a productive connection between friendship and marriage that resonates with contemporary understandings of these relationships.[19] Both Richard Godbeer and Caleb Crain assert that, for nineteenth-century American men, sympathetic friendships could coexist with marriage; young men might help their friends court wives and then expand their homosocial attachments to include their families. Recognizing this conception of heterosexual and homosocial relations as mutually reinforcing draws attention to Cooper's integration of international friendships and domestic romance in *The Prairie*.[20]

Indeed, Cooper depicts a number of friendships—between Ellen and Inez, Paul and Middleton, and Natty and Hard-Heart—that connect characters to each other and the US nation. Their relationships are especially significant because the Bush family threatens Inez's national incorporation by kidnapping her at the moment of her marriage, when Cooper suggests she and other former Spanish colonials would be absorbed into the nation and benefit its future through their wealth. Instead, her captors move her outside of the settlements and the law, thus aligning her with the slaves commonly stolen by Abiram White.[21] By contrast, Inez's friendship with Ellen connects Inez to the settlements and reaffirms her elite social standing. Inez describes Ellen as "having shown so much commiseration and friendship" (173) because she provides the daily care of her companion and promises to live with Inez should the two escape. This promise evinces the women's mutual sympathy; their shared feeling sanctions Inez's marriage to Middleton by demonstrating that she fits into an American community, reducing the apparent difference created by her Creole heritage and Catholicism. While the relationship between these women is afforded relatively little space, it is critical in drawing both female characters into the future of the U.S. nation.

Duncan and Paul likewise rely on their friendship to strengthen their connections to American society. Collaborating in pursuit of their heterosexual relationships brings them together and helps draw Paul, a denizen of the frontier, into settler life (a choice that even Natty affirms).[22] Rather than valorizing an escape from society, Cooper celebrates Paul's and Duncan's contributions to the domestic government in the final chapters. Once returned to American society, the two European American men are differentiated by their class; they share a continued sense of goodwill, but it is marked by inequality, as Duncan confers "patronage" (376) on Paul. Though their friendship strengthens the nation, this relationship is limited to the frontier space where their merit—displayed in their pursuit of Ellen and Inez and their combat against various national enemies and outlaws—creates a temporary sense of equality. In other words, the site of foreign encounter fosters relations that are important to the nation, but that are altered by a return to the settlements.[23]

Perhaps the most significant frontier friendship in the novel is that between Natty and Hard-Heart. The two men play pivotal roles in protecting their band from danger, ensuring that the romantically inclined couples will help forge the national future. Natty and Hard-Heart's friendship is essential to this future because it prompts their collaboration in the interests of the larger group and the nation. Their relationship is based on a mutual respect for their shared capability in navigating warfare and thereby parallels the friendship between Manual and Borroughcliffe. When the Sioux capture the protagonists and Hard-Heart shows himself undaunted by physical pain, Natty declares, "[M]y heart yearns to you, boy, and gladly would I do you good" (278). Their growing affinity culminates in Hard-Heart's choice of Natty as his adoptive father, which attests to the significance of their relationship by associating their elective affinity with the naturalness and strength of bonds of kinship. Moreover, by suggesting that this affective connection results from the shared virtue of stoicism, Cooper evokes Enlightenment arguments about the qualities that inspire sympathy. This resonance suggests that Natty and Hard-Heart's relationship is an ideal friendship.[24] The two men evince the potential for cross-cultural encounters to produce strong attachments, one possible result of US expansion that *The Prairie* portrays amidst other, more violent effects, including the kidnapping of Inez and the deaths of the eldest Bush son and Mahtoree.

Natty and Hard-Heart's relationship models affinity across cultural (particularly, religious) difference. Even in his dying wishes, Natty insists he is distinct from the Pawnee by refusing their funerary customs in preference to Christian rites. Through his reflections on religion, a cosmopolitan perspective begins to emerge: "There is much to be said in favor of both religions, for each seems suited to its own people, and no doubt it was so intended" (382). His comparison of Pawnee and European American cultures suggests Natty's detachment from Christianity through his willingness to assess how its social function compares to that of Pawnee faith and to acknowledge the value of both belief systems. Natty evinces a respect for Pawnee culture on which his friendship with Hard-Heart depends. Their relationship thereby resembles the marriage between Inez and Middleton; though Cooper depicts the husband's Protestantism more sympathetically than the wife's Catholicism, Middleton comes to appreciate that he cannot challenge his wife's faith.[25] Indeed, her desire to convert him strengthens her initial attachment to him (159). While refusing the possibility that Middleton—an embodiment of the national future—will become Catholic, Cooper nevertheless suggests that the affection her faith fosters will benefit the nation. Through marriage to Inez, Middleton ties his "personal merit" (376) to wealth, thus gaining local and national influence. The same mutual respect acquired through and essential to foreign affiliation becomes useful to domestic relations in the context of expansion.

However, even as the elective father-son relation resembles this marriage, the friendship offers a key point of contrast; the greater difference between Natty's and Hard-Heart's faiths lessens the apparent difference within the Catholic and Protestant marriage and provides reassurance of the strength of their union. In *The Prairie*, tension emerges between the desirability of preserving cultural differences and the need to create a strong sense of national cohesion while incorporating new territory. Nonetheless, by creating characters who can maintain their sense of connection and a respect for difference, Cooper suggests that affiliation is as important to the nation as expansion and the assimilation of new citizens. He explores Americans' capacity to forge such relationships with dispossessed and oppressed peoples not only through Natty's relationships in The Leather-Stocking Tales, but also in friendships between European Americans and Africans in novels such as *The Red Rover: A Tale* (1827).

Cooper's characters and their relationships convey enthusiasm for America's participation in a global sphere and its potential influence on the nation and the larger world. Given this engagement in international politics, I suggest we regard Cooper as a "cosmopolitan patriot," to borrow Kwame Anthony Appiah's phrase. Appiah's work challenges the apparent opposition between patriotism and cosmopolitanism by asserting that citizens who love and take pride in the country may also be those who value difference and recognize the potential to be at home beyond the nation. Cooper exemplifies this idea, expressing an interest in drawing on cultural comparison to understand how Americans might improve their nation and the world. In doing so, he evinces both his national pride, through his desire to foster American greatness, and his willingness to move outside the nation to locate beneficial influences and models. In this respect, I build on J. Gerald Kennedy's argument that Cooper "wanted to develop a global (or at least transatlantic) perspective to surmount the parochial nationalism of his American contemporaries,"[26] in order to suggest that Cooper celebrates and hopes to advance his country through comparison and connection to the foreign.

Labeling Cooper a cosmopolitan does not recover his work from its association with imperial expansion and racial hierarchy. Indeed, cosmopolitanism has come under criticism for conferring authority on Western elites who possess the mobility to travel and acquire knowledge of other cultures. As David Simpson argues, there is a paradox in cosmopolitanism; while it is often understood "as respect for and interest in the other, the unknown," this definition "runs against the sense that what marks the cosmopolitan person is *already knowing* what needs to be known."[27] When the cosmopolitan presumes that he possesses greater knowledge than members of the foreign cultures he observes, this affords him a sense of authority to judge others' cultures, reinforcing cultural hierarchies. Indeed, Cooper's desire to spread republicanism, which suggests that Americans have a better understanding of government than the nations he hopes to influence, may evoke justifications for US imperialism. Likewise, *The Pilot*'s representation of Americans as the military equals of the British could be understood as expressing a desire for imperial power, even as the novel asserts the value of republican government.[28] Nonetheless, thinking of Cooper in terms of cosmopolitanism calls attention to the sense of connection to foreign peoples—his complex interests in emulating, influencing, and competing with other nations—that he expressed through his personal friendships, his political advocacy for US involvement in European reform, and his fictional narratives of friendship.

2.

The vitality of friendly sympathy in Cooper's novels from the 1820s becomes all the more apparent when we turn to a later moment in Cooper's career—his 1841 publication of *The Deerslayer*, the final volume in the Leather-Stocking Tales—in which a destructive, dehumanizing version of international encounter emerges.[29] In this narrative, conflict erupts among the French, British, and Native Americans, but it is not productive, as it was in the earlier novels. There is no successful European American marriage at the conclusion to promise the happiness of future generations. Nor does Cooper imagine a broader sense of amity emerging among the nations engaged in battle. However, friendship itself remains an ideal; as Natty insists, "[f]ri'ndship counts for something."[30] *The Deerslayer* celebrates his relationship with Chingachgook, which we might characterize as transnational, rather than international. Natty—while identifying as white and Christian—does not act on behalf of any nation in this novel. He is described as allied with the British (rather than one of them). Therefore, while Natty's friendships cross cultural and racial divisions, because he is not a national representative, these relationships do not evince Americans' ability to navigate foreign affiliations. Rather, Natty and Chingachgook's affinity for one another is exceptional in the novel, and the absence of similar bonds suggests the difficulty of maintaining sympathetic attachments within the context of America's violent history. *The Deerslayer* thus amplifies concerns Cooper's earlier novels raise about the risks of cross-cultural encounter in considering the effects of the conflict among the British, French, American colonists, and Native Americans.

Set on Lake Glimmerglass during the French and Indian War, *The Deerslayer* follows Natty in his efforts to help his Delaware friend Chingachgook free his love interest Wah-ta!-Wah from the "Hurons" or Wyandots who have captured her. Through his friendship with Harry March (or Hurry Harry), Natty becomes involved in protecting the Hutter family—the father, Thomas, and his ostensible daughters, Judith and Hetty—from Wyandot attacks and thereby becomes the subject of Judith's romantic interest. In a series of skirmishes, Natty kills a Wyandot. He acquits himself so well that the tribe condescends to offer him what is in their view "the honor" (473) of marrying the man's widow, the Sumach. However, Natty refuses to "take a wife, under red-skin forms" (472).[31] The conflict escalates as Harry kills a Wyandot woman and the Wyandots kill Thomas Hutter, who reveals on his deathbed that his daughters are adopted and illegitimate. At the novel's close, British troops arrive to defeat the Wyandots, thereby releasing Natty from his captivity and responsibility to protect the Hutters; faced with his impending departure, Judith proposes and is refused. Natty's choice of his "constant friend" over marriage to the ostensibly promiscuous Judith conveys his well-known desire for purity (546). Through this refusal, though, Cooper also critiques the lack of sympathy endemic to American society, which manifests itself in the novel's seductions and murders and finally destroys the fragmented, immoral Hutter family.[32] Cooper thus depicts the sympathy underlying Natty and Chingachgook's friendship as more contained and less contagious than in his earlier novels.

Cooper evokes in *The Deerslayer* the threat that cultural alliances will prove degenerative and spread barbaric forms of violence rather than elevate cultural accomplishments. This concern is most apparent in the question of who should scalp, which surfaces repeatedly in the Leather-Stocking Tales as Cooper interrogates patterns of cultural influence. The act seems diametrically opposed to sympathy because it is associated with taking both pleasure and profit in the death of a fellow human being. Indeed, Natty refuses to join Harry and Hutter's attempts to attack the Wyandot camp at night for easy scalping. Such callous treatment of human life—as something that can be casually taken and converted into revenue—stands in sharp contrast to the sentiment Natty displays when he comforts the first man he kills, Le Loup Cervier, as the Wyandot enemy dies. Nonetheless, Natty does express a desire to scalp that—contrary to Harry's and Hutter's mercenary motives—reveals Natty's strong sympathetic attachment to the Delaware. He admits it is a struggle not to participate in the Delaware traditions of scalping and boasting. After killing Le Loup Cervier, Natty reasons that "the wisest way is not to be boastful" while admitting, "I *should* like Chingachgook to know that I have'n't discredited the Delawares, or my training!" (126). Because of his moving affective response to Le Loup Cervier's death, we can see that Natty's impulse to scalp does not reflect callousness toward life. Rather, Natty's monologue demonstrates his ties to the Delaware while his resistance to this desire reflects his belief that what is acceptable for Native Americans is not for white men. He attempts to justify Native scalping practices by drawing on the language of "gifts," through which he repeatedly offers a rather confusing explanation of racial difference.[33] He thus simultaneously reinforces notions of savage natives and attempts to articulate what we might consider the stance of a cultural relativist.

By labeling scalping a Native American custom, Cooper could initially seem to suggest that frontier life infects American colonists with "savage" practices. Indeed, according to Natty, the cultural exchanges surrounding the practice of scalping threaten white men's identities. He explains his choice not to scalp his enemy by declaring that "not a farthing of such money shall cross my hand. White I was born, and white will I die; clinging to colour to the last, even though the King's Majesty, his governors, and all his councils, both at home and in the colonies, forget from what they come, and where they hope to go, and all for a little advantage in warfare" (125).[34] Whereas Harry distinguishes between Indians and white men based on what he perceives as the former's greater willingness to be scalped, Natty's definition of whiteness divides the races based on the forms of violence they practice, linking scalping to Native Americans and claiming skill with a gun for himself and whites as a whole. Such divisions can advance what Anthony Pagden describes as a stadial theory of civilization, wherein European Americans are at a more advanced and superior stage of development to justify colonial practices.[35] Strikingly though, Natty recognizes that his racial definitions crumble under the weight of white men's behavior, not because his sympathy compromises his identity by linking him to Native Americans—though his monologue about scalping raises this possibility—but because other European colonists lack sympathy for the Native Americans. It is, after all, Harry and Hutter who first advocate scalping in the novel, and Hutter's later death following his own scalping suggests that European Americans' perpetuation of unfeeling violence will be their undoing.

Further, the British and French armies' use of scalping to advance the war exacerbates cross-cultural and international violence and alters the practice of scalping. *The Deerslayer* assigns the European soldiers and kings responsibility for promoting this ostensibly native custom by repeatedly noting that they pay for scalps. For instance, when the Wyandots have Thomas Hutter and Hurry Harry captive, Natty is surprised to learn that they will be scalped rather than returned to the Wyandot lodges. A Wyandot boy explains, "Wigwam full, and scalps sell high. Small scalp, much gold" (231). In this example, cultural exchange is threatening because it inspires mercenary violence. The Europeans' destructive war policy threatens to turn human bodies into money and makes financially expedient the utter lack of sympathy that characters such as Harry experience toward Native Americans.

The depictions of European Americans' attempts to scalp Native women, rather than warriors, foreshadow the novel's final, gory battle; when a British regiment arrives to defeat the Wyandots, the soldiers save Cooper's protagonists only at the price of accidentally killing Hetty, whose status as a "*non compis mentis*" has ensured her safety from the Wyandots throughout the novel. As the treatment of women was often viewed as a measure of a people's degree of civilization, Hetty's death undermines European American claims to superiority.[36] Indeed, Cooper writes, "The scene that succeeded was one of those, of which so many have occurred in our own times, in which neither age nor sex forms an exemption to the lot of a savage warfare" (522). The phrase "savage warfare" here refers to the British use of the bayonet and to American practices of violence in Cooper's own day.[37] It is this sense of savagery, I argue, that interrupts Cooper's earlier vision of American friendship expanding outward to encompass new peoples.

In the context of unfeeling violence, Natty's sympathy for Native Americans becomes the standard against which other characters may be measured. Early in the novel, he claims, "In a state of lawful warfare . . . it is a duty to keep down all compassionate feelin's" (50). Cooper often explores the problems of sympathy in battle; however, as the plot develops, Natty appears remarkable less for his ability to repress his compassion than for the fact that he possesses any compassion to repress. His sympathetic friendships, particularly with Chingachgook, provide him insight into the alterations that cultural contact creates and give the lie to Harry's claims that scalping Indians is equivalent to killing animals, toward which he is also unfeeling.[38] Natty's argument for preserving racial difference offers a way to make sense of cultural/racial differences, such as Native Americans' participation in scalping, without conceding to arguments that they are a lesser species. His often convoluted explanations of difference are radically limited in their persuasive appeal; he cannot stop his companions' various attempts on the lives of the Wyandots, alter their perceptions of Native Americans, or protect the European American women from friendly fire. Still, while *The Deerslayer* complicates the more optimistic representation of American friendship that emerges in Cooper's earlier writing, it continues to treat sympathetic friendships as an ideal, which allows Natty to recognize virtue within a wide swath of his characters. Cooper seems far from certain that such amicable relations characterized the past; nevertheless, he depicts them as essential to creating a "civilized" future for America.[39]

In part, the differences between *The Deerslayer* and earlier novels such as *The Prairie* and *The Pilot* speak to the changes Cooper had witnessed by the time he wrote the last of his Leather-Stocking novels. By the early 1840s, the Supreme Court and state law had consolidated the designation of Native American tribes as "domestic dependent nations," thus radically curtailing, if not entirely eliminating, their sovereignty and seemingly foreclosing the possibility of Native American assimilation. Though earlier texts such as *The Prairie* reflect the ongoing encroachment of Americans into Native lands, the Indian Removal Act—which formally sanctioned breaking a number of treaties with tribes—was not passed until 1830.[40] During the 1830s, Cooper had also observed America limiting its involvement in international alliances following France's July Revolution; Americans resisted supporting or interfering in the foreign nation's attempts at republican reform, despite the two nation's history of affiliation and affinity expressed in agreements such as the 1778 Treaty of Alliance and accompanying Treaty of Amity and Commerce. The Indian Removal Act and the American reaction to the July Revolution might seem quite disparate if we view the former as an act of aggression and the latter as act of neutrality or isolation. Nonetheless, in both instances, Americans refused to participate in the forms of international and cross-cultural affiliation that Cooper's novels laud. Thus, while all of Cooper's novels depict the potential for frontier violence, *The Deerslayer* offers the fullest sense of French and British influence on an American history of violence, in that it presents a genealogy of the violence for which the "age of Jackson" was known.[41] Whereas Cooper's novels from the 1820s evoke cosmopolitan patriotism, we might characterize his novels from the early 1840s as expressing "cosmopolitan despair," the phrase Hsuan Hsu uses to describe Herman Melville's novels. Much as Melville "exposes the inequalities and cultural violence that underlie the dissolution of national boundaries," Cooper acknowledges the cross-cultural violence of American colonial history.[42] This connection between Cooper's and Melville's work reminds us that the trope of international friendship circulated among antebellum authors who took up the question of what international affiliation could reveal about American culture.[43]

Moreover, Melville's representations of the failure of sympathy highlight Cooper's more mixed—and at times downright celebratory—response to the possibilities of affiliation. Cooper's recurring scenes of self-sacrificing friendship promise that there are alternatives to national violence. Therefore, while there are shifts in Cooper's writing over the course of his career, we should also consider the consistency with which he allows for the possibility of cross-cultural sympathy. Though the mordant narrative that emerges in *The Deerslayer* refuses to reconcile tensions between international friendships and national loyalties, it nonetheless has much in common with his earlier novels.

Both Cooper's more optimistic and his grimmer explorations of sympathy's capacity to transcend national divisions arise within his narratives of international conflict. For instance, *The Last of the Mohicans: A Narrative of 1757* (1826), perhaps his best-known novel today, explores how the transnational friendship between Natty and Chingachgook is strengthened through their collaboration amidst conflicts among the French, British, and Native Americans. The two men frequently display the importance of their attachment, whether on the trail of an enemy, in combat, or mourning over a grave. The contests at the center of this novel and so many of Cooper's historical romances not only create the possibility for cross-cultural contact but also foster potential ambiguities about the relationships between participants in these conflicts. Readers are encouraged to wonder whether characters will forge friendships or marriages that unite disparate peoples, whether they will develop political alliances, and even whether they will share the same afterlife. As Jonathan Lamb argues, "[S]ympathy thrives in situations of comparative powerlessness in which the function and tendency of social roles is no longer directly apparent to those who fill them."[44] Cooper's emphasis on sites of conflict and warfare allows him to respond to the shifting historical and social context of the colonial and early national periods. By insisting that Americans can develop strong affinities for foreign peoples and vice versa, Cooper picks up on the potential for such destabilizing moments to foster sympathy and then employs feeling to reconsider international relations.

To return briefly to *The Pilot*, it is worth noting that, when Alice Dunscombe objects to John Paul Jones's choice to cut his ties with God, king, and family, she expresses concerns about the breakdown of loyalty that remained important to Americans in the 1820s. These issues would continue to trouble the United States during the nineteenth century, especially when sectional divisions grew into the Civil War.[45] The radical changes to social and political structures that threaten loyalty in turn render sympathy powerful, as Cooper suggests by imagining how Jones's mistreatment by Britain and subsequent loss of national loyalty allow him to be moved by sympathy for the American Revolutionaries. In this break from older, hierarchical social structures, individuals have the opportunity to redefine their relations to the world by forging elective affinities with their equals. Cooper's fiction participates in the larger process of reconceptualizing these relationships by exploring Americans' friendships with a range of foreigners. His novels illuminate how the broader nineteenth-century literary archive and the tropes of friendship that emerge throughout it speak to Americans' aspirations, fantasies, and anxieties regarding the nation's emergent connections to and influence on the world.

NOTES

I would like to thank Robert Levine and the anonymous readers of *LEAR* for their generous comments on earlier drafts of this essay.

1. See Fiedler, *Love and Death*, and Schweitzer, *Perfecting Friendship*.

2. Foster, *The Coquette*, 24.

3. See, e.g., Child's *Hobomok* (1824), Warner's *The Wide, Wide World* (1850), and Douglass's *The Heroic Slave* (1853).

4. Smith, *Theory of Moral Sentiments* (1759), 265; Hume, *Treatise of Human Nature* (1740), 403.

5. See Crain's *American Sympathy*; Godbeer's *Overflowing of Friendship*; and Schweitzer's *Perfecting Friendship*.

6. See Schweitzer, *Perfecting Friendship*.

7. For example, Smith's *Theory of Moral Sentiments* is often cited for its exploration of the relation between sympathy and the nation (though he briefly considers the extent to which sympathy can exist between nations). Centuries later, theorists of nationalism remain interested in the mechanisms that inspire a sense of fellow feeling among citizens, as in Benedict Anderson's *Imagined Communities*.

8. Schweitzer, for instance, reads Cooper's narratives of amicable relationships as justifying European American land appropriation; she argues in *Perfecting Friendship* that

Cooper imagines these lands as a kind of inheritance bequeathed by a dying people to a more advanced civilization. By contrast, Barbara Alice Mann challenges the association of Cooper with racism by emphasizing that many of his contemporaries criticized his fiction as overly sympathetic to Native Americans; see Mann, "Race Traitor."

9. See Cooper, *Gleanings in Europe: England* (1837) and *Notions of the Americans* (1824).

10. Cooper, *Letter to Gen. Lafayette.* Anne C. Loveland discusses the tension between Cooper's vision of American influence in spreading democracy and those who saw democracy as particularly suited to America in "James Fenimore Cooper and the American Mission." The Monroe Doctrine of 1823 also speaks to the arguments against American intervention in Europe; as Daniel Walker Howe writes, "[I]n a gesture of reciprocal isolationism the United States resolved that it would not intervene in European wars or 'internal concerns'" (*What Hath God Wrought?*, 115).

11. See Cooper, *Gleanings in Europe: France* (1837).

12. Renan, "What Is a Nation?," 19.

13. James Crane briefly comments on Manual and Borroughcliffe's friendship in "Love and Merit in the Maritime Historical Novel." However, he interprets the American-British relationship as part of Cooper's larger emphasis on the value of the US republic, which he suggests wins out over the Old World traditions. By contrast, I assert that Cooper establishes Americans as the equals of the British, with whom Americans can engage in productive exchange.

14. Cooper, *The Pilot*; 151. Subsequent references to this edition will appear parenthetically in the text.

15. See Person, "Cooper, 1789–1851," and Franklin, *Cooper: The Early Years.*

16. Crain writes, "[A]s a metaphor and model for citizenly love, romantic friendship was more congenial to republican ideology than either filial or marital relationships. Romantic friendship was egalitarian. It could bind men without curtailing their liberty" (*American Sympathy*, 5).

17. Cooper, *The Prairie*, 156. Subsequent references to this edition will appear parenthetically in the text.

18. Rebecca Lush offers an extended analysis of how Inez functions as a site of desire through which Cooper can define the nation's racial and cultural borders. As she notes, while Cooper does not always deny the possibility of intermarriage, neither does he imagine a happy and productive union between European Americans and Native Americans in his novels; see Lush, "'Louisianian Lady.'"

19. Fiedler describes Natty and Chingachgook's friendship as "the pure marriage of males—sexless and holy, a kind of counter-matrimony, in which the white refugee from society and the dark-skinned primitive are joined till death do them part" (*Love and Death*, 211).

20. See Crain, *American Sympathy*, and Godbeer, *Overflowing of Friendship.* Mann's examination of Jane Austen's influence on Cooper has pointed the way for this analysis, attesting that his fiction likewise affords considerable importance to sisterly relationships, including female friendships. Mann thereby challenges the misconception that Cooper's most significant writing is about men's relationships that are predicated upon the exclusion of women in her "Aunt Jane and Father Fenimore."

21. Cooper foregrounds the connection between Inez and slaves, depicting a criminal who steals slaves to resell them as also selling Middleton knowledge of Inez's whereabouts. In effect, she has become part of the system of slave trade and theft.

22. Natty asserts that it is Paul's duty to consider his betrothed's preference for life within the settlements, despite his preferences for the frontier.

23. Dana Nelson reads the absence of white male friendship in Cooper's fiction as a reflection of the economic pressures placing men in competition in "Cooper's Leatherstocking Conversations." Here, though, the frontier permits new relations through an escape, not from intraclass competition, but from class divisions.

24. Jonathan Lamb notes that stoicism was "a topos in primitivism," used by Michael de Montaigne and Gottfried Wilhelm von Leibniz, as well as by Adam Smith, and that, for Smith in particular, "such stoicism in the face of painful death is the primary qualification for sympathy among civilized people" (*Evolution of Sympathy*, 71).

25. Specifically, Cooper suggests that Inez's priest opportunistically uses her disappearance "in the impending warfare of faith" (162) rather than responding sympathetically and heroically, like Middleton.

26. See Appiah, "Cosmopolitan Patriots"; Kennedy, "Cooper's Quarrel with America," 92.

27. Simpson, "Limits of Cosmopolitanism," 54.

28. Some critics contest the association of Cooper's work with inclusiveness and respect for difference, instead arguing that he naturalizes the displacement of Native Americans and that he expresses nativist fears about immigration. See Person, "Historical Paradoxes," and Gladsky, "Cooper and American Nativism."

29. Critics who argue that Cooper presents a bleak vision of America often draw on his later works, including the last two volumes of the Leather-Stocking Tales. It is the considerable attention to this series and Natty's role within it that has led scholars such as Fiedler to argue that Cooper depicts ideal friendship as something that can exist only in an escape from society and marriage.

30. Cooper, *The Deerslayer*, 273. Subsequent references to this edition will appear parenthetically in the text.

31. Cooper acknowledges that the practice of allowing a captive and enemy to marry into the tribe was "by no means unusual among the Indians." However, he suggests that the Wyandots view this instance of the practice as conferring an honor on Natty because he is "a pale face" (473).

32. Juliet Shields, in "Savage and Scottish Masculinity," reads Natty's refusal of Judith as reflecting his lack of sentiment. However, it is more appropriate to attribute the failure of feeling to those men who attempt to seduce Judith. They fail to show any concern for their effect on her. Indeed, her lover, Captain Warley, remarks near the close of the novel, "I do suppose there *are* women in the colonies, that a captain of Light Infantry need not disdain" (525), his supposition attesting that he has yet to meet a colonial woman he does not disdain. Therefore, I argue that Cooper represents a lack of sympathy as a problem, not particular to the frontier, but characteristic of European American civilization.

33. Natty's understanding of racial difference is often hard to pin down, as he alternately attributes the differences he observes to nature and habits or learned custom through his use of the unstable term "gifts." For instance, he refers to the "gifts" belonging to his "religion and colour" as opposed to "ways that God intended for another race" (85–86), but later in the novel asserts that "gifts come of sarcumstances" (439). Yet what remains consistent is his apparent certainty that some difference is to be expected and accepted across racial/national identities.

34. Mann offers an overview of British and American policies regarding scalping both during and after the French and Indian War that suggests Natty's criticism of the governors and kings echoes eighteenth-century responses to policies and practices. Mann writes of British Lieutenant-Governor Henry Hamilton ("The Famous Hair Buyer General") that "Hamilton was widely reviled by Americans for offering scalp bounties, and he did collect and forward scalps to headquarters, but it was Governor Frederick Haldiman who authorized paying scalp bounties and the Crown that ultimately authorized the policy of providing scalp bounties" (*Washington's War on Native America*, 115). Cooper reminds us, through Natty's protest, that the highest levels of European government were implicated in the violence of scalping.

35. See Pagden's *European Encounters with the New World.*

36. Shields, "Savage and Scottish Masculinity," 145.

37. Cooper's direct condemnation of British and American "savagery" sets *The Deerslayer* apart from even those earlier texts such as *The Last of the Mohicans* (1826) that represent considerable violence, for these earlier texts emphasize the moral failings of the French above and beyond those of the British. Magua does criticize the British treatment of Native Americans; he blames them for Native Americans' use of alcohol and therefore labels Colonel Munro a hypocrite for publicly whipping him as punishment for drunkenness. Nonetheless, we do not see the same degree of British participation in violence against the undefended in *The Last of the Mohicans* as in *The Deerslayer*. This distinction supports my larger argument that there is a shift between Cooper's representations of international relations in the 1820s and the 1840s.

38. Various contemporary accounts of European American raids on Native Americans record similar attitudes, and note that the conflation of Native Americans and animals became a frequent justification for casual acts of violence. For example, John Heckwelder's *Narrative of the Mission of the United Brethern* (1820) records that settlers around the Ohio River "would rove through the country in search of land, either to settle on, or for speculation; and some, careless of watching over their conduct, or destitute of both honour and humanity, would join a rabble, (a class of people generally met on the frontiers) who maintained, that to kill an Indian, was the same as killing a bear or a buffalo, and would fire on Indians that came across them by the way" (130). Heckwelder records how a collapse of the distinctions between the human and the animal was used to justify violence; this resembles the attitudes we see Hurry Harry express. Like Cooper, Heckwelder condemns this attitude as inhumane.

39. While Nelson similarly argues that Cooper depicts interracial friendships as an important site of fellow feeling, she suggests that, "[f]or Cooper, there is seemingly no such public agenda [as there is for Harriet Beecher Stowe]: for him, interracial feeling does certainly change and define individual people, but he does not explicitly

engage it to change national destiny by showing us characters using it to influence political outcomes" ("Cooper's Leatherstocking Conversations," 143). I build on this assertion to argue that Cooper is demonstrating the limits of friendship's ability to effect change in an unfeeling culture.

40. Indian Removal, as Howe argues, constituted a more formal, federal stance on the long-held debates about whether Native American tribes could remain sovereign or assimilate into the nation by denying federal protection to those who remained and thereby denying them access to the vast bulk of rights afforded white citizens in places such as Georgia (*What Hath God Wrought?*, 348).

41. Ibid., 411.

42. Hsu, *Geography*, 155.

43. For instance, see Melville's depictions of interracial and international friendship in *Moby-Dick; or The Whale* (1851) and *Typee: A Peep at Polynesian Life* (1846).

44. Lamb, *Evolution of Sympathy*, 1.

45. See Duquette, *Loyalty*.

BIBLIOGRAPHY

Anderson, Benedict. *Imagined Communities: Reflections on the Origin and Spread of Nationalism*. New York: Verso, 1983.

Appiah, Anthony. "Cosmopolitan Patriots." In *Cosmopolitics: Thinking and Feeling beyond the Nation*, edited by Pheng Cheah and Bruce Robbins, 91–114. Minneapolis: University of Minnesota Press, 1998.

Child, Lydia Maria. *Hobomok*. Edited by Carolyn Karcher. New Brunswick: Rutgers University Press, 1986. Kindle book.

Cooper, James Fenimore. *The Deerslayer or, The First War-Path*. Historical introduction and explanatory notes by James Franklin Beard; text established by Lance Schachterle, Kent Ljungquist, and James Kilby. Albany: State University of New York Press, 1987.

———. *Gleanings in Europe: England*. Historical introduction and explanatory notes by Donald A. Ringe and Kenneth W. Stange; text established by James P. Elliott, Kenneth W. Staffs, and R. D. Madison. Albany: State University of New York Press, 1982.

———. *Gleanings in Europe: France*. Historical introduction and explanatory notes by Thomas Philbrick; text established by Thomas Philbrick and Constance Ayers Denne. Albany: State University of New York Press, 1983.

———. *The Last of the Mohicans: A Narrative of 1757*. Historical introduction by James Franklin Beard; text established with explanatory notes by James A. Sappenfeld and E. N. Feltskog. Albany: State University of New York Press, 1983.

———. *Letter to Gen. Lafayette*. Edited by Robert E. Spiller. New York: Columbia University Press, 1931.

———. *Notions of the Americans: Picked up by a Traveling Bachelor*. Text established with historical introduction and textual notes by Gary Williams. Albany: State University of New York Press, 1991.

———. *The Pilot: A Tale of the Sea*. Edited with historical introduction and explanatory notes by Kay Semour House. Albany: State University of New York Press, 1986.

———. *The Prairie: A Tale*. Edited with historical introduction by James P. Elliott. Albany: State University of New York Press, 1985.

Crain, Caleb. *American Sympathy: Men, Friendship, and Literature in the New Nation*. New Haven, CT: Yale University Press, 2001.

Crane, James. "Love and Merit in the Maritime Historical Novel: Cooper and Scott." *Sullen Fires across the Atlantic: Essays in Transatlantic Romanticism*. Web. 25 April 2011.

Douglass, Frederick. *The Heroic Slave*. *Autographs for Freedom*. Edited by Julia Griffiths. Miami, FL: Mnemosyne, 1969.

Duquette, Elizabeth. *Loyalty: Bonds of Nation, Race, and Allegiance in Nineteenth-Century America*. New Brunswick, NJ: Rutgers University Press, 2010.

Fiedler, Leslie. *Love and Death in the American Novel*. Rev ed. New York: Stein and Day, 1966.

Foster, Hannah. *The Coquette*. Edited by Cathy Davidson. New York: Oxford University Press, 1987.

Franklin, Wayne. *James Fenimore Cooper: The Early Years*. New Haven, CT: Yale University Press, 2007.

Gladsky, Thomas. "James Fenimore Cooper and American Nativism." *Studies in the American Renaissance* (1994): 43–53.

Godbeer, Richard. *The Overflowing of Friendship: Love Between Men and the Creation of the American Republic*. Baltimore, MD: Johns Hopkins University Press, 2009.

Heckewelder, John. *A Narrative of the Mission of the United Brethren*. Philadelphia: McCarty and Davis, 1820. *GoogleBooks*.

Howe, Daniel Walker. *What Hath God Wrought?: The Transformation of America, 1815–1848*. New York: Oxford University Press, 2007.

Hsu, Hsuan. *Geography and the Production of Space in Nineteenth-Century American Literature*. New York: Cambridge University Press, 2010.

Hume, David. *A Treatise of Human Nature*. Edited by Ernest C. Mossner. New York: Penguin, 1969.

Kennedy, J. Gerald. "Cooper's Europe and His Quarrel with America." In Person, *Historical Guide*, 91–122.

———. "National Narrative and the Problem of an American Nationhood." In *A Companion to American Fiction 1780–1865*, edited by Shirley Samuels, 7–19. Malden: Blackwell, 2004.

Lamb, Jonathan. *The Evolution of Sympathy in the Long Eighteenth Century*. London: Pickering and Chatto, 2009.

Loveland, Anne C. "James Fenimore Cooper and the American Mission." *American Quarterly* 21.2 (1969): 244–58.

Lush, Rebecca. "'Louisianian Lady': Racial Ambiguity, Gender, and National Identity in Cooper's *The Prairie*." *Literature in the Early American Republic* 2 (2010): 153–71.

Mann, Barbara Alice. "Aunt Jane and Father Fenimore: The Influence of Jane Austen on James Fenimore Cooper." *Literature of the Early American Republic* 1 (2009): 221–53.

———. *George Washington's War on Native America.* Westport, CT: Praeger, 2005.

———. "Race Traitor: Cooper, His Critics, and Nineteenth-Century Literary Politics." In Person, *Historical Guide*, 155–85.

Melville, Herman. *Moby-Dick; or the Whale.* Edited by Andrew Delbanco. New York: Penguin, 2002.

———. *Typee: A Peep at Polynesian Life.* Edited by John Bryant. New York: Penguin, 1996.

Nelson, Dana. "Cooper's Leatherstocking Conversations: Identity, Friendship, and Democracy in the New Nation." In Person, *Historical Guide*, 123–54.

Pagden, Anthony. *European Encounters with the New World: from Renaissance to Romanticism.* New Haven, CT: Yale University Press, 1993.

Person, Leland S., ed. "James Fenimore Cooper, 1789–1851: A Brief Biography." In Person, *Historical Guide*, 27–57.

———. ed. *A Historical Guide to James Fenimore Cooper.* New York: Oxford University Press, 2007.

———. "The Historical Paradoxes of Manhood in Cooper's *The Deerslayer.*" *Novel* 32.1 (1998): 76–98.

Renan, Ernest. "What Is a Nation?" Trans. Martin Thom. In *Nation and Narration*, edited by Homi K. Bhabha, 8–22. New York: Routledge, 1994.

Schweitzer, Ivy. *Perfecting Friendship: Politics and Affiliation in Early American Literature.* Chapel Hill: University of North Carolina Press, 2006.

Sedgwick, Catharine Maria. *Hope Leslie, or Early Times in Massachusetts.* Edited by Carolyn Karcher. New York: Penguin, 1998.

Shields, Juliet. "Savage and Scottish Masculinity in *The Last of the Mohicans* and *The Prairie*: James Fenimore Cooper and the Diasporic Origins of American Identity." *Nineteenth-Century Literature* 64.2 (2009): 137–62.

Simpson, David. "The Limits of Cosmopolitanism and the Case for Translation." In *Transatlantic Literary Studies: A Reader*, edited by Susan Manning and Andrew Taylor, 53–57. Edinburgh: Edinburgh University Press, 2007.

Smith, Adam. *The Theory of Moral Sentiments.* New York: Penguin, 2010.

Warner, Susan. *The Wide Wide World.* New York: Feminist Press, 1987.

Cooper's Revision of Paradise Lost *and of Romantic Satanism in* The Last of the Mohicans

Donna Richardson
St. Mary's College of Maryland

INTERPRETERS have long recognized *Paradise Lost* (1667) as a source for *The Last of the Mohicans* (1826), but they have underestimated the complexity of the ways in which Cooper adapts this source, and therefore the sophistication of Cooper's commentary on the American version of the fall from Eden. Many have noted that Cooper compares his villain, the Huron warrior Magua, to "the Prince of Darkness brooding on his own fancied wrongs."[1] The only detailed analysis of Miltonic allusions in the novel, however, is a 1980 essay by Robert Milder, who concludes that Cooper "do[es] justice to the Indians' legitimate grievances against the white man, while at the same time affirming his belief in the superiority of white civilization." Milder argues that Cooper uses a Miltonic "unified pattern organized around the idea of a New World 'fall'" to create an uneasy apologetic for an American republic purportedly grounded in law, agrarianism, and a Christian ethic. According to Milder, Magua justifies his vengeance against the father of his captive, Cora, by relating a personal history that reflects "the vengeance of the Indian race against the white man," who is "wholly responsible for despoiling a New World paradise." Chingachgook, the "good Indian," relates with "passive resignation" nearly "the same story" of how Europeans have "corrupted the Indian through drink, driven the Indian from his lands, and hastened the process of genocide by entangling the Indian in his own European

Literature in the Early American Republic: Annual Studies on Cooper and His Contemporaries
Volume 6, 2014. Copyright © 2014 by AMS Press, Inc. All rights reserved.

quarrels." But by comparing Magua with Satan and Shylock, Cooper "presents the Indians' revenge as compromising their claims to justice and even survival."[2]

Many recent interpreters share Milder's conclusion that Cooper rationalizes white hegemony.[3] Milder's analysis, however, effectively demonstrates that Cooper is more insightful about the problems with European civilization than these interpreters suggest. In the manner of Geoffrey Rans, who argues that Cooper uses the romance genre only to show the problems with its ideals,[4] Milder argues that Cooper uses *Paradise Lost* to show how the Europeans have brought upon themselves a moral fall that compromises the Christian righteousness of any future American republic. For Milder, Hawk-eye is not a viable ethical alternative; Hawk-eye's insistence that he is "without a cross," while literally referring to his pride in unmixed ancestry, is also a pun implying that Hawk-eye is, according to Milder, "not a Christian" ethically, despite professing Christianity, in the sense that Hawk-eye acts according to the vengeful, "irredeemably pre-Christian" ethic of the Indians. As a representative of "Christian idealism," Cora is ineffectual in playing Portia to Magua's Shylock because she invokes Christian mercy for wrongs committed by her supposedly Christian culture.[5] Yet there is a contradiction built into Milder's construal of Cooper: If Cooper does use the Miltonic allusions in this way, he is guilty of sanctioning the very ideologies he criticizes. If Magua is in the position of Satan, then the Europeans he rebels against are in the position of God. The allusions would implicitly deify the Europeans who caused the fall and deny that Native Americans might present a positive alternative to, rather than merely an accusation of, European culture.

But Cooper's use of Miltonic allusions represents a more consistent and complex cultural analysis than Milder and recent critics recognize. In *Atlantic Double-Cross*, Robert Weisbuch argues that Cooper and other Americans are "friendly, even worshipful" in their relation to British forebears such as Milton, but "with the English Romantics," the Americans engage in a "complex, subtle argument similar in its revisionary rites to the argument those very English Romantics take up in relation to Milton."[6] While I agree with Weisbuch's latter point, I will argue that Cooper follows the English Romantics in revising Milton's ideas in addition to revising the Romantics themselves. A well-read man who later met Walter Scott, William Godwin, and Samuel Taylor Coleridge,[7] Cooper emulates their portrayal of satanic human characters who are more justified than Milton's Satan in rebelling against authority, especially when that authority is the imperfect will of other people. Rather than making Magua a satanic primitive who opposes a more advanced culture identified with Milton's God, Cooper casts him as a Romantic satanic rebel who, like Frankenstein's Creature, justly criticizes human authorities who have tried to play God and have thereby violated the very ideals of law, governance, and morality by which they justify their dominance. The plot supports Magua's indictment; the best institutional representatives of Europe, Munro and Montcalm, act as if with the authority of God but impose hypocritical laws and disrespect others' codes of justice, thus creating righteous anger in Native Americans that would require Christ-like self-sacrifice to redeem.

Cooper further follows the British Romantics in affirming that Milton's Christian ethic provides a necessary corrective to satanic rebellion, precisely because, in the absence of any sufficiently knowable divine authority, all sides in human conflicts deify their own values and demonize their opponents. In such conflicts as those of Prometheus with Jupiter, Caleb Williams with Falkland, Beatrice Cenci with her father, and Frankenstein with his Creature, neither side is entirely wise or righteous, yet each assumes either the authority of an affronted God or the self-righteous victimization of Satan—in fact, the opponents usually combine or switch these roles. Though these British writers range from Unitarians to atheists, they all imply that these mutually destructive foes should instead take on the role of Christ by recognizing their own fallibility, forgiving that of others, and finding what common ground exists in their values and experiences. Cooper, who is at the more traditionally Christian end of this spectrum, similarly suggests that more than one side in this complex conflict of nations is guilty of satanic accusation; while Magua makes Munro personally responsible for every European institutional flaw, Hawk-eye projects all the imperfections of man in a state of nature, including some of his own, onto Mingo imps and devils.

Although Magua and Hawk-eye try to demonize and resist some individual or group as embodying the unjust God or depraved devils who oppose them, neither they nor their opponents have the self-awareness to be sufficiently representative, responsible agents of the particular ideological forces in the American conflict. Cooper revises the discourse of Romantic satanism by dramatizing its operation on a more collective, intercultural level than appears in British Romantic works, in which the conflict, whether psychological, political, or mythic, is represented literally as a duel between at least potentially empowered subjectivities. Cooper suggests the collective version of satanic self-deification is ethnocentrism, which, like individual self-idolatry, is a universal failing affecting all cultures and which only appears more clearly in the state of nature that is the American wilderness. Individual characters who confront this ethnocentrism in themselves and others remain implicated in language practices, personal prejudices, and institutional injustices in ways they could never fully comprehend or control, particularly in cultural conflicts with more than two clearly defined opposing sides.

Cooper suggests that, to redeem this ideological fall, Christian self-sacrifice on a personal level is necessary but not sufficient; it is also necessary to respect the codes and practices of other cultures besides those of Europe and to integrate the values of all the cultures involved. This necessity is most evident when the Christian idealism Cora represents is put before a more legitimate tribunal than Magua to answer for wrongs done in the name of her values. As in several British Romantic works, a trial reinterprets Satan's temptation of Eve on a more human level; a satanic prosecutor manipulates an imperfect embodiment of institutional authority by demonizing the defendant and deploying his own hypocrisies against him, thereby tempting the defendant as well as the institution into becoming, or remaining, as self-deifying as himself. In Cooper's novel, the institutional authority has more legitimacy than the more traditional European ones in British Romantic works because it represents the practices of a group more sinned against than sinning—the relatively impartial and righteous judicial procedures of the neutral Delawares. But in this trial, Magua initially distorts the definition of justice by pandering to the victimization, as well as the ethnocentrism, felt by the Delawares and by demonizing all Europeans as gluttonous, bigoted, mercenary people without honor, thereby influencing Tamenund and the other

Delawares to discount all of Cora's pleas for mercy based on the more noble aspects of the European values she represents. The actions of the European men, including Hawk-eye, only confirm Magua's accusations. Cooper implies that justice to redeem this fall requires some individual who, unlike Hawkeye, is a man *with* a cross in two related figural senses—someone willing to bear the cross of self-sacrifice by being more fully cross-cultural, not only in personal relationships such as friendship and marriage but also by respecting the codes of justice in different cultures. Ironically, the character who comes closest to such redemption is Uncas—someone who is not "with a cross" in either literal sense (Christian or mixed race). His culturally impartial justice and his personal sacrifices create a model that does reconcile the Delaware people and that could motivate Cooper's readers to act on, rather than merely eulogize, the best aspects of the Native American culture he represents.

1. The British Romantic Reinterpretation of Milton

Milton's literary successors use his depiction of Satan to explore the psychology of individual human characters, but as belief in the authority and comprehensibility of Milton's God wanes during the eighteenth century, these characters evolve from sinners against a just God to representatives of and rebels against self-serving human constructions of authority.[8] Milton's Satan initially enriches the psychological· depiction of individual human villains, for example, Samuel Richardson's attractive and appalling seducer Lovelace in *Clarissa* (1748). But gothic novels soon begin to depict satanic human characters as villainous representatives of church and state, signifying that traditional institutions themselves are satanic insofar as they reflect their representatives' desire to play rather than to serve God. Romantics such as William Blake and Percy Shelley more fundamentally revalue Milton's Satan by intimating that humans have no Miltonic certainties but instead are born into a fallen state of perception wherein they become misguided and outcast for simply acting on their nature. Hence, their condition is more like that of Milton's Satan than of his Adam, and whatever ideologies of authority may be responsible for aggravating their fallen state deserve rebellion rather than obedience. In Godwin's *Caleb Williams* (1794), a model for *Frankenstein* and the poetry of Percy Shelley, this authority comprises two competing sociopolitical ideologies. Both the protagonist and his nemesis Falkland try to live by what each believes is the best ideal in his society (Enlightenment truth seeking and feudal chivalry, respectively). But these imperfect ideals fail them, first blinding them to their own weaknesses and making them vulnerable, then enabling them to become egomaniacal and criminal in self-defense. In more metaphysically-oriented Romantic works, the satanic characters' rebellion questions whether any religion sufficiently justifies the ways of God to man. In *The Rime of the Ancient Mariner* (1798), the Mariner, who is the prototype for many figures such as the characters in *Frankenstein* (1818), strikes back at the powers underlying nature because he initially experiences only the storm blasts of life, with their resulting psychic coldness and isolation, insufficiently mitigated by such small bits of love and hope as the companionship of the albatross. His incomplete redemption reveals a providential universe, but one that includes such uncertainties as the dice rolling that determines his fate. Lord Byron's heroes and Mary Shelley's Frankenstein blame the universe because they have acted on the best principles they could discover but have fallen irrevocably into disaster and criminality. Frankenstein's Creature sums up their experiences by turning on his imperfect creator and accusing him of his own crimes: "I ought to be thy Adam; but rather I am thy fallen angel, whom thou drivest from joy for no misdeed."[9]

But though they use a satanic character to interrogate Milton's theology, these authors, whose religious positions range from Unitarianism and pantheism to atheistic materialism, still retain some version of Milton's Christian ethic. Most British Romantic writers follow Coleridge in condemning satanic characters as egomaniacs who are all the more dangerous for such virtues as their steadfast will and resistance to pain or fear.[10] In the conflicts of Caleb Williams and Falkland, each thinks he is the righteous instrument of the best social ideal, and, like Frankenstein and his Creature, each alternately casts himself as an abused Satan and as a disrespected God. As I have argued elsewhere,[11] in Percy Shelley's *The Cenci* (1819), both Beatrice and her father similarly cast each other as Satan and themselves in different, but equally self-idolizing, images of God's power without God's love. From a more transhistorical perspective, even Percy Shelley's "type of the highest perfection of moral and intellectual nature," Prometheus, is, as Shelley says in his preface, more similar to Satan than to any other literary character.[12] Prometheus takes on the roles of a victimized Satan and a disobeyed God in his conflict with Jupiter, only to discover that in doing so he has adopted Jupiter's accusatory self-righteousness and cursed those he loves as well as himself.

These works suggest that when there is no sufficiently knowable divine truth or righteousness, it is all the more important that imperfect antagonists should act like Christ rather than like either Jehovah or Satan; they should admit error, forgive others' errors, love others' good intentions, and appreciate whatever common principles can be found in their respective ideals. Caleb Williams belatedly comes to this realization in the trial that ends the novel (in the more positive of the alternative endings). The Ancient Mariner finds some redemptive relation to nature when he takes responsibility for the consequences of his rebellion, sees himself as no better than the things he scorned in nature, and empathizes with those things. Walton achieves a less complete epiphany at the end of *Frankenstein.* By listening to both Frankenstein and the Creature, by admitting his pursuit of glory has endangered his men, and by realizing he has thus contradicted his boast that he will "kill no albatross,"[13] Walton achieves some perspective on the metaphorical albatross killing that each of the main characters has done. Percy Shelley's Laon and Cythna, and more successfully their representative "type" Prometheus, learn that their sacrifice can at least set an ideal of love and resistance to tyranny. They may not fully compensate for past failures or prevent future ones, but they can know that they have set, as Cythna says, a "type of peace" to inspire those who "come / Behind."[14]

2. The New World Babel and the Original Cultural Sin

In *The Last of the Mohicans*, Cooper depicts this dynamic of Romantic satanism more collectively, as it is manifested in the confrontation of cultures. The opening of the novel, as well as the 1831 preface, indicates that America could never have been an Eden; its exceptionality is only to be a more natural and therefore more clear-cut exhibition that all cultures, like all individuals, are morally fallen. Though he is a Christian who, like Coleridge, later becomes more conservatively so,[15] Cooper questions human ability to know divine purpose at least as much as Coleridge does in *The Rime of the Ancient Mariner*.[16] In the first paragraph, Cooper also seems, like Coleridge, to believe that if untamed nature ultimately does reveal some providential pattern, it initially aggravates more than it tempers the satanic aspects of human nature. To survive in the wilderness, Europeans learn to "emulate . . . the patience and self-denial of the practiced native warriors" in a struggle that teaches them to "overcome every difficulty." But conflict with nature, like the Ancient Mariner's encounter with the storm blast, provokes desire on all sides for "vengeance" while also promoting the more calculated institutional aggression of developed societies, the "cold and selfish policy of the distant monarchs of Europe" (11). As Cooper suggests in his 1831 introduction, "nations" as well as individuals manifest their fallen state through their "pretensions" of superiority to others:

> Like nations of higher pretensions, the American Indian gives a very different account of his own tribe or race from that which is given by other people. He is addicted to over-estimating his own perfections, and to undervaluing those of his rival or his enemy; a trait which may possibly be thought corroborative of the Mosaic account of the creation. (6)

The plight of Native Americans is but one instance of all the cultural conflicts in which fallen humanity manifests its ethnocentrism. Cooper may elsewhere defend the United States, including its treatment of Native Americans, against European critics. But in *The Last of the Mohicans*, he depicts the epic past on which this republic is based as a fallen world in which the ethnocentrism on all sides destroys the possibility of what could have been a greater transatlantic culture combining the best traditions of many nations.

This besetting sin is manifested in the uses of language by all sides in the conflict. Cooper's narration opens later in Genesis than Milton's—metaphorically, at the Tower of Babel, the epitome of collective sin, rather than in Eden. The lake of the Horican, where the territorial conflicts take place, has borne many names, each one reflecting only a single language and set of cultural values. The French named the lake "du Saint Sacrament" for their practice of converting others by baptism; the English called it Lake George to assert the dominance of their monarchy (11–12). Neither Hurons nor Mohawks, the major allies of the French and English, respectively, have original claim to this frontier, which was once Mohican land. It is a fitting irony that Cooper makes up a fictitious name of his own, since no name of the lake has any more Adamic primacy than the differing hegemonic practices of the cultures that currently claim and name it.

Although the narrator's initial meditation is more critical of the Europeans, the first dramatic scene depicts both Europeans and Native Americans displaying a Babel of ethnocentrism in their speech and in their behavior. The narrator's turgid opening paragraphs are limpid compared with the first words of dialogue, uttered by the singing-teacher David Gamut, who sets new standards for monocultural tone-deafness. Desiring to accompany Major Heyward's party to Fort William Henry, Gamut tries to strike up a conversation with Magua, the guide, using Heyward's warhorse as a pretext. His fatuousness masks, even to himself, the ulterior purposes of his bombast—to find an escort, as well as to parade his travel experience, education, and biblical knowledge. None of his posturings means anything to Magua, who expresses his own sense of superiority through a contemptuous silence. As the party assembles and heads into the woods, Magua further indulges his disdain, as well as his treacherous plans, by pretending to understand less English than he does and by muttering insults in his own language, insults that he then inaccurately translates into English. Alice, meanwhile, voices to Heyward her qualms about Magua in the ornamental language of drawing-room flirtation while Heyward responds by anatomizing Magua in third person, as if Magua could not understand him, and shows complete ignorance of British wrongdoing by minimizing Magua's previous confrontation with her father. Cora is the only one who addresses straightforwardly the issues of communicating with and trusting someone from another culture; she confronts both Heyward and Alice, "coldly," about their judgments based on Magua's skin color and "manners" (21).

As these Europeans are inducted into the wilderness, the New World seems to be a less fallen version of Babel, a version in which the Europeans could experience a redemptive immersion in other languages and cultures. Alice, like her father, does not speak French; David Gamut is monolingual; and none of them speaks any native language. By contrast, their rescuer, Hawk-eye, who was raised by the Delawares, acts as their cultural interpreter, in the role of Milton's archangel Raphael.[17] Hawk-eye believes that Europeans can learn much from Native Americans, whose character and language are less corrupted by satanic deceit than European tongues:

> I'm an admirator of names, though the Christian fashions fall far below savage customs in this particular. The biggest coward I ever knew was called Lyon; and his wife, Patience, would scold you out of hearing in less time than a hunted deer would run a rod. With an Indian, 'tis a matter of conscience; what he calls him-self, he generally is—not that Chingachgook, which signifies big serpent, is really a snake, big or little; but that he understands the windings and turnings of human nature, and is silent, and strikes his enemies when they least expect him. (57)

It would seem that such linguistic integrity entails linguistic adaptability; all major Native American characters speak at least one European language, as well as several native tongues. But as the novel proceeds, it appears that, except for Hawk-eye and the Mohicans, the better a person knows any language, the more prone he is to use it for deception. Montcalm, like Magua, pretends not to speak English in order to gain advantage over others (164). Heyward uses his French to fatally mislead the French sentry outside Fort William Henry (136–37). Magua, the most multilingual character, rhetorically manipulates everyone; like Satan in Pandemonium, he repeatedly stirs the Hurons to demonic violence. Cooper suggests that just as Milton's serpent uses his purportedly new acquisition of language to tempt Eve, fallen humanity uses both first and acquired languages to deceive others, rather than to comprehend the windings and turnings of others' customs. As Montcalm says, with unintended irony, "There is a vast difference between understanding and speaking a foreign tongue" (164). Montcalm means that it is easier to comprehend than to speak a second language. Cooper suggests that it is easier to speak a language than to inhabit and appreciate the culture it represents.

In the one amicable, truly multilingual and cross-cultural dialogue in the novel, the only two characters who can confront the mutual responsibility of their peoples for the Native American fall are also unwilling to redeem this fall by sacrificing their personal sense of cultural superiority, particularly through intermarriage. Hawk-eye's first words to Chingachgook rationalize the fall of Delaware culture according to the all-too-familiar argument that stronger cultures inevitably take over weaker ones; he contends that Chingachgook's people took the land from the Algonkians and Iroquois just as the Europeans have taken it from them. Chingachgook agrees that this is an inevitable, natural reality, like the cycle of the seasons, and describes with pride how his people in their time had driven "the Maquas into the woods with the bears" (32). But neither of them thinks that this is an ideal state of things, and each is willing to concede that his side is not blameless. Chingachgook counters Hawk-eye's argument by replying that Europeans' use of superior technology is less than honorable because guns require less skill and courage than traditional weapons. Although Hawk-eye argues that a good bowman can shoot faster than a muzzle-loading frontiersman, he concedes that "there is reason in an Indian" and "my people have many ways of which, as an honest man, I can't approve." Since "every story has its two sides," he asks for Chingachgook's account. On his part, Chingachgook acknowledges that his people mistook alcohol, Cooper's version of the forbidden fruit, for spiritual experience and "foolishly" sold their land to the Dutch (31–33). Later, when Hawk-eye relates the oral annals of past conflicts, he will lay some of the blame for dispossession on "the deviltries of the Dutch," who tricked the Delawares into disarming themselves (127). The two men concede that all bear responsibility for the injustices inherent in the rise and fall of empires.

Yet on a more intimate level, each man is isolated by feelings of ethnic superiority. Chingachgook prides himself on being "an unmixed man" of "the blood of the Sagamores," which will die out when his son dies ("my boy is the last of the Mohicans," 33). Unable to conceive that his tradition could continue mingled with another peoples', he pronounces the doom foreshadowed by the title of the book before any action occurs to cause it. His increasing lack of agency reflects his fatalism in the novel, to the point where he ironically becomes indistinguishable from a beaver as he passively awaits the rescue attempts by the other warriors. Hawk-eye, despite criticizing the settlements for their "womanish" ways, false learning, and injustice toward native peoples, views his white skin with "secret satisfaction" (31). As Milder observes, Hawk-eye's incessant descriptions of himself as a man "without a cross" figuratively express the racism that prevents him from intermarrying and suggest that his actions frequently fall short of Christian ideals. But this pun also unites these attitudes, implying that such ethnocentricity *is* the original sin. The two men achieve a detached perspective on justice at the expense of any personal involvement that might redeem the fall both lament.

Colonel Munro's example, however, shows that such personal crossing of cultural barriers, though necessary, is insufficient to deal with the larger issues of multicultural justice. As Munro tells Heyward, he is not an uncritical exponent of British colonialism. Munro has done what no other Christian in the novel is willing to do; he married a woman from a different ethnic background and has a mixed-race child. But transcending such cultural divides with one person is easier than understanding and negotiating with the institutional practices of an entire culture—whether one's own or another's. To emphasize this point, Cooper makes the man who has an interracial family, and who openly criticizes the "unnatural union" of his Scottish homeland with a "trading nation" (159) that traffics in slaves, also the authority figure who motivates Magua's revenge by enforcing that nation's law with Old Testament harshness. Unlike the accused authorities in British works, Munro is never confronted by his Satan; he does not even know what he has done, so he represents more generally how difficult it is to see one's actions as part of a collective cultural process. His inability to comprehend or control this process is further shown by the fact that his spirit is broken, not by the massacre and Magua's recapture of his daughters, but by the cold and selfish policies carried out by his fellow British officer, General Webb.

In the second debate over the Native American fall, Magua exposes the enormity of European ethnocentrism, thereby echoing the Creature's criticism of Frankenstein and the logic of other satanic figures. It is crucial to Cooper's purpose that Magua chooses Cora to hear his views; if he simply wanted to avenge himself by an exercise of power, it would have been more effective to terrorize the delicate and helpless Alice. But Magua wants what he considers justice, not merely the satisfaction of a personal vendetta, although like most satanic characters he is unable or unwilling to avoid conflating the two. According to the practices of his people, Magua plans to marry Cora, thus replacing the wife he lost with someone from the culture that deprived him of his family. Furthermore, he respects as well as desires Cora, saying that "the Great Spirit" has given her the "wisdom" to resist temptations such as alcohol, and he infers that only she has both the judgment to understand him and the courage to articulate the defense her father would have made. Magua tells Cora that Munro, like Milton's God, "made a law" against drunkenness, but he, or at least other Europeans whose policy he represents, created the temptation in the first place: "[I]s it justice to make evil and then punish for it!" In the form of alcohol, Europeans introduced a forbidden fruit in which no God can be found, only the bitter knowledge of the Europeans' injustice, even if, as Chingachgook learns, it can also provide awareness of one's own culpability. Cora initially defends her father, but after hearing Magua's argument, she admits to herself, if not to Magua, that this punishment was "imprudent severity" that she does not know how to "palliate." Magua argues further that Munro did not just punish him; he flogged him on the back, thus not only imposing his culture's laws with excessive severity, but also disrespecting another culture's codes of justice (103).

Magua indicts a justice so fallen that, although its wrongs do not excuse his Old Testament vengeance, no individual European can achieve the Christ-like self-sacrifice that would be necessary to redeem it. For Magua, getting "what a Huron loves—good for good—bad for bad" means that Cora will not simply be "within reach" to suffer physically when he is feeling the shame of his scars. Cora, whom Magua calls "the heart of Munro," will realize Magua is doing the same thing to her that her father did to Magua—righteously acting on his culture's version of justice while violating another's. Cora exhorts Magua to show Munro "how an Indian can forgive an injury," but she cannot turn the other cheek and accept the challenge of converting Magua by example, as his wife, and proving that her Christianity is less hypocritical than European law while also saving her sister and Duncan. Cora understands what is at stake; she says to Magua, "[Y]ou mingle bitterness with my prayers; you stand between me and my God!" and she cannot "bow down this rebellious, stubborn pride of [hers], and consent" to—or even articulate to Alice—the condition upon which Alice's and Duncan's lives depend (104, 108–9).

It would be unfair to claim that Cooper blames Cora; as an individual, she is a disempowered victim who is pressured by the wrongs of both sides to exhibit a level of self-sacrifice virtually impossible for anyone but Christ himself. But in principle, Cooper makes it clear that the proximate cause of her death, as well as Uncas's, is her inability to follow through on the most demanding of Christian principles. Magua carries her off to marry her, but when she refuses to go any further, he raises his knife to kill her. Ironically, she loses heart when rescue is audibly closing in; Uncas calls out "Cora! Cora!" and Hawk-eye follows with "Courage, lady; we come—we come." Although Magua stops the other Hurons from killing her and cannot bring himself to do the deed, his action precipitates Uncas's hastily throwing himself at Magua to save her. Magua stabs Uncas while another Huron, no longer inhibited by the preoccupied Magua, kills Cora. Magua's hesitation, plus the fact that Cora would have been rescued in a few more minutes, suggests that a sufficient exercise of Christian principle could have contributed to redeeming both cultures. If Cora could not bring herself to reform Magua by marrying him, she could have held out until Uncas and the others could save her. The circumstances of her death underline the vexed question of whether Cooper implies that Cora would or should have married Uncas, had they lived.[18]

The massacre at Fort William Henry is, in consequence, a disaster of biblical proportions for which European self-righteousness bears as much responsibility as Native American rebellion against it. The massacre, as David Gamut exclaims, is a "jubilee of the devils" in which the Hurons perform such "hellish rites" (177) as drinking blood and smashing babies against rocks. But Cooper lays the ultimate responsibility on the Europeans by casting the massacre as their Judgment Day; they hear Magua's vengeful whoop with a "curdling horror at the heart" (177) and a "dread" similar to "that which may be expected to attend the blast of the final summons" (176). Cooper shows his limitations by his casting only one side in the role of Satan, when plenty of Europeans were equally instigators of revenge out of proportion to their perceived wrongs. Ideally, Cooper would have balanced Magua's violence against that of a Falkland or Frankenstein, a Fort William Henry against a Pequot massacre (as he does more successfully in *The Wept of Wish-Ton-Wisht*). But Cooper is far ahead of his time by suggesting the degree to which the Europeans drive their "Creature" to act like Satan by representing themselves as false gods. Montcalm completes the forging of the satanic rebel by making a separate peace with Munro according to European standards while disregarding Huron custom. Montcalm explains to Magua that the French have achieved their purpose by driving the "English squatters" off their land, a property-ownership view of war alien to Magua. Montcalm simply overrides Magua's objections, calling himself the Huron's "Canadian father" and telling Magua he should "prove" his authority with his people "by teaching his nation how to conduct towards our new friends" (170, 169).[19] Both English and French leaders act as though their cultural values are divine absolutes, but their behavior proves them rather less righteous and certainly less self-aware than Milton's deity. It is appropriate that, during the massacre, Alice cries out in vain to any "Father—father" ("Come to us, Father, or we die!") while her father, though passing "at no great distance," is too "bent on the high duty of his station" to hear her (176–77). Even men such as Munro and Montcalm, whom Cooper characterizes as the best exponents of European institutions, are often incapacitated and sometimes corrupted by their cultural roles.

The second half of the novel suggests that this fall could be partly redeemed, but only by one who sacrifices his ethnocentricity on a personal and institutional level. Like Scott's "Jewess" Rebecca in *Ivanhoe* (1819), Cora is a "dark lady" who represents more than a role model for individual women; she symbolizes a multicultural ideal of European potential (Rebecca's beliefs are closer than any Christian character's to Scott's own). Cora is the "heart" of the best principles her father represents, but she is held hostage to the consequences of New World injustices committed in the name of these principles.

Such ideals are often characterized by female images[20] because, among other traits, they are vulnerable—requiring self-sacrifice seldom fully achieved by those who try to uphold them and discounted as ineffectual or hypocritical when their proponents fail to live up to them. The captivity-and-rescue story in the second half of the book questions whether, and how, the ideals Cora represents can be redeemed from the sins in which all sides have become complicit.

3. Uncas: The Man with a Cross

Although Cooper's later novels may have portrayed Natty Bumppo as a mythic hero, Cooper takes pains to point out in the 1831 preface to *The Last of the Mohicans* that Natty "betray[s] the weaknesses as well as the virtues both of his situation and of his birth," including the "prejudices" of "civilized life" (7). The Shakespearean epigraph of the novel, "Mislike me not, for my complexion, / The shadowed livery of the burnished sun" (5), reinforces Cooper's condemnation of such prejudices and suggests that the true protagonist is the character also designated by the title. Though Uncas is neither Christian nor of mixed ancestry, Cooper presents him as the only one willing to bear the cross of sacrificing his monocultural identity, as well as his life, to save Cora and the principles she represents.

Uncas has as much pride as Chingachgook in his traditions; according to the warrior code, he is fearless and loyal to his companions. From his father, he learned more self-restraint than the garrulous Hawk-eye; hence he has less false pride and prejudice and is a better, more impartial observer (his self-possession is reflected in understated characterization, perhaps the reason interpreters have not analyzed him at much length). When Hawk-eye chastises him for excessive enthusiasm in rescuing the sisters, Uncas refrains from talking back to him, although, as Heyward realizes, Uncas has "suppressed passions that were ready to explode, as much in compliment to the listeners, as from the deference he usually paid to his white associate." In fact, Uncas is better than Hawk-eye at keeping his feelings from interfering with his ability to observe and judge others objectively. When Hawk-eye rails at "them careless imps, the Mohawks," for having muddied a spring and thrown away the cup left there for everyone's use, Uncas "silently extended towards him the desired gourd, which the spleen of Hawk-eye had hitherto prevented him from observing, on a branch of an elm" (119). There are a variety of incidents in which Uncas treats Hawk-eye with tolerant forbearance, most notably when he refrains from critiquing Hawk-eye's mediocre impersonation of a bear. Yet Uncas combines Mohican self-control and good sense with a young man's emotional openness to another culture, particularly its female representatives, and he learns to evaluate it better than either his father or Hawk-eye. By combining his traditions with his feelings, Uncas is repeatedly the one best able to track the sisters when they are captured. The first time, only Uncas can find the trail because he alone notices the unusual gait of their horses; the second time, he is the one able to find Cora's veil, as well as her footprints.

Unlike Munro, who is attracted only by an individual rather than by the culture from which she is remotely descended, Uncas is also drawn to the more ideal aspects of European values Cora represents. Uncas's appreciation of Cora's qualities makes him respond in a more chivalric manner than is typical in his culture's treatment of women; he attends her wants like a courtly suitor, with an "instinctive delicacy" that "den[ies] his habits, we had almost said his nature" (114–15). His behavior at Glenn's Falls suggests that he understands the spirit of Cora's Christian self-sacrifice better than his father or Hawk-eye. The latter learn from the Europeans only what they can use for survival, such as the sound of a horse's scream, or Cora's argument, when they run out of gunpowder, that instead of sacrificing themselves they should leave the sisters and return later. As Hawk-eye says, Cora's argument has not only "reason" in it but also "the spirit of Christianity." Chingachgook sees the natural reason of Cora's argument, agrees, and swims away. Hawk-eye hesitates only briefly, and ironically on principle grounded in his not having a "cross" ("what might be right and proper in a red skin, may be sinful in a man who has not even a cross in his blood to plead for his ignorance"); he is affected more by the "disgrace" of having run out of powder than by any Christian scruples, and he is at least as reluctant to abandon his gun as to abandon Cora.[21] But Uncas intends to stay, until Cora pleads with him on the grounds of her feelings (she does not wish to be responsible for his capture), and he leaves with great reluctance (78–79). Uncas's learning to combine the best of both cultures is most evident when he observes the sisters' reunion after their first captivity:

> Uncas stood, fresh and blood-stained from the combat, a calm, and apparently an unmoved looker-on, it is true, but with eyes that had already lost their fierceness, and were beaming with a sympathy, that elevated him far above the intelligence, and advanced him probably centuries beyond the practices of his nation. (115)

Cooper's condescending language is mitigated by the fact that he has severely questioned the "practices" of European nations, and none of the Europeans seems as willing as Uncas to advance "beyond" the "practices" of his or her own culture.

It is therefore not surprising that, after the massacre, Uncas is the only man who fully commits himself to rescuing both Cora and what she represents. The other men disguise themselves to rescue Alice from the enemy Huron camp, or to help Uncas after the Hurons capture him, interacting underhandedly with native society only for the purpose of escaping from it with their original identities and relationships, not to mention their lives, intact. Duncan, the southern slave-owner, is focused on extricating the passive, traditional European womanhood Alice represents and taking her away from the wilderness. To do so, he practices the most egregious deceptions; he pretends to be a French ally, he paints his face to appear more open and simple than he is, he professes to honor the customs of his hosts, and worst of all, he disguises himself as a healer. But he has no interest in his hosts' customs or language, much less in their well-being, and when taken to help a dying Huron woman, he ignores her to search for Alice. Hawk-eye can do no better than disguise himself in a shaman's bear suit and use trickery to help Alice and Uncas escape. The bear suit reveals rather than conceals his true identity: he masquerades as a creature of the forest, who infiltrates Native American culture but remains a white "man without a cross" inside. David Gamut, tricked out after his capture in a fool's motley of cultural castoffs, uses his *tabu* of feeble-minded piety to get away with helping Uncas escape. Cooper credits this descendant of the Puritans with courage; David even takes up a slingshot, becoming a comic version of his Old Testament namesake. In fact, because of his willingness to sacrifice himself for Uncas, David comes closer than any other white character to cultural redemption, saving the man who might have served as its model. But David's various disguises are superficial overlays to a religious identity that cannot appreciate, much less assimilate to, other cultures. It is fitting that Uncas judges Heyward, Alice, Munro, David, and Hawkeye free to go. Not only have they escaped Magua according to the rules of capture; the versions of European values they represent are free of desire to become part of another culture.

But Cooper has made Magua deposit Cora for safekeeping with the Delawares and thereby has rendered her rescue more complex because it is more difficult to redeem what she represents from the legitimate anger of the Delawares—epitomized by the centenarian chief Tamenund. Given the wrongs done to them, native peoples will kill the albatross, rejecting the nobler but more vulnerable representations of European culture, whether individuals such as Cora or compromised ideals such as those of Christianity. As in *Caleb Williams*, Cooper's novel climaxes in a trial scene where a satanic character deploys his opponent's own hypocrisies against him and what he represents.[22] When Magua comes to the Delaware camp for what he calls the "justice" of reclaiming Cora as well as those who escaped him, the Delawares initially hearken to Magua's diabolical eloquence because his description of the "heart" of the white people confirms their common experiences and panders to their sense of righteous victimization:

> [Europeans are] dogs to their women, and wolves to their slaves . . . [with] tongues like the false call of the wild-cat . . . his heart teaches him to pay warriors to fight his battles . . . His gluttony makes him sick. God gave him enough, and yet he wants all. Such are the pale-faces." (301)

Magua further casts all evil onto the Europeans and absolves the Native Americans of responsibility by describing the two kinds of people as separately created races. Influenced by Magua's arguments, Tamenund then discounts Cora's pleas for "mercy!"— and her reminder that her father once was merciful to Tamenund—because all the ancient Sagamore can remember is the big picture, in which the Delaware have lost everything to the "thirst" of which even the "justest white men" were guilty. Tamenund does not heed Cora's further plea to identify with the paternal feelings of her father and release Alice because he identifies himself as father "of a nation." From this larger perspective, the Europeans are a "proud and hungry race" who "claim, not only to have the earth, but that the meanest of their colour is better than the Sachems of the red man" (304, 305). Ironically, Tamenund accuses the whites of deserving no mercy because they are guilty of the ethnocentrism most immediately represented to him by Cora's rejection of Magua:

> "The dogs and crows of their tribes," continued the earnest old chieftain, without heeding the wounded spirit of his listener, whose head was nearly crushed to the earth, in shame, as he proceeded, "would bark and caw, before they would take a woman to their wigwams, whose blood was not of the color of snow." (305)

Cora's "shame" ambiguously includes her victimization by this prejudice, as a person of mixed race, and the fact that her rejection of Magua now seems likely to condemn her sister as well as herself.

The white males only vindicate Magua's and Tamenund's condemnations by the ways in which they try to redeem Cora from Magua's "justice." Duncan, ironically called "The Open Hand," tries to bribe Magua, as he did at Glenn's Falls, and again makes circumstances worse by disrespecting Magua's motives. Hawk-eye, who has just displayed his willingness to sacrifice his life by winning a shooting match in a "headlong wish to vindicate his identity" (298), says he is not willing to sacrifice himself in an "unequal exchange" for any woman, even the "best woman on the frontiers" (314). He acts like an Old Testament Lot, bargaining for Cora's life by offering to spend a season *hors de combat*, then raising the ante by throwing in his treasured rifle, and finally by offering his life in exchange for Cora. His wavering prompts Magua to reject his offer; despite a moment of hesitation, Magua satanically prides himself on having, unlike Hawk-eye, "but one mind" with a purpose "fixed forever." Magua, with "bitter irony," makes the implications of the men's bargaining explicit when he tells Tamenund that Cora will ultimately overcome her objections and marry him because she comes from a "race of traders" who bargain for their honor rather than make any sacrifices for it. Ironically, it is they, rather than he, who act like Shylock. To complete the undermining of European principle, Duncan disrespects Delaware law by yelling after the departing Magua, "These Delawares have their laws, which forbid them to detain you; but I—I have no such obligation!" (316).

As Cora says to Tamenund, the only one who has a right to speak convincingly in favor of justice toward the captives is Uncas, one who has honored both cultures—"one of thine own people" (316). Uncas confronts his enemies and his Delaware kinsmen undisguised, doing his best to save both female captives as well as the rescuers while honoring Indian customs. When caught by the Hurons, he exhibits courage in the face of their torture and thus wins their respect, in painful contrast with the Huron coward Reed-That-Bends. Escaping from the Hurons, Uncas then shows a different kind of courage when facing his cousins, the Delawares; he refuses to dissimulate about his support for his white comrades. When the Delawares accuse him of having become a dog of the white men, Uncas makes the "biting, and perhaps merited, retort" that the Delaware are themselves "dogs that whine" for the scraps offered by the French. His status as a Mohican Sagamore is confirmed not only by his tortoise tattoo but also by his courage in the face of false accusations against himself and others. Uncas defends Hawk-eye against Magua's unjust charge of killing Delaware warriors and tells Tamenund that, according to the rules of captivity, none of the whites except Cora is Magua's prisoner. But he also upholds the honor and safety of the Delawares, as well as the partial justice of Magua's accusations, by letting Magua take Cora, according to the "inviolable laws of Indian hospitality" (305). As soon as the demands of these laws are fulfilled, Uncas raises a war party and sacrifices his own life in an attempt to save Cora, with his attempt denoting that some European ideals are still worth emulating and worth dying to redeem. His courage and impartial dispensing of justice reveal the relative merits of Magua's, Cora's, and his own motives, so that his people support and share in his attempt to free Cora.

Uncas is the exemplar of what Americans could be—if the depths of cultural sin were not initially so great and the consequent sacrifices demanded so extreme. The Delawares, personified in the women who lament over the mingled graves of Cora and Uncas, honor their union in the Delaware afterlife, thereby indicating that their deeds do reconcile the feminine heart of Native American justice to a potential union of cultures. But the ending implies that only native peoples, and rare Europeans such as Munro, will accept such a possibility in this life. The "heart-broken" Munro asks Hawk-eye to tell the Delaware women that "the Being we all worship, under different names, will be mindful of their charity; and that the time shall not be distant, when we may assemble around his throne, without distinction of sex, or rank, or color!" Hawk-eye doubts the Delaware women will understand "the efficacy" of these words, presumably because he doubts they will ever believe in a Being on a "throne" (347). But it is he who doubts the spirit of these words—that gender, class, and ethnic distinctions could ever be meaningless in this world. Perhaps the ultimate ironic meaning of the title is that, if more descendants of the Europeans pursued the spirit of Milton's Christian ethic beyond Milton's Christian doctrine, and applied this spirit to cultures as well as to individuals, Uncas might not be the last of the Mohicans. As with Percy Shelley's Laon and Cythna, Uncas's sacrifice may be a "type of peace" that is too belated to save either his people or the possibility of a truly transatlantic culture, but that could enlighten and motivate the American republic to mitigate further cultural catastrophes.

NOTES

1. Cooper, *The Last of the Mohicans*, 284. Subsequent references to this edition will be cited parenthetically in the text. Robert Lawson-Peebles ("The Lesson of the Massacre of Fort William Henry," 136), lists the handful of critics who have mentioned Milton in relation to *The Last of the Mohicans*. None of them except Milder engages in discussions more than a page or two long. They include John P. McWilliams Jr., whose essay "Red Satan: Cooper and the American Indian Epic" cites few specific Miltonic allusions, despite its title, and Joel Porte (*Romance in America*, 39–41), who says that the epic elements in this novel are all Homeric, except the descriptions of Magua, which are derived from Milton.

2. Milder, "New World Fall," 409–10, 413.

3. Ian Haywood argues that the "hyberbolic violence" on all sides serves a role similar to the casting of Magua as Satan; white violence expresses Cooper's "liberal guilt and anxiety about the inevitability of war-fuelled progress," but the extreme violence of the "bad" Indians ultimately justifies their annihilation. Haywood concludes that "Cooper's

narrative solution to this ideological problem was to transfer primitive Indian virtues to the new breed of white American hero: the frontiersman, a hybrid figure who polices the border between the civilized and the 'savage,' and whose *raison d'être* is the continuing conquest of the American wilderness" (*Bloody Romanticism*, 172–74). The 2006 reading anthology *Transatlantic Romanticism*, edited by Lance Newman, Joel Pace, and Chris Koenig-Woodyard, more brusquely dismisses Cooper as an "apologist for American national expansion"; Natty Bumppo is a "'white Indian' who models the reinvigoration of an exhausted Euro-American culture by the absorption of Native American cultural vitality," a "symbolic incorporation" that is a "way of simultaneously mourning and excusing imperialist expansion and Indian removal" (649). Kate Flint, in *The Transatlantic Indian*, cites as a matter of consensus Jane Tompkins's assessment that Cooper uses sensationalism and sentimental stereotypes to create "nostalgia for Indianness . . . even as they affirm the impossibility of union with the 'dusky' race and acquiesce in its extermination" (139). Tompkins actually goes further; she concludes that Cooper uses polarized stereotypes and "grotesque concatenations of events" to "explicitly reject" a "vision of the brotherhood of man" (*Sensational Design*, 111) and to enforce a racism whose purpose is "preserving the system as a whole from the disruptive influences of an alien culture" (118).

4. Rans, *Cooper's Leather-Stocking Novels*, 106. John Morsellino, "Cooper and Creole Democracy," argues that Cooper is sufficiently critical of European values, and of Hawk-eye's racism, to portray Cora as a lost ideal of creole democracy that might augment and correct such values. However, Rans finds Cooper "unable to resolve" historical contradictions (xvi), and Morsellino sees Cora's death merely as a "senseless" underscoring of "the senselessness of . . . prejudice" (82), whereas I will argue that Cooper finds a tentative multicultural resolution in the actions of Cora and Uncas.

5. Milder, "New World Fall," 419–20, 427–28.

6. Weisbuch, *Atlantic Double-Cross*, xv.

7. Cooper's encounter with Coleridge is recounted in Earl Leslie Griggs's, "James Fenimore Cooper on Coleridge." Cooper's letters from Europe include many to, from, and about Sir Walter Scott. In the letter of 7–13? November 1826, Cooper records meeting Scott, who "treated [him] like a younger brother" (Cooper, *Letters and Journals*, 1:170). For Cooper's meeting with Godwin, see Henry Walcott Boynton, *James Fenimore Cooper*, 176–77. Cooper's epigraphs also show his intimate familiarity with contemporary British poets, including those in the Godwin-Shelley circle.

8. My rendering of British Romantic satanism differs substantially from the recent work of Peter A. Schock, who tries to correct what he sees as an ahistorical twentieth-century tradition of interpreting Romantic satanism exclusively as the metaphysical rebellion of individual subjectivity, on the part of both poet and protagonist (*Romantic Satanism*, 4–6). While his shift of focus back onto the general, political side of Romantic satanism is a welcome corrective to previous criticism, Schock goes too far in the opposite direction. He focuses on mythic political representations (e.g., Satan as "an expression of group identity") as if they were abstractions *independent from* and incommensurate with individual subjectivity when the explicit philosophy of Godwin, echoed by Percy Shelley and others, is that political representations are the *sum of* individual ones and can therefore be figured by depicting individual

subjectivities (Godwin's "political justice" is the sum of what he calls improved individual perceptions; his human characters are types of historical ideologies, just as Percy Shelley's Prometheus is the "type" of the multiple great minds throughout history). Schock constructs his argument primarily top-down, from the authors' abstract ideas in their political nonfiction, and deals with few of the individual human representations of Satan in these authors' fictional works. When he does, he sees the individual human characters (e.g., Beatrice Cenci) as essentially innocent satanic victims rebelling against entirely bad institutional ideologies (e.g., the warped Catholicism of her father) when in fact the human characters on both sides of the conflict are cast in the roles of both Satan and God, thus implying the more ironic political dialectic I describe above.

9. M. Shelley, *Frankenstein*, 90. Such statements epitomize Romantic satanism in many other Romantic works, especially in the nexus of the Godwin-Shelley family's writings. In a note to *Queen Mab*, Percy Shelley has Adam rather than Satan question whether it was just of God to create him with an imperfect character and then punish him for a deed God predicted forty years before creating him (*Complete Works*, 1:146).

10. Peter McInerney, "Satanic Conceits in *Frankenstein* and *Wuthering Heights*" (9–12), points out the error of many critics in thinking that Romantic writers merely glorify satanic rebels; he argues that Coleridge's criticism in *The Statesman's Manual* of Napoleon and other historical figures epitomizes the moral ambiguities most British Romantics depict in satanic characters. Coleridge's central statement in this work is that, in such men, "the Will becomes satanic pride and rebellious self-idolatry in the relations of the spirit to itself, and remorseless despotism relatively to others; the more hopeless as the more obdurate by its subjugation of sensual impulses, by its superiority to toil and pain and pleasure; in short, by the fearful resolve to find in itself alone the one absolute motive of action, under which all other motives from within and from without must be either subordinated or crushed" (*Complete Works*,1:458).

11. Richardson, "The *Hamartia* of Imagination," 220–22.

12. P. Shelley, *Shelley's Poetry and Prose*, 207.

13. M. Shelley, *Frankenstein*, 33.

14. P. Shelley, *Poetical Works*, 129.

15. Donald A. Ringe, *James Fenimore Cooper* (150), succinctly summarizes the evolution of Cooper's religious beliefs. He says that Cooper consistently believes the restraints necessary to maintain democracy "must come through a religious view of the world." Cooper's early novels suggest that a Romantic sublime may be adequate to instill spiritual awe and humility in such characters as Hawk-eye, but in later novels, the "actual adherence to the principles of the Christian religion" is necessary. Ringe suggests that this shift begins as early as *The Prairie*, with the depiction of characters such as Ishmael Bush who are insensitive to natural religion. As I will suggest, the puns directed at Hawk-eye's being "without a cross" imply that Cooper is foregrounding this tension already in *The Last of the Mohicans*—that despite Hawk-eye's natural reverence and professed Christianity, he does not act as fully on a Christian ethic as someone who is not doctrinally Christian (Uncas) or as several characters who are (Cora and David).

16. McWilliams argues that Cooper's *Notions of the Americans* presents a "harmony" among "civil, moral, divine, and natural law," but only as an unreachable

ideal: "Elsewhere, Cooper is forever detecting flaws in the scheme or in man's abilities to realize it. Most obviously, the divine law to which Cooper appeals can never be comprehended by man . . . the principles of divine law form a credo to which Cooper and Natty Bumppo can only appeal with futile longing" (*Political Justice*, 20).

17. Steven Blakemore has recognized that Cooper's implicit references to Babel reflect "a world irrevocably fallen" and that Cooper establishes a hierarchy in which some languages are more corrupted than others. Although such a hierarchy may indeed exist, Blakemore makes too sharp a distinction between the "Edenic language of the Delawares and the fallen languages of the French and English" ("Strange Tongues," 39). The quotations Blakemore uses from Cooper actually suggest that *all* Indian languages, not just Delaware, are truer to nature than the white languages—but also that none of them is what Blakemore calls "prelapsarian," merely superior to the corruption of European usage, because in Cooper's Babel neither nature nor human nature is prelapsarian. Speaking the "purest" language in the novel does not keep Chingachgook from expressing in it the sense of ethnic superiority at the heart of the American fall, or from acknowledging his peoples' complicity in losing their land, specifically by drinking the forbidden fruit. Hawk-eye, moreover, refers incessantly to his being "without a cross" whether he is speaking in Delaware or in English.

18. Elsewhere, in *The Deerslayer*, for example, Cooper makes this problem with Christian ideals apply equally to male Europeans, as when Deerslayer shows himself unwilling to compensate for killing a native woman's husband by marrying her and caring for her children (though he has offered to provide for the recently orphaned Hutter sisters, to whom he owes no such obligation). When the woman's insulted brother then throws a tomahawk at him, Deerslayer, despite claiming to possess white Christian "gifts," quite literally, as Hetty Hutter says critically, "returns evil" for evil by throwing the brother's tomahawk back at him. The description of his doing so even includes a "red spot" on each cheek, neither of which he turns to his attacker (*The Deerslayer*, 471-473, 484-486). According to McWilliams, Cooper suggests that the letter of Christian nonviolence is an ideal that is not survival-worthy in a violent natural world—one must slay human attackers as well as deer to survive. McWilliams thinks that, by killing, Deerslayer "commits a sin by absolute standards" but that "morally he does not fall, because his values remain unaltered" (*Political Justice*, 284–86). This is close to my argument that the Christian ethic Cooper adapts from the British Romantics implies that, although humans are imperfect, they should still strive to approximate an ideal of imitating Christ. I would, however, argue that for Cooper all humans are fallen, and that Deerslayer's failings also include his refusal to take responsibility for his victim's survivors. Culturally in *The Last of the Mohicans*, and individually in *The Deerslayer*, Cooper still holds people responsible for the injustices they, or their fathers, have wrought in their fallen state. In both Cora's and Deerslayer's cases, the ideal redeeming response would be to face cultural or personal responsibility and bear the cross of intermarriage. In both cases, failure to do so results in others' deaths, leaves one with no descendants, and leaves behind no model of conduct that could sufficiently compensate for past violence.

19. Montcalm's hypocrisy is especially blatant; like William Shakespeare's Henry V before Harfleur, he claims divine authority while failing to take responsibility for

the violence unleashed by his actions, and he lifts not a finger to resist the massacre. Montcalm's meditation after speaking with Magua directly echoes the sentiments, and the rationalizations, of Shakespeare's Henry V in his speech before Harfleur and in his act 4, scene 1 "Ceremony" soliloquy. After the massacre, Hawk-eye calls Montcalm to account on Judgment Day and pronounces a Miltonic judgment that applies as well to Munro, Magua, and all others responsible: "Nothing but vast wisdom and onlimited [*sic*] power should dare to sweep off men in multitudes . . . for it is only the one that can know the necessity of the judgment; and what is there short of the other, that can replace the creatures of the Lord" (183–84).

20. Haywood documents numerous British and American graphic representations, both sentimental and satirical, of "the abused female body" (162) as a symbol of national violation in the Romantic era. But the figures Hayward documents are limited to power-gendering of the female as completely helpless (indeed, limbless) and physically vulnerable to aggression by other countries, gendered as male. Ideals such as justice, freedom, and liberty are also more positively, if still traditionally, gendered as female, signaling at once the value of emotion in these ideals and their consequent vulnerability. Representations roughly contemporaneous with Cooper's novel include the blindfolded goddess of Justice with her scales before the Supreme Court; paintings of European revolutionary movements such as Eugene Delacroix's "Liberty Leading the People"; and, later in the century, the Statue of Freedom atop the US Capitol, as well as the Statue of Liberty.

21. Hawk-eye uses similar words and behavior while saving himself later, at the expense of another helpless but more self-sacrificing Christian, David Gamut. To help Uncas escape from the Hurons, Hawk-eye offers to sacrifice himself—though he knows Uncas will not accept his offer. It is David who volunteers to stay behind disguised as Uncas, to convince the Hurons that Uncas is still their captive. Ironically, Hawk-eye escapes in David's clothes and tells David that he is getting a "great convenience" from the exchange of garments. The switch of identities endangers David's life but gives him the moral "convenience" of becoming the protector while Hawk-eye becomes the fool. Hawk-eye is impressed by, though not motivated to emulate, David's exhortation to forgive the Hurons if they kill him. In language like that he used to address Cora at Glenn's Falls, Hawk-eye gives David advice on how to survive until Hawk-eye can rescue him and says that David's forgiveness is "a principle . . . different from the law of the woods! And yet it is fair and noble to reflect on . . . It is what I would wish to practyse [*sic*] myself, as one without a cross of blood, though it is not always easy to deal with an Indian, as you would with a fellow christian [*sic*]." Hawk-eye admits that David is right from the perspective of "eternity," but "much depends on the natural gifts, and on the force of temptation" (274). Although he may ultimately volunteer to sacrifice himself for another if the person is of sufficient personal importance to him, his willingness to bear such crosses is repeatedly, and confessedly, less Christian than that of either David or Cora.

22. The configuration of these trials varies considerably. In novels such as Godwin's *Caleb Williams* (1794) and Scott's *Ivanhoe* (1820), as well as in long poems such as Percy Shelley's *The Revolt of Islam* (1817) and *The Cenci* (1819), there are many trials or tribunals presided over by a reigning hegemony, which rules with various degrees

of human imperfection—at best, the British legal system; at worst, entirely satanic, self-idolizing representatives of organized religion such as the Pope, the Iberian Priest, or the Templar Grand Master. In most, the satanic institution itself accuses someone of satanic rebellion for defying its righteous authority; in *Caleb Williams*, Caleb and Falkland provoke trials against each other by exchanging accusations. In most of these cases, the institutional representative either convicts the rebel or morally destroys him, or both, by exploiting publicly or exposing to the rebel himself the self-idolatry in the rebel's most ideal version of himself. Caleb and Falkland try to convince the British jury system that the other, rather than himself, represents the ideology that unjustly sets itself above society; by doing so, each one confirms rather than challenges the authority of the adversarial, accusatory justice system itself. The situation in Cooper involves less complex psychology, but more complex expression of collective responsibility. Magua tries to convince a relatively just Native American authority, in the form of Tamenund and the neutral Delawares, that he and they are entirely righteous in condemning every aspect of European values, even the better ones represented by Cora, as wholly responsible for their fall, and the behavior of the white males only reinforces his accusations. In the British works, whether the rebel reinforces the existing system or manages to change it depends on the degree to which the accused rebel admits his responsibility to himself and others and is willing to sacrifice himself by exposing the whole truth about his motives and deeds. In Cooper's novel, the outcome is swayed by the intervention of a character with the courage to see the good and bad in his own, as well as another, culture; emotionally engage with the good; and sacrifice his ethnocentrism to a more multicultural ideal, even at the price of his life.

BIBLIOGRAPHY

Blakemore, Steven. "Strange Tongues: Cooper's Fiction of Language in *The Last of the Mohicans.*" *Early American Literature* 19.1 (1984): 21–41.

Boynton, Henry Walcott. *James Fenimore Cooper.* New York: Century, 1931.

Coleridge, Samuel Taylor. *The Statesman's Manual.* In *The Complete Works of Samuel Taylor Coleridge*, edited by W. G. T. Shedd. 7 vols. New York: Harper and Brothers, 1853.

Cooper, James Fenimore. *The Deerslayer or, the First War-Path.* Historical introduction and explanatory notes by James Franklin Beard; text established by Lance Schachterle, Kent Ljungquist, and James Kilby. Albany: State University of New York Press, 1985.

———. *The Last of the Mohicans: A Narrative of 1757.* Historical introduction by James Franklin Beard; text established with explanatory notes by James A. Sappenfield and E. N. Feltskog. Albany: State University of New York Press, 1983.

———. *The Letters and Journals of James Fenimore Cooper.* Edited by James Franklin Beard. 6 vols. Cambridge, MA: Belknap Press of Harvard University Press, 1960–68.

Flint, Kate. *The Transatlantic Indian, 1776–1930.* Princeton, NJ: Princeton University Press, 2008.

Griggs, Earl Leslie. "James Fenimore Cooper on Coleridge." *American Literature* 4.4 (1933): 389–91.

Haywood, Ian. *Bloody Romanticism: Spectacular Violence and the Politics of Representation, 1776–1832*. New York: Palgrave MacMillan, 2006.

Lawson-Peebles, Robert. "The Lesson of the Massacre of Fort William Henry." In *New Essays on* The Last of the Mohicans, edited by H. Daniel Peck, 115–38. New York: Cambridge University Press, 1992.

McInerney, Peter. "Satanic Conceits in *Frankenstein* and *Wuthering Heights*." *Milton and the Romantics* 4 (1980): 1–15.

McWilliams, John P., Jr. *Political Justice in a Republic: James Fenimore Cooper's America*. Berkeley: University of California Press, 1972.

———. "Red Satan: Cooper and the American Indian Epic." In *James Fenimore Cooper: New Critical Essays*, edited by Robert Clark, 143–61. New York: Vision Press, 1985.

Milder, Robert. "*The Last of the Mohicans* and the New World Fall." *American Literature* 52.3 (1980): 407–29.

Morsellino, John. "Cooper and Creole Democracy." In *James Fenimore Cooper: His Country and His Art*, edited by Hugh C. MacDougall and Steven Harthorn, 79–83. Oneonta: State University of New York College at Oneonta, 2005. http://exterma;.oneonta.edu/cooper/articles/suny/2005suny-morsellino.html (accessed 28 August 2011).

Newman, Lance, Joel Pace, and Chris Koenig-Woodyard, eds. *Transatlantic Romanticism: An Anthology of British, American, and Canadian Literature, 1767–1787*. New York: Longman, 2006.

Porte, Joel. *The Romance in America: Studies in Cooper, Poe, Hawthorne, Melville, and James*. Middletown, CT: Wesleyan University Press, 1969.

Rans, Geoffrey. *Cooper's Leather-Stocking Novels: A Secular Reading*. Chapel Hill: University of North Carolina Press, 1991.

Richardson, Donna. "The *Hamartia* of Imagination in Shelley's Cenci." *The Keats-Shelley Journal* 44 (1995): 216–39.

Ringe, Donald A. *James Fenimore Cooper*. Boston: Twayne, 1962.

Schock, Peter A. *Romantic Satanism: Myth and the Historical Moment in Blake, Shelley, and Byron*. New York: Palgrave Macmillan, 2003.

Shelley, Mary. *Frankenstein*. Edited by Joanna M. Smith. Boston: Bedford Books of St. Martin's Press, 1992.

Shelley, Percy Bysshe. *The Complete Works of Percy Bysshe Shelley*. Edited by Roger Ingpen and Walter E. Peck. 10 vols. New York: Charles Scribner's Sons, 1928.

———. *Shelley: Poetical Works*. Edited by Thomas Hutchinson. New York: Oxford University Press, 1970.

———. *Shelley's Poetry and Prose*. Edited by Donald Reiman and Neil Fraistat. New York: Norton, 2002.

Tompkins, Jane. *Sensational Design: The Cultural Work of American Fiction 1790–1860*. Oxford: Oxford University Press, 1985.

Weisbuch, Robert. *Atlantic Double-Cross: American Literature and British Influence in Age of Emerson*. Chicago: University of Chicago Press, 1986.

Narratives of Extinction: James Fenimore Cooper and the Last Man

John Hay
University of Nevada, Las Vegas

"THOU wilt here read of the acts of the extinct race." Although this declaration comes from the narrator of Mary Shelley's apocalyptic novel *The Last Man*, published in January 1826, it could have easily appeared in the preface to another novel published that same month: James Fenimore Cooper's *The Last of the Mohicans* (1826). In his own preface, Cooper establishes the narrative as an account of the last days of a vanishing people, whose "glory shone the brightest as they were about to become extinct."[1] Simultaneously then, and on both sides of the Atlantic, writers such as Shelley and Cooper were beginning to employ what literary critic Patrick Brantlinger calls an "extinction discourse."[2] Reflecting the growing acceptance among natural philosophers of the principle of biological extinction, this discursive form became a means of describing the eradication of organic populations.

As early as 1813, the influential English translation of Georges Cuvier's *Essay on the Theory of the Earth* announced that some "races even have become extinct, and have left no memorial . . . except some small fragments which the naturalist can scarcely recognise."[3] Over the next fifteen years, a veritable vogue developed in British literary circles for tales of the "Last Man," a romantic hero witnessing the death throes of the human race, and Mary Shelley's novel epitomized the theme. In the United States, Cooper's depiction of a vanishing Native American presence similarly showcased this figure of finality.

Literature in the Early American Republic: Annual Studies on Cooper and His Contemporaries
Volume 6, 2014. Copyright © 2014 by AMS Press, Inc. All rights reserved.

The Last of the Mohicans has commonly been classified as a historical romance, operating in the same mode as Walter Scott's *Waverley* (1814), yet I argue that the novel should be read, like Shelley's, as a narrative of prospective extinction.[4]

Questions about the novel's mode might be traced back to the novelist himself: "It was not the intention of the author to write a historical romance," claimed Cooper's daughter Susan in her introduction to the fiftieth-anniversary edition of *The Last of the Mohicans*. As Richard Slotkin notes, while Scott's historical romances usually follow the "reconciliationist model of history," ending with a marriage between a hero and a heroine who represent opposing factions (such as Highland and Lowland Scots in *Rob Roy* [1817], or pro-Norman and anti-Norman Saxons in *Ivanhoe* [1819]), conflict in *The Last of the Mohicans* ends with "elimination."[5] Cooper was interested in depicting inevitable termination, not in resolving historical tension, and the novel exemplified the era's transatlantic fascination with the "last of the race." In this essay, I contend that Cooper's work, like Mary Shelley's, contributed and responded to a growing cultural acceptance of extinction. Furthermore, as novelists, both Shelley and Cooper faced formal literary challenges in crafting their narratives of extinction. For British authors, and especially Shelley, "lastness" entailed a problematic literary zone that ultimately concludes only in ambiguity and mediated regression as characters face the impossibility of narrating the end of history. What for Shelley was a narratological conundrum, however, became for Cooper a key ideological concept of the American frontier, one that allowed white settlers to establish narrative continuity with a region's threatened Native American history. The figure of the Last Man, oddly enough, holds open the doors that an extinction discourse aims to close.

1. *Witness to Extinction: The Last Man*

At the end of Mary Shelley's *The Last Man*, which describes the steady elimination of the human race by a worldwide plague at the end of the twenty-first century, two men and a girl, the last three survivors on earth, sail from Venice toward Athens in the hopes of living in "beatific union" (344). When a storm in the Adriatic Sea leads to shipwreck,

Lionel Verney, now the last man alive, washes ashore near Ravenna. Verney immediately compares himself to "that monarch of the waste," Robinson Crusoe: "We had both been thrown companionless—he on the shore of a desolate island: I on that of a desolate world" (349). Yet unlike Crusoe, who faced the challenge of building a home in a new world while hoping for rescue, Verney wanders through the palaces of the old world, doomed to a life of solitude. He envies the possibility of human contact granted to Defoe's hero, who "had fled from his fellows, and was transported with terror at the print of a human foot," whereas Verney "would have knelt down and worshipped the same" (350).[6]

Bereft of contemporaries, Verney has the hope of contact only via his historical imagination. He therefore travels to Rome, which is everywhere "replete with relics of ancient times" (359). Here, recalling passages of classical literature amid their original settings, Verney finds consolation, "a medicine for my many and vital wounds" (360). Yet mere contemplation of the past is not enough: "The generations I had conjured up to my fancy, contrasted more strongly with the end of all—the single point in which, as a pyramid, the mighty fabric of society had ended, while I, on the giddy height, saw vacant space around me" (361). After obtaining paper and ink by scavenging through Roman homes, he sets down the personal history that ultimately constitutes the novel's narrative. The conclusion of this narrative reveals Verney's plan to sail across the Mediterranean and, eventually, around the world. Verney claims to have relinquished the hope of discovering other survivors, but the very construction of the narrative seems to be a communicative act toward some future reader, the "tender offspring of the re-born world" (341).

Despite this gesture to possible future regeneration, Verney's story remains chilling for its depiction of ultimate solitude and secular apocalypse, a bleak vision of a lonely figure passing through a wrecked and meaningless world. Verney's ordeal may in fact reflect Mary Shelley's own despair; shortly before composing the novel, she had grieved the loss of three of her children, her husband, and a close friend (Lord Byron), remarking in her journal, "The last man! Yes I may well describe that solitary being's feelings, feeling myself as the last relic of a beloved race, my companions extinct before me." And indeed, critics have long viewed *The Last Man* as a roman à clef, the title figure symbolic of Mary Shelley herself and the characters Adrian and Lord Raymond functioning as thin fictionalizations of Percy Shelley and Lord Byron, respectively.[7]

Yet the novel is also the culmination of a contemporaneous literary vogue for Last Man tales. The popular Scottish poet Thomas Campbell's poem "The Last Man" became the subject of a public debate within English periodicals in 1825 when Francis Jaffrey, writing for the *Edinburgh Review*, suggested that Campbell borrowed the idea from Byron's poem "Darkness" (1816). Campbell responded by insisting that he had personally suggested the idea of the Last Man to Byron years earlier and finally decided to publish his own work when he heard that Thomas Lovell Beddoes was composing a dramatic poem on the subject. The next year, when Shelley's novel was published, there appeared several other works titled *The Last Man*, including a popular satirical poem by Thomas Hood, a painting by John Martin, and an anonymously penned fragment in *Blackwood's Edinburgh Magazine*.[8]

Unfortunately for Shelley, this vogue soon passed, and her novel was skewered by the critics; one reviewer, after noting that the idea of the Last Man had "already tempted the genius of more than one of our poets," pronounced her work "the offspring of a diseased imagination."[9] The novel also failed to impress a general audience, and following a pirated Philadelphia edition in 1833, it remained out of print until 1965.[10] When scholars began seriously reevaluating Mary Shelley's works in the 1980s and 1990s, her reputation grew from the "author of *Frankenstein*" to a key figure of the British Romantic movement, and recent criticism of *The Last Man* has been prolific. The novel, previously valued only as a veiled portrayal of Shelley's circle, has been reframed as both a critique of British nationalism in a period of imperial expansion and a record of cultural anxieties regarding an increasingly global economy.[11]

But why did the figure of the Last Man suddenly become so prominent in the 1820s? The immediate geopolitical context might suggest a reaction to the aftermath of the recently concluded Napoleonic Wars (and perhaps the image of the lonely exiled emperor on Saint Helena) or the ongoing Greek Revolution. The *geological* context, however, offers a much stronger clue. The professional acceptance of biological extinction occurred very swiftly in the early nineteenth century, and the leading figure associated with this new idea was undoubtedly Georges Cuvier. The "Preliminary Discourse" to Cuvier's *Recherches sur les ossemens fossiles de quadrupèdes* (1812) was translated into English as an *Essay on the Theory of the Earth* in 1813 and reprinted many times over the next two decades. Cuvier's central claim was that the history of the earth is characterized by violent catastrophes—"great and terrible events"—that destroyed "numberless living beings" and in many cases led to the extinction of species.[12] While the specific nature of these calamities was open to debate (potential causes included comets, floods, and volcanic activity), Cuvier stressed that their operation would be sudden and widespread, destroying entire populations. Furthermore, he insisted that the structures of many fossil organisms differed greatly enough from those of living animals to indicate a record of entire species no longer in existence. Cuvier's popularity ensured a wide circulation for his theories, and it has been suggested that, by the time of his death in 1832, his "geological conclusions" had reached "educated readers virtually everywhere in the Western world."[13]

In fact, Cuvier's argument for biological extinction had become quickly accepted long before his death. In the December 1819 issue of the London-based *Monthly Review* (the same journal that would later accuse Mary Shelley of possessing a "diseased imagination"), an article on George Bellas Greenough's *Critical Examination of the First Principles of Geology* (1819) insisted that extinction could finally be considered a well-known truth. The idea that "the world was [once] inhabited by genera and species of animals that no longer exist on our planet," wrote the reviewer, could be counted among the "inductions from facts which are admitted by all geologists."[14] Earlier generations had faced two major obstacles to believing in extinction. The first was the concept of divine design; especially within the Protestant tradition, extinction suggested a miraculous and pointless snap in the Great Chain of Being, an accidental flaw in God's universal narrative. The second obstacle regarded the exploration of the earth. Until the beginning of the nineteenth century, there persisted a reasonable possibility that species known only through fossilized remains might yet be found living and thriving in other corners of the globe. Cuvier helped to solidify the case for extinction by arguing that large fossil quadrupeds—such as the woolly mammoth—were both anatomically distinct from living species and unlikely to be still surviving on earth while remaining undiscovered.[15] As the investigations of naturalists covered more territory around the world, living specimens of fossilized species could no longer be hypothetically displaced into unexplored regions.

Once biological extinction was established as a recurring phenomenon throughout natural history, the earth's crust became a vast record of entire species meeting their ultimate demise. That the permanent annihilation of biological forms was simply part of the natural order suggested a problem for human history: if *homo sapiens* was just one species among many, then the prospect of extinction loomed as a kind of secular apocalypse.[16] The end of humanity, in other words, might not coincide with the end of the earth. Furthermore, humanity's collapse could result from a seemingly arbitrary nature rather than from a divine plan. The end could come about quickly or, perhaps worse, gradually; a disaster might destroy many but not all, and a lingering remnant might perish without hope of social renewal. Thus the figure of the Last Man—in Thomas Campbell's words, "a being witnessing the extinction of his species"—became a distinct possibility.[17] He would be the chief protagonist in a narrative of extinction.

The Last Man finds himself alone in a world in which a grand design is no longer perceptible but the marks of history—the ruins of the past—are everywhere visible.[18] The apocalypse offers neither communal redemption nor the revelation of ultimate meaning. Yet, all the same, the Last Man's position at the end of history grants him the vision and authority to reflect on the totality of human endeavor. "Time and experience have placed me on an height from which I can comprehend the past as a whole" (209), Lionel Verney thus declares. Like the owl of Minerva—and unlike the phoenix—the Last Man flies at dusk and enjoys both an all-encompassing gaze and the final word on human history. This very authority, however, is threatened by Verney's words themselves, as the truly Last Man must be a being without an audience.[19]

Shelley's novel illustrates the supreme difficulty of the Last Man literary theme: How to narrate the end of history? Verney is the novel's narrator; sitting alone amid the ruins of Rome in the twenty-first century, he records his story, leaving it for any potential postapocalyptic readers to come. Yet Shelley's primary audience lived in the nineteenth century, a temporal disparity bridged only through a feat of narrative sleight of hand. In the "Author's Introduction" to the novel, Shelley's 1826 "Author" wanders through Roman ruins and enters a mysterious cave. Upon finding "piles of leaves" and "fragments of bark" that display written characters, she claims to have discovered the prophetic Sibylline leaves (3). These writings are scattered scraps of several different languages, and, through "solitary labours," the Author translates and collates them, slowly assembling the narrative that forms the novel. She notes her own influence on the finished account: "Doubtless the leaves of the Cumaean Sibyl have suffered distortion and diminution of interest and excellence in my hands. My only excuse for thus transforming them, is that they were unintelligible in their pristine condition" (4).

The narrative of Lionel Verney is thus triply mediated: first, by an unknown power that transports his words from his future manuscript into the spiritual realm; next, by the divine intuition of the multilingual ancient Sibyl; and finally, by an Author working through "long hours of solitude" with "unintelligible" fragments (5). Shelley presents her contemporaries with an account of the distant future by claiming that it was translated from a work of antiquity, thus creating what one critic calls a "vertiginous literary experiment."[20] All these layers of mediation obscure an underlying paradox: the Last Man is necessarily a figure outside of narrative, a figure existing beyond the limits of literary mimesis. His condition is defined by the very inability to communicate. So while Verney's position at the end of time grants him the authority to interpret the total human drama, to "reveal the meaning of the enigma, whose explanation closed the history of the human race," his attempt to communicate his vision to future human readers threatens the very historical authority he enjoys as the Last Man (333). Recognizing this predicament, Verney himself questions his own act of authorship and realizes that his narrative is *not* primarily designed for readers in the future. Rather, Verney composes his history both for himself and, bizarrely, for readers *in the past*.

In his youth, Verney had been an orphan, an "unlettered savage" (23) tutored and brought into intellectual maturity by Adrian, the Earl of Windsor. In developing the ability to read and write, he discovered the delights of authorship: "I acquired new sympathies and pleasures. . . . Suddenly I became as it were the father of all mankind. Posterity became my heirs" (120). In the aftermath of the global plague, faced with a barren world without posterity, Verney initially turns to authorship not as an act of communication—he severely doubts that other survivors exist to read his manuscript—but rather as an "opiate," an active recollection of friends and family that preserves his sanity in the midst of extreme solitary conditions. He escapes from "the lonely state of singleness" that surrounds him "by perceiving and reflecting back the grouping and combined colouring of the past" (209). The narrative is a means of maintaining psychological cohesion; Verney retains his humanity by affirming his identity in its historical relation to the (past) community to which he belonged.[21]

Rather than addressing his account to future readers, Verney begins his manuscript with the words, "Dedication to the illustrious dead. Shadows, arise, and read your fall! Behold the history of the Last Man!" (364). In a reversal of his earlier conception of authorship as a means of communicating with "posterity," he now understands his narrative to be a message for the dead. Normally this would be a futile task, but the structure of the novel actually fulfills Verney's intention: the audience that reads his account—a nineteenth-century audience—will indeed be dead by the time that Verney is born in the late twenty-first century. Of course, this looping of history, by which the author of the future can speak to the reader of the past, still threatens Verney's claim to be the Last Man. The Last Man is by definition the only human to witness the end of history, and his ultimate solitude "brings him to the edge of narrative's capacity to preserve and communicate experience."[22] At the completion of the manuscript, Verney realizes the impossibility of conveying his condition to an imaginary other: "How express in human language a woe human being until this hour never knew! How give intelligible expression to a pang none but I could ever understand!" (365).

Verney's frustration is warranted, as the translation of his words onto the Sibylline leaves will indeed render them "unintelligible."

In the end, the Last Man is an object of imagination. He can only be constructed, never reconstructed. A figure of total solitude and ultimate perception, he can communicate only with himself. Due to the extremity of his isolation, only another—perhaps a god—can speak for him, a possibility realized only in imaginative fiction. As the limit point of history, the Last Man is also the limit point of literature. He can exist only as a monument, not as a subject, because his vision of the world at its end is untransmittable. As a literary figure, the Last Man, exemplified in Lionel Verney, is finally characterized by unintelligibility and repeated mediation.

2. The Last Man in America

Lionel Verney is obviously the title character of Shelley's novel, and he even declares in bold capitals, "I was the LAST MAN" (348). But who is the last of the Mohicans? Critics have long disagreed over which character should be considered the "hero" of Cooper's simultaneously published novel: there is Duncan Heyward, the white military officer rewarded in the end with a promising marriage; Hawk-eye (Natty Bumppo), the scout who helps shuttle the others through the wilderness; and Uncas, the young Mohican characterized by courage and bravery but fated to a violent death.[23] The specific identity of the title character, however, has been relatively unexamined. When Hawk-eye and his two Mohican companions, Chingachgook and his son Uncas, make their appearance in the third chapter, Chingachgook declares that his boy is "the last of the Mohicans" (33). Yet those familiar with Cooper's earlier novel *The Pioneers* (1823) could read this declaration with ironic suspicion, as that previously published story had offered a seventy-year-old Chingachgook as "the last of his family, and his particular tribe."[24] The inevitability of Uncas's death in *The Last of the Mohicans* is thus foreshadowed by his absence in *The Pioneers*. Following Uncas's funeral, the elderly Delaware chief Tamenund, in the last line of the novel, laments that "he has lived to see the last warrior of the wise race of Mohicans" (350). Like the novel's title, Tamenund's declaration is artfully ambiguous; is he referring to Uncas, over whose funeral he has just presided, or to Chingachgook, who stoically stands to the side like a "blazed pine, in a clearing of the pale-faces" (349)? In either case, the conclusion of the novel is also, it seems, the conclusion of a race of people.

Shelley and Cooper both offer narratives of extinction, but while Shelley imagines the end of the human species, Cooper confines his work to the passing of a race. Scholars have recently begun to note that Cooper's frontier tales were often bound up with the convoluted disçourse of race, a discourse that in America was especially pertinent to the institution of slavery.[25] As Southerners became ever more defensive of slaveholding practices, racial discourse in the 1820s and 1830s increasingly turned to "scientific" accounts that categorized human beings into essentially separate subspecies and often speculated about the possibility of polygenesis, the independent origination of distinct human races. Such essentialist accounts of race tended to assume the desirability of racial purity, a desire seemingly shared by Cooper's Natty Bumppo, a self-proclaimed "man without a cross." Ezra Tawil has argued that racial ambivalence in Cooper's work (specifically in *The Pioneers*) reflects the process by which "an emergent racialist discourse" was displacing "an older model of difference," as the strict divisions of biological essentialism supplanted the looser divisions of observable kinds.[26] *The Last of the Mohicans* specifically has been a site for the critique of attitudes toward racial mixing; the ending of the novel is well known for the death of the racially tainted Cora (who is partially descended from African slaves), and Cooper has conventionally been accused of "killing her off" in order to deny her sexual union with any of her potential male matches (Uncas, Magua, or Duncan).[27]

Yet I propose that another kind of racial crisis is at the center of the novel: biological extinction. Cooper's conflict between whites and Indians may be suggestive of the most controversial issue of his era—slavery—but the phenomenon of the "vanishing Indian" does not apply to a slave population that continued to grow throughout the author's lifetime. The passing of the Native Americans gained significance in Cooper's day because, due to the growing belief that human races were determined by genuine biological barriers, the Indians were increasingly perceived as a case of impending biological extinction.

The professional geological acceptance of a theory of extinction was broadcast to Cooper and other Americans to the same degree as it was to the British Romantic writers who crafted Last Man tales. Cuvier's *Essay on the Theory of the Earth* was published in New York in 1818, and appended to it were some "Observations on the Geology of North America" by Cooper's acquaintance Samuel L. Mitchill. Also, the same article from the *Monthly Review* covering Greenough's *Critical Examination of the First Principles of Geology* (and announcing the well-known truth of extinction) was reprinted in the June 1820 issue of the short-lived New York quarterly *The Literary and Scientific Repository*, which was edited by Cooper's friend Charles Kitchel Gardner. Cooper would have been very familiar with this journal, as he contributed several anonymously authored reviews during its brief run (1820–22).[28] In addition to these materials, Cooper may have read an account of the burgeoning "Last Man" theme in British letters. English periodicals such as the *Edinburgh Review* were very popular in the United States, and the *Museum of Foreign Literature and Science*, published monthly in Philadelphia and New York, included in its June 1825 issue an article titled "Mr. Campbell's Last Man," which reprinted the poet's letter of response to the accusation of thematic borrowing.[29]

While *The Last of the Mohicans* might at first seem merely to be accounting for the passing of a single tribe, Cooper's Mohicans—"the greatest and most civilized of the Indian nations" (3)—function as a synecdoche for vanishing Indian populations in general, whose numbers were indeed plummeting during the early nineteenth century. Accordingly, in an 1831 introduction to the novel, Cooper remarked that the Mohicans were simply the first to suffer "the seemingly inevitable fate of all these people" (6–7). As a marker for a group Cooper's contemporaries increasingly understood to be biologically distinct, the Mohicans represented a genetic population on the brink of destruction rather than a "primitive" state of society to be ushered into civilization. The new racial discourse imposed theoretically insurmountable barriers between Native and Euro-Americans, a concept reflected in the Leather-Stocking Tales; thus, in *The Prairie* (1827), Dr. Obed Bat rejects an offer to take an Indian wife on the grounds that "all admixture of the varieties of *species* . . . interrupt the harmony of nature." This version of "natural harmony" suggests a proto-Darwinian emphasis on selective rather than cooperative survival; Fiona Stafford thus endorses *The Last of the Mohicans* as "the first novel to deal with the essentially modern tragedy of extinction," crediting Cooper with anticipating geologist Charles Lyell's realization that biological extinction can be the result of inter-species competition rather than ecological catastrophe.[30]

Of course, the tendency of white Americans like Cooper to view the Indians as Other (on account of both their social and their physiological differences) was counterbalanced by the urge to see in the Indians a basis for white American self-identity. Many scholars have suggested that colonial and early-republic Americans understood the unique American "character" to occupy a seat of dialectic tension between the savage Indian of the western frontier and the refined European of the eastern shore.[31] The "loss" of the Native Americans through removal and extinction was thus the loss of a key element of the American character and even a potential threat to the coherence of the republic. The solution was to retain the Indian in history; like the Romans in Europe, the Indians could serve as foundational "Ancients," shoulders upon which modern Americans could stand. Their history could be assimilated into "American" history even as their still-living representatives acted as impediments to US national desires.

No one embraced this solution more strongly than Cooper's contemporary Henry Wadsworth Longfellow. In response to European critics who insisted that a national literature could not develop in a country whose landscape inspired few associations with a deep and living history, Longfellow sought to appropriate the "ancient history" of the Indians as fertile soil for a mature American poetry. Writing in 1824, long before penning his 1855 national epic *The Song of Hiawatha*, Longfellow explains the historical and cultural boon that the Indians will grant to white Americans when they finally vanish:

> As population advances westward, the plough-share turns up the wasted skeleton; and happy villages arise upon the sites of unknown burial-places. And when our native Indians, who are fast perishing from the earth, shall have left forever the borders of our wide lakes and rivers, and their villages have decayed within the bosoms of our western hills, the dim light of tradition will rest upon those places, which have seen the glory of their battles, and heard the voice of their eloquence;—and our land will become, indeed, a classic ground.[32]

For Longfellow, the Indians have the *potential* to be the ancient Romans of America, but they can become so only posthumously, when they will deserve veneration after "perishing from the earth." Their potential for glory will be realized only in death and burial. Meanwhile, in this account, the westward-moving pioneers are not warring with Indians; they are digging up ancient history, discovering America's past as they go.

Cooper was less enthusiastic than Longfellow about the death of the Indians, but he shared the same desire to claim their history for the young American nation. He thus faced the problem of achieving appropriation without assimilation, of claiming an Indian heritage without belonging to an Indian bloodline. The provisional literary solution to this difficulty of historical transmission is the Last Man, a theme that emerged in conjunction with the trope of the vanishing Indian in US literature. *The Last of the Mohicans* was published in the midst of other similar titles; *Tadeuskund: The Last King of the Lenape*, by Nicholas Hentz, appeared in 1825, and John Augustus Stone's drama *Metamora; or, The Last of the Wampanoags*, one of the most popular plays in antebellum America, was first performed in 1829. As a mediating figure between conquered and conquering, a spokesman for and embodiment of a people, the last of the race holds the keys to an entire history. He can offer some "last words" and effectively deliver the eulogy for a dying population. But in Cooper's hands, the Last Man is not a mediator but rather endlessly mediated. Cooper's Last Man cannot be fixed with any certainty, the very authority of his lastness being therefore questionable. In other words, unlike the British Last Man, the last of the tribe can speak to the agents (i.e., the white settlers) responsible for his destruction—and yet, just like Lionel Verney, the "Last of the Mohicans" is no simple authority on history but rather a figure, represented only with difficulty, whose unintelligible words require repeated translation.

3. Interminable Lastness

An answer to the question, "Who is the last of the Mohicans?" might be provided by allowing the novel's title to refer to a plural rather than singular Last: Chingachgook and Uncas are together the last of the Mohicans. Chingachgook's eventual death was portrayed in *The Pioneers*, and Uncas's death in *The Last of the Mohicans* simply (re-)emphasizes the termination of the bloodline. The difficulty of describing a single character as "last" is underscored by the plurality of names belonging to every character in the novel. Cooper's practice of naming in the first three Leather-Stocking Tales (*The Pioneers*, *The Last of the Mohicans*, and *The Prairie*) defies any attempt to attach "lastness" to a single character, as a proliferation of names frustrates the identification of authoritative finality. "Chingachgook," Hawk-eye explains, is Delaware for "Big Serpent" (or "Great Snake"), and the enemy Mingo Indians of *The Last of the Mohicans*, having sided with French Canadian soldiers, refer to him as "le Gros Serpent." Yet in *The Pioneers*, Chingachgook is known to the white settlers of Templeton as "John Mohegan." The settlers provided him with the Christian "John" while Delaware Indians in the region styled him "Mohegan," a "national name" that "recalled the idea of a nation in ruins"—a name, furthermore, that he self-applies. At this point, Chingachgook *is* the Mohican tribe, and his Delaware name has shifted from that of a warrior to that of a monument.[33]

"Uncas" is an even more problematic name. The Mingoes refer to Chingachgook's son as "le Cerf Agile," a name whose English translation ("the bounding deer") is the cause for some debate in *The Last of the Mohicans* (91). "Uncas" is a kind of general name for a Mohican warrior; the Mohicans, according to Cooper's mythology, were a noble strain of the larger Delaware people, and "Uncas" operates as a regal family name, usually replaced by a more specific nickname (like "Chingachgook") when a warrior has established himself.[34] Thus, like "Mohegan," "Uncas" is a name signifying both the individual and the entire tribe simultaneously. In the novel's climactic recognition scene, Uncas reveals himself and describes his lineage to the ancient Delaware chief Tamenund. This elderly chief, upon hearing the name Uncas, confuses the young Mohican for his similarly named great-great-grandfather. When Uncas reminds the old chief that all his old ancestors have died, Tamenund experiences "a flash of recognition," restoring "him, at once, to a consciousness of the true history of his nation" (310).

The name "Uncas," with its potential for designating so many figures, thus consolidates the "true history" of the Mohican people.[35]

Furthermore, the use of this name facilitates the white appropriation of Indian history without sexual union. Uncas's death unambiguously leaves his father Chingachgook as the last surviving Mohican, and readers looking back to *The Pioneers* might recall the character of John Mohegan as a pitiful, aging, childless man who never stopped mourning the death of his son and found consolation only in alcohol and, finally, death. And when Cooper returned to the Leather-Stocking Tales with *The Pathfinder* in 1840 (after taking a thirteen-year hiatus following the publication of *The Prairie* in 1827), he reaffirmed Chingachgook's lastness: in that novel, which is set shortly after the time of *The Last of the Mohicans*, Natty Bumppo explains, in regard to Chingachgook, that "no shoot of the old Mohican stem remains." Yet readers of *The Pathfinder*, if they had been following the series, would have had reason to doubt that the Mohican family tree was mere dead wood. In *The Prairie*, set in 1805 posterior to the events of all the other Leather-Stocking Tales, Captain Duncan Middleton reveals to Natty Bumppo not only that he is the grandson of Duncan Heyward but also that he possesses the middle name "Uncas." Heyward, it seems, had begun a family tradition to keep alive the name of the young Mohican warrior who had helped him and his bride-to-be, and now "Uncas," Middleton explains, is a name "likely to be handed down, as an heir loom among the rest of his descendants."[36] Symbolically, through name, Duncan Heyward's descendants have adopted themselves into the Mohican lineage. Chronologically, Chingachgook died in the late eighteenth century as "Mohegan," the last of his tribe. Yet, unbeknownst to him, the name of his deceased son—a name, like "Mohegan," signifying his entire tribe—lived on in the bloodline of a white family. The Mohicans endure in a name, not of the melancholy alcoholic who died in the 1780s but of the young warrior who died in the 1750s. Alice Munro, Duncan Heyward's future wife, had looked upon Uncas as a "relic" (53); she and her husband have since acquired the relic and handed it down as an heirloom, preserving the history of an entire tribe in their family nomenclature. In this way, the Heywards (and Middletons) have become Mohican heirs, grafting a shoot onto what Natty Bumppo thought was a dead stem.[37]

Adding to this prospect of corporeal extinction is the threat that the Mohican dialect is likewise at the vanishing point, so part of the claim to lastness in Cooper's work is also linguistic. But like Verney's narrative, originally unintelligible, repeatedly translated and mediated, the words of the last of the Mohicans appear to the reader removed by several orders of narrative intervention. As with *The Last Man*, *The Last of the Mohicans* reveals a problem of communicability. Uncas seems to possess the historical authority of the Last Man, an ability to "comprehend the past as a whole" made visible when he provides the elderly Tamenund with "a consciousness of the true history of his nation." In this case, Uncas's authority derives partially from his speech alone; Tamenund first recognizes the presence of a strange "voice" at his ear speaking "with the tongue of a Delaware" (307–8). The speech, of course, would be unintelligible to the average non-Delaware reader in its "original" form. The narrator must render it in English, an aspect of translation that Cooper's critics have generally overlooked. Much of the dialogue in the Leather-Stocking Tales is purportedly translated from an Indian language by a narrator who attempts to preserve, "as far as possible, the tone of thought of each interlocutor, as well as the peculiarities of manner."[38] If Natty Bumppo seems to alternate between a backwoods vernacular and a loftier, more poetic dialect, it is probably because he alternates between speaking in English and speaking in Delaware (or in one of the other myriad Indian dialects at his command). Similarly, the narrator's translation of Uncas's Mohican voice renders it into archaic English (using, for example, "thou" and "thine"), suggesting its obsolescence and proximity to extinction. Of Uncas's white companions, the only one who can understand his words is the illiterate Hawk-eye, who can translate Mohican speech into English but cannot transcribe it into text.

But Natty is not available to offer either Cora or the reader a translation when Uncas addresses Tamenund near the end of the novel. Uncas's words are then translated by a disembodied narrator, who records the speech in English for the reader but cannot, of course, clarify the dying Mohican dialect for Cora, who is actually present to hear it. In fact, *only* the impersonal narrator can render this speech into English; none of the listeners in the novel would be competent for the task. Cooper's narrator, like Mary Shelley's introductory author, must therefore perform the task of recording a voice that derives its very character from the fact that it could not be recorded.

In further resemblance to Shelley's editor of the Sibylline leaves, Cooper's narrator finds in the Last Man a figure whose words are not only unrecordable but also unintelligible, as he denies the possibility of translating faithfully "the comprehensive and melodious language" (319) that Uncas employs. Contraposed to Uncas's indecipherable native eloquence is Chingachgook's primal and incomprehensible utterance following his son's death. At Uncas's funeral, the other characters offer respectful silence while the father delivers a barely audible "monody" for his son: "The strains rose just so loud, as to become intelligible, and then they grew fainter and more trembling, until they finally sunk on the ear, as if borne away by a passing breath of wind" (345). Readers might recall Chingachgook's own death scene in *The Pioneers*, the Mohican "chanting a kind of low dirge . . . [in] deep and remarkably guttural tones" as he waits to be consumed by a forest fire. His last words are not even "words" but rather "tones"; while the former could perhaps be translated with difficulty, the latter defy expression in written language. Chingachgook's death in that earlier novel further displays the ultimate inability to transmit the experience of a Last Man, as the inscription on his headstone misspells his name as "Chingagook." Natty expresses mild disappointment when realizing that the moniker was recorded incorrectly: "The name should be set down right, for an Indian's name always has some meaning in it."[39] Of course the difference between "Chingachgook" (which means Big Serpent) and "Chingagook" (which is meaningless) is noticed only by Natty, the sole remaining character who speaks the dying (or perhaps at this point, dead) Mohican language.

Indeed, Natty Bumppo himself could stake a claim to being the last of the Mohicans. The chaste Natty, a "man without a cross," refuses to mix his blood with another's and dies without propagating his seed. However, despite his repeatedly stated antipathy toward racial crossing, Leather-Stocking weaves his own character and fate into that of the Mohicans. As he puts it, he has "the gifts of a Delaware grafted on a Christian stock." His individual "roots" thus remain white and Christian, merely enhanced (and never reproduced) by talents developed as a hunter and a scout among the Indians. Yet his formal childhood adoption by the Mohicans, when he was "engrafted into the tribe with full and solemn ceremony," ensures a communal if not biological bond.[40] By associating himself with the Indian camps and their languages, and by dissociating himself from the white settlements, Natty yokes his destiny to the vanishing Indian. He becomes not only a mediating figure between the Last Man and a future audience but also a Last Man himself. Following Uncas's burial, Chingachgook begins to cry, "I am alone," but Hawk-eye interrupts him ("No, no!") with a pledge of undying friendship, thus assuring him that the last of the line is not doomed to solitude (349). Natty, while continuing to deny any impurity in his "white" blood, affirms his kinship with Chingachgook and Uncas as brother and uncle. Chingachgook's death therefore leaves Natty Bumppo as the last of the tribe with which he had aligned himself. This slippery status of the Last Man—at times signifying Uncas, Chingachgook, or even Leather-Stocking—thus undermines the novel's maintenance of racial purity and distinct biological categories. The quality of "lastness" slides across racial boundaries and refuses to remain fixed to one character.[41]

"I am without kith or kin in the wide world!" Natty Bumppo announces in his famous death scene in *The Prairie*, continuing with his declaration that "when I am gone there will be an end of my race." Who are the members of Natty's "race"? Perhaps simply the Bumppo family (never depicted in any of the novels) or perhaps the Mohicans, but the term is finally ambiguous; it may instead signify the class of frontiersmen to which Natty belongs. Natty dies facing the western sunset, in an echo of the last line of *The Pioneers*, which had explained the old hunter's departure from Templeton, New York: "He had gone far towards the setting sun,—the foremost in that band of Pioneers, who are opening the way for the march of the nation across the continent."[42] Yet this line must be understood ironically; Natty opposes the "march of civilization" that brings the "wasty ways" of the settlements to the pure, virginal wilderness. He flees west as a refugee from civilization, not as its trailblazer. He runs the risk of being remembered as first rather than last, a vanguard member of the civilization he despises rather than a man of nature who has hitched his wagon to the dying Indians.

As a narrative of extinction, *The Last of the Mohicans* (in its relation to the Leather-Stocking Tales more broadly) produces an ambiguity of termination similar to that of Mary Shelley's *The Last*

Man. For both Cooper and Shelley, this ambiguity deflects the historical authority vested in the Last Man. Shelley's imaginative text reveals the necessary limitations to recording the end of history. In Cooper's hands, the uncertainty of the last allows white settlers to claim a kind of ancestry and continuity with the very people they are displacing and destroying, to appropriate Indian history so as to justify the "inheritance" of their territory. And yet, this same uncertainty pushes back against the biological understanding of race that initially points to extinction. For both authors, being last—witnessing the end and having the final say—remains unfinished work.

NOTES

1. Shelley, *Last Man*, 312; Cooper, *Last of the Mohicans*, 3. Subsequent references to these editions will be cited parenthetically in the text.

2. Brantlinger, *Dark Vanishings*, 1. My essay builds on the work of several recent critics who suggest that Cooper's work was influenced by a growing cultural acceptance of extinction. Fiona J. Stafford (in *Last of the Race*), Brantlinger (in *Dark Vanishings*), and Jonathan Elmer (in *On Lingering* and "Vaulted Over") have each included remarks on both Cooper and Shelley (as well as other writers of Last Man tales) in their separate studies on the literature of extinction and the "last of the race" theme.

3. Cuvier, *Essay*, 17. This popular English translation was republished in 1815 and 1817. For an account of the translation and reception of Cuvier's work in England and America, see Martin J. S. Rudwick, *Georges Cuvier*, 254–57.

4. My use of the term "narrative of extinction" extends from Wai-chee Dimock, *Empire for Liberty*, 118.

5. Susan Fenimore Cooper, "Introduction," xxii; Slotkin, "Introduction," xiii.

6. "The Last Man," claims W. Warren Wagar in *Terminal Visions*, "is an anti-Crusoe, conquered rather than conquering, crushed by his solitude, and sure of his defeat" (17).

7. Shelley, *Journal*, 193. Sir Timothy Shelley, Mary's father-in-law, had forbidden her to write a biography of his son, so the thinly veiled fictionalizations in *The Last Man* afforded her a way of bypassing this injunction. A useful study for such an investigation of the novel's sources is Walter Peck's "The Biographical Element."

8. Jaffrey, Rev. of *Theodric*, 284. For a detailed critical treatment of the Last Man vogue in early nineteenth-century British literature, see A. J. Sambrook, "A Romantic Theme."

9. *Monthly Review*, Unsigned review of *The Last Man*, 334, 335.

10. Hugh J. Luke Jr., the editor of the 1965 reprint, saw the novel as ultimately flawed but believed that a Cold War audience would approach the text with a different attitude than Shelley's contemporaries: "Anyone who has lived with the possibility of

instantaneous and complete obliteration of human society . . . can hardly dismiss the theme of *The Last Man* as a merely grotesque one" ("Introduction," viii).

11. Lee Sterrenburg long ago argued that Shelley was engaging with and rejecting contemporary attitudes toward revolution (notably those of Burke, Godwin, and Carlyle) ("Anatomy"). More recently, Charlotte Sussman, in "'Islanded in the World,'" has linked the novel to British concerns over emigration and population management, and Elmer, in "Vaulted Over," views the spread of plague in the novel as a critique of imperial England's sovereign agency. Mark Canuel, in "Acts, Rules," sees in the novel "the formation of less restrictive patterns of social cooperation" (151–52) that would later "characterize the logic of the liberal state," and Hilary Strang, in "Common Life," finds Shelley struggling with the biopolitics of democratic equality.

12. Cuvier, *Essay*, 17, 16. The historian of science William Whewell would later label this outlook on geological history "catastrophism."

13. Rudwick, *Georges Cuvier*, 257.

14. *Monthly Review*, Unsigned review of *A Critical Examination*, 378. Greenough was at that time President of the Geological Society of London.

15. Laudan, *From Mineralogy to Geology*, 150–51. Arthur O. Lovejoy explored the eighteenth-century consensus that the different species of life on earth formed a "Great Chain of Being," together representing the totality of biotic potential. This model was altered, but not dismantled, in the face of overwhelming evidence for extinction, resulting in what Lovejoy calls the "temporalization of the Chain of Being," a belief that only the totality of natural history could account for a complete chain of life-forms (*Great Chain of Being*, 244).

16. Indeed, in *The Last Man*, Verney exclaims that the "species of man must perish" (322).

17. Campbell, quoted in Paley, "Apocalypse without Millennium," 107.

18. "The very idea of a last man," writes Stafford, "is impossible in a culture that adheres firmly to a sudden, divinely orchestrated ending of the entire race" (*Last of the Race*, 18).

19. As Morton D. Paley puts it, "The authenticity of Verney's narrative is predicated on his being *Last*, a condition that precludes by definition his having readers" ("Apocalypse without Millennium," 121).

20. Ruppert, "Time and the Sibyl," 144. In the early nineteenth century, the act of setting a tale in the future was often achieved only via difficult narratological maneuvering; see Alkon, *Origins of Futuristic Fiction*. Writing of *The Last Man* in a letter to a friend, Shelley exclaimed, "You can form no idea of the difficulty of the subject . . ." (*Letters*, 1:510).

21. "Like Crusoe's journal," explains Stafford, "the narrative of the Last Man is self-authenticating: writing matters to the writer" (*Last of the Race*, 223). Similarly, Samantha Webb identifies Verney's use of narrative "as consolation rather than as exchange" ("Reading the End," 132).

22. Sussman, "'Islanded in the World,'" 298.

23. If Duncan is the hero of the novel, Natty Bumppo is certainly the hero of the Leather-Stocking series. Uncas, despite a legitimate claim to being the titular

character of the novel, has not often been considered the hero. For an important exception, see Donald Darnell, "Uncas as Hero." Geoffrey Sanborn makes a strong case that Magua, usually understood to be the devilish villain, should be seen instead as the novel's tragic hero (*Whipscars and Tattoos*, 37-72). According to Jonathan Arac, in his *American Literary Narrative*, "By the irony of history, none of the participants in *The Last of the Mohicans* is the hero so much as are Cooper's chosen readers, the Americans who are the actual possessors of the continent for which the British, French, and Indians believed themselves to be struggling" (10).

24. Cooper, *Pioneers*, 85.

25. Cassandra Jackson reads Cora as a linking figure between American slavery and Indian Removal, embodying a historical burden that the frontier myth seeks to eliminate (*Barriers between Us*, 9–29). In *The Making of Racial Sentiment*, Ezra Tawil contends that the politics of racial difference (often between white and Native American characters) in novels such as *The Pioneers* worked to solidify a theory of racial essentialism that could be applied to black slavery. Bill Christophersen, building off of Tawil's work, claims that *The Last of the Mohicans* resonates with fears of slave rebellion stoked by the Missouri Crisis and Denmark Vesey's failed 1822 rebellion ("Missouri Crisis"). As early as 1960, Leslie A. Fiedler claimed that miscegenation was the "secret theme" of *The Last of the Mohicans* and of the Leather-Stocking Tales more broadly (*Love and Death*, 202).

26. Tawil, *Making of Racial Sentiment*, 81. Barbara Alice Mann persuasively contends that Natty Bumppo, despite his repeated proclamations, is a character of mixed blood in her "Race Traitor."

27. Axelrad, "*The Last of the Mohicans*," 38. Allan M. Axelrad here defends Cooper against the "received wisdom" that the author killed off Cora and Uncas over a belief that they were racially unsuitable for marriage.

28. See Cooper, *Early Critical Essays*.

29. "Mr. Campbell's Last Man."

30. Cooper, *The Prairie*, 221; Stafford, *Last of the Race*, 260. Despite his doctoral accreditation, Dr. Obed Bat largely plays the role of a fool, and his opinions should not be taken as Cooper's own.

31. Classic elaborations of this idea can be found in Roy Harvey Pearce, *Savagism and Civilization*; Richard Slotkin, *Regeneration through Violence*; and Philip J. Deloria, *Playing Indian*.

32. Longfellow, *Poems and Other Writings*, 794.

33. Cooper, *Pioneers*, 85. As Natty insists, "Old John and Chingachgook were very different men to look on," the Mohican chief being, when "in the middle of manhood, . . . taller than now by three inches" (155).

34. In Cooper's *The Deerslayer*, Natty explains that "Chingachgook" is just a nickname: "Uncas is his ra'al name—all his family being called Uncas, until they get a title that has been 'arned by deeds" (138).

35. In *The Wept of Wish-Ton-Wish* (1828), Cooper's next novel after *The Prairie* (1827), the ancestral Mohican Uncas plays the villain against the heroic Narragansett chief Conanchet in the 1760s.

36. Cooper, *Pathfinder*, 79; *Prairie*, 113.

37. Cooper was very familiar with this tactic of appropriating a name. In 1826, the same year in which he published *The Last of the Mohicans*, James Cooper legally became James Fenimore Cooper, adopting his mother's maiden name. The Fenimores had no male heir, so Cooper took the name for himself and continued the line in the appellation of his descendants, who would also share the name "Fenimore Cooper." Cooper, *Letters and Journals*, 5:200–02; see also Franklin, *Cooper: The Early Years*, 510–13.

38. Cooper, *Pathfinder*, 463. More recently, scholars have begun to recognize the complex interweaving of dialect and translation that Cooper was representing within his novels; see, e.g., Rosenwald, *Multilingual America*, 20–47.

39. Cooper, *Pioneers*, 410, 452.

40. Cooper, *Pathfinder*, 121; *Deerslayer*, 555. The latter anecdote was added posthumously by Cooper's daughter Susan, though she likely derived it from her father.

41. Thomas Philbrick declared that *The Last of the Mohicans* is centered on ambiguities, that "the lines that distinguish races, nationalities, and occupations . . . are crossed and blurred" ("Sounds of Discord," 34).

42. Cooper, *Prairie*, 383; *Pioneers*, 456.

BIBLIOGRAPHY

Alkon, Paul K. *Origins of Futuristic Fiction*. Athens: University of Georgia Press, 1987.

Arac, Jonathan. *The Emergence of American Literary Narrative, 1820–1860*. Cambridge, MA: Harvard University Press, 2005.

Axelrad, Allan M. "*The Last of the Mohicans*, Race Mixing, and America's Destiny." In *Leather-Stocking Redux; Or, Old Tales, New Essays*, edited by Jeffrey Walker, 33–56. New York: AMS Press, 2011.

Brantlinger, Patrick. *Dark Vanishings: Discourse on the Extinction of Primitive Races, 1800–1930*. Ithaca, NY: Cornell University Press, 2003.

Canuel, Mark. "Acts, Rules, and *The Last Man*." *Nineteenth-Century Literature* 53 (1998): 147-70.

Christophersen, Bill. "*The Last of the Mohicans* and the Missouri Crisis." *Early American Literature* 46 (2011): 263–89.

Cooper, James Fenimore. *The Deerslayer or, The First War-Path*. Historical introduction and explanatory notes by James Franklin Beard; text established by Lance Schachterle, Kent Ljungquist, and James Kilby. Albany: State University of New York Press, 1987.

———. *Early Critical Essays, 1820–1822*. Edited by James F. Beard Jr. Gainesville, FL: Scholars' Facsimiles and Reprints, 1955.

———. *The Last of the Mohicans; A Narrative of 1757*. Historical introduction by James Franklin Beard; text established with explanatory notes by James A. Sappenfield and E. N. Feltskog. Albany: State University of New York Press, 1983.

———. *The Letters and Journals of James Fenimore Cooper*. Edited by James Franklin Beard. 6 vols. Cambridge, MA: Belknap Press of Harvard University Press, 1960–68.

———. *The Pathfinder; or The Inland Sea*. Edited with historical introduction by Richard Dilworth Rust. Albany: State University of New York Press, 1981.

———. *The Pioneers, or the Sources of the Susquehanna; A Descriptive Tale*. Historical introduction and explanatory notes by James Franklin Beard; text established by Lance Schachterle and Kenneth M. Andersen Jr. Albany: State University of New York Press, 1980.

———. *The Prairie: A Tale*. Edited with historical introduction by James P. Elliott. Albany: State University of New York Press, 1985.

Cooper, Susan Fenimore. "Introduction." In *The Last of the Mohicans, or, A Narrative of 1757*, by James Fenimore Cooper, ix–xxxviii. Boston: Houghton, Mifflin, 1876.

Cuvier, Georges. *Essay on the Theory of the Earth*. Translated by Robert Kerr. 1813. Reprint, Farnborough, UK: Gregg International Press, 1971.

Darnell, Donald. "Uncas as Hero: The *Ubi Sunt* Formula in *The Last of the Mohicans*." *American Literature* 37 (1965): 259–66.

Deloria, Philip J. *Playing Indian*. New Haven, CT: Yale University Press, 1998.

Dimock, Wai-chee. *Empire for Liberty: Melville and the Poetics of Individualism*. Princeton, NJ: Princeton University Press, 1989.

Elmer, Jonathan. *On Lingering and Being Last: Race and Sovereignty in the New World*. New York: Fordham University Press, 2008.

———. "'Vaulted Over by the Present': Melancholy and Sovereignty in Mary Shelley's *The Last Man*." *Novel* 42 (2009): 355–59.

Fiedler, Leslie A. *Love and Death in the American Novel*. New York: Criterion Books, 1960.

Franklin, Wayne. *James Fenimore Cooper: The Early Years*. New Haven, CT: Yale University Press, 2007.

Jackson, Cassandra. *Barriers between Us: Interracial Sex in Nineteenth-Century American Literature*. Bloomington: Indiana University Press, 2004.

[Jaffrey, Francis]. Rev. of *Theodric, a Domestic Tale*, by Thomas Campbell. *Edinburgh Review* 41 (1825): 271–87.

Laudan, Rachel. *From Mineralogy to Geology: The Foundations of a Science, 1650–1830*. Chicago: University of Chicago Press, 1987.

Longfellow, Henry Wadsworth. *Poems and Other Writings*. Edited by J. D. McClatchy. New York: Library of America, 2000.

Lovejoy, Arthur O. *The Great Chain of Being: A Study of the History of an Idea*. 1936; New York: Harper, 1960.

Luke, Hugh J., Jr. "Introduction." In *The Last Man*, by Mary Shelley, vii–xviii. Lincoln: University of Nebraska Press, 1965.

Mann, Barbara Alice. "Race Traitor: Cooper, His Critics, and Nineteenth-Century Literary Politics." In *A Historical Guide to James Fenimore Cooper*, edited by Leland S. Person, 155–85. Oxford: Oxford University Press, 2007.

Monthly Review. Unsigned review of *A Critical Examination of the First Principles of Geology*, by G. B. Greenough. *Monthly Review* 90 (1819): 376–93.

———. Unsigned review of *The Last Man*, by Mary Shelley. *Monthly* Review 1 (1826): 333–35.

"Mr. Campbell's Last Man." *Museum of Foreign Literature and Science* 6 (1825): 585–87.

Paley, Morton D. "*The Last Man*: Apocalypse without Millennium." In *The Other Mary Shelley: Beyond* Frankenstein, edited by Audrey A. Fisch, Anne K. Mellor, and Esther H. Schor, 107–23. New York: Oxford University Press, 1993.

Pearce, Roy Harvey. *Savagism and Civilization: A Story of the Indian and the American Mind.* Rev. ed. Berkeley: University of California Press, 1988.

Peck, Walter E. "The Biographical Element in the Novels of Mary Wollstonecraft Shelley." *PMLA* 38 (1923): 196–219.

Philbrick, Thomas. "*The Last of the Mohicans* and the Sounds of Discord." *American Literature* 43 (1971): 25–41.

Rosenwald, Lawrence Alan. *Multilingual America: Language and the Making of American Literature.* New York: Cambridge University Press, 2008.

Rudwick, Martin J. S. *Georges Cuvier, Fossil Bones, and Geological Catastrophes: New Translations and Interpretations of the Primary Texts.* Chicago: University of Chicago Press, 1997.

Ruppert, Timothy. "Time and the Sibyl in Mary Shelley's *The Last Man*." *Studies in the Novel* 41 (2009): 141–156.

Sambrook, A. J. "A Romantic Theme: The Last Man." *Forum for Modern Language Studies* 2.1 (1966): 25–33.

Sanborn, Geoffrey. *Whipscars and Tattoos:* The Last of the Mohicans, Moby-Dick, *and the Maori.* New York: Oxford University Press, 2011.

Shelley, Mary. *Frankenstein; or, The Modern Prometheus.* 1818; New York: Norton, 1996.

———. *The Last Man.* 1826. Edited by Anne McWhir. Peterborough: Broadview, 1996.

———. *The Letters of Mary Wollstonecraft Shelley.* Edited by Betty T. Bennett. 3 vols. Baltimore, MD: Johns Hopkins University Press, 1980–88.

———. *Mary Shelley's Journal.* Edited by Frederick L. Jones. Norman: University of Oklahoma Press, 1947.

Slotkin, Richard. "Introduction to the 1831 Edition." In *The Last of the Mohicans*, by James Fenimore Cooper, ix–xxviii. New York: Penguin, 1986.

———. *Regeneration through Violence: The Mythology of the American Frontier, 1600–1860.* Middletown, CT: Wesleyan University Press, 1973.

Stafford, Fiona J. *The Last of the Race: The Growth of a Myth from Milton to Darwin.* Oxford: Clarendon Press, 1994.

Sterrenburg, Lee. "*The Last Man*: Anatomy of Failed Revolutions." *Nineteenth-Century Fiction* 33 (1978): 324–47.

Strang, Hilary. "Common Life, Animal Life, Equality: *The Last Man*." *ELH* 78 (2011): 409–31.

Sussman, Charlotte. "'Islanded in the World': Cultural Memory and Human Mobility in *The Last Man*." *PMLA* 118 (2003): 286–301.

Tawil, Ezra. *The Making of Racial Sentiment: Slavery and the Birth of the Frontier Romance.* New York: Cambridge University Press, 2006.

Wagar, W. Warren. *Terminal Visions: The Literature of Last Things.* Bloomington: Indiana University Press, 1982.

Webb, Samantha. "Reading the End of the World: *The Last Man*, History, and the Agency of Romantic Authorship." In *Mary Shelley in Her Times*, edited by Betty T. Bennett and Stuart Curran, 119–33. Baltimore, MD: Johns Hopkins University Press, 2000.

Notes on Contributors

ALLAN M. AXELRAD, Professor Emeritus of American Studies at California State University, Fullerton, is the author of *History and Utopia: A Study of the World View of James Fenimore Cooper* (1978), plus a variety of articles and book chapters on Cooper. He is currently working on a book titled "The American Author: James Fenimore Cooper and *The Leather-Stocking Tales.*"

MATTHEW J. C. CELLA, Assistant Professor of English at Shippensburg University, has published articles and reviews in *ISLE, Western American Literature*, *MELUS*, and *Great Plains Quarterly.* His *Bad Land Pastoralism in Great Plains Fiction* (2010) was a finalist for the 2011 Great Plains Distinguished Book Prize.

JOHN HAY is an Assistant Professor of English at the University of Nevada, Las Vegas. His current project, "The Postapocalyptic Frontier: Uncanny Historicism in the Nineteenth Century," reveals the ways in which frontier accounts in nineteenth-century American literature prefigure later postapocalyptic fictions.

JILLMARIE MURPHY, Assistant Professor of English and American Literature at Union College, is the author of *Monstrous Kinships: Realism and Attachment Theory in the Nineteenth- and Early-Twentieth Century Novel* (2011); the coeditor, with Ronald A. Bosco, of *Hawthorne in His Own Time* (2007); and a contributor to *The Oxford Handbook of Early American Literature* (2008).

Donna Richardson, Professor of English at St. Mary's College of Maryland, is the author of *Visual Paraphrasing of Poetry* (1992), essays on Shelley and other nineteenth-century poets, and most recently, "The Can of Ail: A. E. Housman's Moral Irony" (2010).

Tyler Roeger, doctoral candidate at the Pennsylvania State University, counts among his dissertation and research interests gothic fictions, constructions of space, and the social and imaginative possibilities of urban environments in early American and antebellum print.

Lance Schachterle has overseen the publication of seven works by Cooper since becoming editor-in-chief of "The Writings of James Fenimore Cooper" (www.wjfc.org) in 2002. For this series of critical texts, he has co-edited *The Pioneers, The Deerslayer, The Spy,* and *The Bravo*, and is currently working on *The Chainbearer.* He has also published on Cooper in *LEAR, Nineteenth-Century Literature, Studies in Bibliography, Textual Cultures*, and elsewhere.

Sarah Sillin, doctoral candidate in the Department of English at the University of Maryland, is currently completing a dissertation titled "Global Sympathy: Representing Nineteenth-Century Americans' Relations to the World."

Steven Carl Smith, Assistant Professor of History at Providence College and named 2012 Malkin New Scholar by the Bibliographical Society of America, has held fellowships from the McNeil Center for Early American Studies, the American Antiquarian Society, the Library Company of Philadelphia, the New York Public Library, the Gilder Lehrman Institute of American History, and the New York State Library. His broader research is a social history of the early New York publishing trade that examines the set of economic relationships and shared cultural practices that bound printers, booksellers, and their readers and contributors together and provided the arena for both political debate and literature production.

Megan Walsh, Assistant Professor of English at St. Bonaventure University, has published in *Early American Literature* and the Blackwell

Companion to Benjamin Franklin. She is currently completing a book manuscript titled "A Nation in Sight: Book Illustration and American Literature, 1770–1830."

Index

Thoreau, Henry David, 70
    Walden, 186n18
Thornton, John, 45

Watts, Steven, 28n9, 106n7, 107n18
Wayne, Caleb, 7, 23
Weaver, William Woys, 133n24
Webb, Samantha, 264n21
Webster, Noah, 138, 140–41,
Weems, Mason Locke (Parson), 47, 50–51, 59nn16 and 23